A CALL
TO ACCOUNT

A CALL
TO ACCOUNT

Empirical Evidence and Reference Guide

Original interviews used in *Does Your Vote Count?*

EDITED BY
CRISS HAJEK

BREAKOUT EDUCATIONAL NETWORK
IN ASSOCIATION WITH
DUNDURN PRESS
TORONTO · OXFORD

Publisher: Inta D. Erwin
Copy-editor: Amanda Stewart, First Folio Resource Group
Designer: Bruna Brunelli, Brunelli Designs
Production Editor: Amanda Stewart, First Folio Resource Group
Printer: Webcom

National Library of Canada Cataloguing in Publication Data

A call to account/edited by Criss Hajek.

One of the 16 vols. and 14 hours of video which make up the
    underground royal commission report
A companion to Does your vote count? by Paul Kemp
Includes bibliographical references and index.
ISBN 1-55002-432-9

    1. Canada — Politics and government. 2. Federal government —
Canada. I. Hajek, Criss. II. Title: underground royal commission
report.

JL75.C22 2002   320.971   C2002-902312-2

1   2   3   4   5   07   06   05   04   03

Printed and bound in Canada.
Printed on recycled paper. ♻
www.dundurn.com

Excerpts from the interviews featured in *A Call to Account* can also be found in its companion piece, *Does Your Vote Count?*, by Paul Kemp

Exclusive Canadian broadcast rights for the *underground royal commission* report

intelligent television

Check your cable or satellite listings for telecast times

Visit the *urc* Web site link at:
www.ichanneltv.com

The *underground royal commission* Report

Since September 11, 2001, there has been an uneasy dialogue among Canadians as we ponder our position in the world, especially vis à vis the United States. Critically and painfully, we are re-examining ourselves and our government. We are even questioning our nation's ability to retain its sovereignty.

The questions we are asking ourselves are not new. Over the last 30 years, and especially in the dreadful period of the early 1990s, leading up to the Quebec referendum of 1995, inquiries and Royal commissions, one after another, studied the state of the country. What *is* new is that eight years ago, a group of citizens looked at this parade of inquiries and commissions and said, "These don't deal with the real issues." They wondered how it was possible for a nation that was so promising and prosperous in the early 60s to end up so confused, divided, and troubled. And they decided that what was needed was a different kind of investigation — driven from the grassroots 'bottom,' and not from the top. Almost as a provocation, this group of people, most of whom were affiliated with the award winning documentary-maker, Stornoway Productions, decided to do it themselves — and so was born the *underground royal commission*!

What began as a television documentary soon evolved into much more. Seven young, novice researchers, hired right out of university, along with a television crew and producer, conducted interviews with people in government, business, the military and in all walks of life, across the country. What they discovered went beyond anything they had expected. The more they learned, the larger the implications grew. The project continued to evolve and has expanded to include a total of 23 researchers over the last several years. The results are the 14 hours of video and 16 books that make up the first interim report of the *underground royal commission*.

So what *are* the issues? The report of the *underground royal commission* clearly shows us that regardless of region, level of government, or political party, we are operating under a wasteful system ubiquitously lacking in accountability. An ever-weakening connection between the electors and the elected means that we are slowly and irrevocably losing our right to know our government. The researchers' experiences demonstrate that it is almost impossible for a member of the public, or in most cases, even for a member of Parliament, to actually trace how our tax dollars are spent. Most disturbing is the fact that our young people have been stuck with a crippling IOU that has effectively hamstrung their future. No wonder, then, that Canada is not poised for reaching its potential in the 21st century.

The *underground royal commission* report, prepared in large part by and for the youth of Canada, provides the hard evidence of the problems you and I may long have suspected. Some of that evidence makes it clear that, as ordinary Canadians, we are every bit as culpable as our politicians — for our failure to demand accountability, for our easy acceptance of government subsidies and services established without proper funding in place, and for the disservice we have done to our young people through the debt we have so blithely passed on to them. But the real purpose of the *underground royal commission* is to ensure that we better understand how government processes work and what role we play in them. Public policy issues must be understandable and accessible to the public if they are ever to be truly addressed and resolved. The *underground royal commission* intends to continue pointing the way for bringing about constructive change in Canada.

— Stornoway Productions

Books in the *underground royal commission* Report

"Just Trust Us"

The Chatter Box
The Chance of War
Talking Heads Talking Arms: (3 volumes)
No Life Jackets
Whistling Past the Graveyard
Playing the Ostrich

Days of Reckoning
Taking or Making Wealth
Guardians on Trial
Goodbye Canada?
Down the Road Never Travelled
Secrets in High Places
On the Money Trail

Does Your Vote Count?
A Call to Account
Reflections on Canadian Character

14 hours of videos also available with the *underground royal commission* report.
Visit Stornoway Productions at www.stornoway.com for a list of titles.

TABLE OF CONTENTS

INTRODUCTION

No matter how we citizens feel or think about government, it is the most important institution in our lives, affecting what we earn, what we buy, how we are educated — virtually everything we do. So how do we make government accountable to *us*? How do we monitor, for example, what it does with the money we pay into it in the form of taxes — $170 billion annually? Well, we elect members to represent us in Parliament to be our voice, our accountability instrument. But what happens when Parliament fails to hold the government to account? What happens when the very institution that is supposed to represent us becomes dysfunctional?

I did not begin this assignment by asking myself these questions. I approached the task of converting these television interviews into a text format with organizational detachment. And then something happened: I began to realize that the individuals interviewed here had an important message for every Canadian citizen. The relevance of Parliament is under threat; our collective voice is steadily becoming a whisper.

The essays in *A Call to Account* originated as hours of videotaped footage. This material was recorded between November 2000 and July 2001 for a series of television documentaries exploring governance. Many of the people featured in this book were interviewed a number of times during this period, and in many instances the material presented is a compilation of several interviews. These interviews contributed greatly to the insights Paul Kemp draws in his book *Does Your Vote Count?* However, as Kemp used only a portion of the transcripts, it is important to present them in their entirety, a resource of empirical data.

The people interviewed in *A Call to Account* are from all walks of public life — members of Parliament, Cabinet ministers, senators, journalists, lobbyists, advisors, civil servants and even a former prime minister. Their points of view are varied, but all come to the table with a passion to present their philosophies about governance and the country they serve. Our country.

This discussion should inspire even the least civic minded among us to examine and re-examine our government in terms of accountability. The citizens of Canada have an obligation to question, challenge and demand accountability of the representatives that they elect to govern. It is our duty and it is indeed our call.

Criss Hajek
April 2002

PART ONE

The Members of Parliament
— A View from the Trenches

Chapter 1
The Independent

JOHN NUNZIATA

John Nunziata established the law firm Nunziata, Anand and has enjoyed a prominent career in political life spanning over 20 years. He began at age 23 as an alderman in the City of York. In 1984 he was first elected to the House of Commons, as a Liberal MP representing York South–Weston. Mr. Nunziata held three consecutive terms as a Liberal MP. However, in 1996 he was expelled from the Liberal caucus for voting against the government's budget, and was forced to seek re-election to the House of Commons as an independent MP in the 1997 election. He was successful, earning a distinction achieved by only a few individuals since Confederation. He was defeated by less than 1,500 votes, losing in the 2000 election to Liberal Alan Tonks. He has served on numerous committees, boards and commissions, led a number of task forces and travelled extensively as a member of various Canadian delegations. Mr. Nunziata recently joined Mandrake, one of Canada's leading recruiting firms.

The following interview was conducted two weeks prior to the 2000 election.

TOPICS:
Life as an Independent MP
Team Player or Trained Seal: Life on the Back Bench
Concentration of Power
Plurality and Rewards
Electioneering
Getting Elected Versus "Doing the Right Thing"
Effectiveness as an Independent
Delivering the Goods Outside the Government
Reaction to "Vote-Buying"
Reflections on Leaving the Government Back Bench

Life as an Independent MP

It's those encounters; those brief encounters over the years that came together in the last election and that allowed me to win as an independent. I feel good about it. People understand the process. They refer to me as a fighter.

They like what I did with Jean Chrétien when I told him that he tried to hoodwink the people of Canada in 1993 by promising to scrap the GST. People have long memories. They remember and I'm hearing a lot of thank yous. People are saying, "Thank you for all the great work you've done for the community and for us personally."

Team Player or Trained Seal: Life on the Back Bench

People know who I am and they know that I have a track record of speaking out on their behalf. I'm not going to be a trained seal in Ottawa. I'm not going to be silent on the back bench. People are so fed up with the political parties and the leaders that they want someone who is going to be their representative. They know that, as my slogan says, "I'm going to do what's right."

"Team" is code for a trained seal and synonymous with team-trained seal. My opponent has said he's going to toe the party line and kiss Mr. Chrétien's ring when he's required to do so. He will bow down and do all the things necessary to be a good little MP in order to be in the good books, so that he might get on the right committee. If being a team player means being a trained seal and an irrelevant government backbencher, then who wants to be one?

Concentration of Power

The fact is, there is no team in Ottawa. When you're on the government side, power is concentrated in the hands of half a dozen people, half of whom are not elected. All the power rests with the Prime Minister's Office and everything else is window-dressing. Pierre Trudeau referred to MPs as nobodies 50 yards off the Hill and Mr. Chrétien has turned MPs into nobodies, even his MPs, right on the floor of the House of Commons.

I think the role of government members is understood. I remind you again of what Pierre Trudeau said: MPs are nobodies. Until we change the power structure in Ottawa, until we take power away from the non-elected people in the Prime Minister's Office, until we take it away from Eddie Goldenberg and Jean Pelletier and the power corporation within the Prime Minister's Office, we will continue to have a system that's very severely flawed, undemocratic and dictatorial.

Half a dozen people run this country, half of whom are non-elected. That's the reality. Everything else is, as I said, window-dressing. So for anyone to suggest that Cabinet ministers or lowly members of Parliament have any influence, that's nonsense. I've been there, I've been in opposition, and I've been in government.

Caucus meetings are nothing more than giant focus groups where MPs come to Ottawa. It's a bitch session for MPs. They can complain and they can squawk but ultimately the leader makes the decision. Decisions are taken in advance. I can't tell you the number of initiatives the government took without reference to the caucus when I was in the government caucus. MPs would read about these initiatives in the newspapers or see them on television even before there was any discussion whatsoever. So as far as influence is concerned, it's all phony influence. The only people that have influence are these half a dozen people.

Let's take the budget, for example. Government members see the budget for the first time when everyone else sees it, when Peter Mansbridge and Mike Duffy see it. That's the first time they see the budget, and in terms of having influence, they don't have any more influence than any other citizens' group that might bring forward their concerns. They can express their concerns at caucus but the government listens more to the opposition than they do to their own government members. They're very sensitive to the headlines every day and to what the opposition is saying.

Plurality and Rewards

I can't help but chuckle at what's happening in the United States with regard to their election. We have a worse system in Canada than the Electoral College system in the United States. In the 1997 election, 62 percent of those who voted, voted against the Liberals. So Jean Chrétien, with 38 percent of the popular vote, has 100 percent of the power. That's hardly an expression of the will of the people.

He exercises that power in a dictatorial fashion, punishing MPs that don't toe the party line. We all know what happens. If you're not a good boy, or a good little girl, then instead of going on one of the more sexy committees, like the justice committee or the finance committee or foreign affairs, you're put on the library committee. If you're not a good little boy or girl, you're not going to go on any foreign trips and you're not going to get invited to 24 Sussex for a state visit. In other words, MPs are punished if they don't toe the party line. I know that. I've been there, done that and got the T-shirt.

Electioneering

I found it interesting that Brian Tobin, my old buddy, came to the riding last week arguing that they need a team player, that they need someone in the caucus room presumably in order to be able to deliver something. Now here's a man who is a good buddy of Jean Chrétien and formerly a friend of mine until his visit. He sat around the Cabinet table, yet under his watch they devastated Atlantic Canada with the EI (employment insurance) cuts. I mean, what hypocrisy. He couldn't convince the prime minister not to make those horrible, devastating cuts. As a result, they lost dozens of seats in Atlantic Canada in the 1997 election.

In politics, I've come to learn that you never know who your friends are. Brian Tobin refused to debate with me, which is quite astounding. Brian Tobin, a great orator, the great debater, the great saviour, refused to debate. Captain Canada was afraid to talk about the health cuts that the Liberal government made. He was afraid to talk about the little influence he had when Jean Chrétien decided to eviscerate Atlantic Canada as far as the EI payments were concerned. There was a lot of press coverage that followed.

Getting Elected Versus "Doing the Right Thing"

There are two different responsibilities as an MP. A huge part of the job is the constituency work, where each of us becomes an ombudsman for our constituents. We deal with constituency problems, whether it is immigration or EI or helping with pensions or helping with government-related problems. I take the approach that if they come to me for help, whether it's provincial, municipal or federal, I'm there to try to sort their problems out, try to point them in the right direction. So that's a big responsibility.

I represent about 110,000 people from all different walks of life and nations and countries. It's an interesting group of people: people that I grew up with, people I trained as a hockey or baseball coach, people I went to school with at Rockcliffe or Runnymede Collegiate, people that have been involved in politics, all kinds of different people. I think my relationship with the community is pretty close. I can walk down a street and know people by name or I can go into a local shopping plaza and people certainly know who I am.

As far as being a representative, I consider it my legal and moral responsibility to represent the people of this riding in Ottawa — not the reverse. My responsibility is not to sell government policy to the riding or to simply be another vote in order to ensure that the government gets its way on every piece of legislation. My view has always been that where the best interests of the riding conflict with the position of the political party, the riding's views should always lead the way.

We know that that doesn't happen generally. Being outside of the party system and in the House of Commons, I can do that very simply. As an independent I have far more power than a government back-bencher. I can ask questions in the House of Commons virtually when I want — and very rarely the set-up questions that government members often ask.

I've asked more questions in the House of Commons than all the Toronto MPs combined. I mean the tough questions, holding the government accountable on issues like the Human Resources Development Canada(HRDC) scandal, child pornography, the hepatitis C issue, poverty in Toronto, homelessness in Toronto, the waterfront issue in Toronto. I consider that to be pretty powerful. The freedom, in order to be a true representative of the people in the riding, is pretty significant.

Effectiveness as an Independent
I'm pretty damn effective as an independent. I can focus public attention on issues. I have a national media profile, which means that when

I go to bat for a particular group or organization, the media reports on it. I ask people, when I do radio interviews, to call their members of Parliament so I can focus public attention and build the pressure.

When you look at the government's moves with regard to reforming the criminal justice system, I think it's because people like me and others have moved the agenda. The Canadian Police Association has endorsed me and the readers of NOW magazine voted me the best MP in Toronto three years running. Obviously I'm effective and people see it.

Delivering the Goods Outside the Government

If it's a question of delivering democracy and delivering representation, then I'm doing it in spades. A government member will never be able to deliver that. You're talking about government money. York South–Weston is one of the better-funded ridings in all of Toronto.

The fact is, the system today is much different than it was, especially in Ontario under the Trudeau years, where every minister was given a pot of money to distribute to government supporters and government members. Now it's done very fairly; it's done on a per capita basis, whether it's HRDC funding, summer student funding or all the economic development funding. I have organizations in this riding, such as the Learning Enrichment Foundation that receives millions of dollars a year. The Black Creek Business Development Association is another example.

The bureaucrats know that if I'm not treated fairly here in York South–Weston, they're going to see it on the news that night or read about it in the newspapers. We're dealt with fairly and that's all I'm asking. I go flat out for my constituents and I deliver. I can give you a list of all the different organizations that have been funded in the last three and a half years and you can compare them to all the other different ridings. It also begs the question, as Metro chairman and as the mayor of the City of York, what did Alan Tonks ever deliver to this area? A big, fat goose egg. If anything, he's failed at all his attempts to deliver, whether it's at the Greater Toronto Services Board or at Metro Council or as mayor of the City of York.

Reaction to "Vote-Buying"

I think it's a turn-off. It happens in Atlantic Canada and it happens to a certain degree in Western Canada. It happens in the prime minister's riding. But for as many voters as it may attract in a particular locale, it turns off a whole lot of other people because they know that the government is trying to buy votes with their money. It's not that way in Toronto.

The prime minister promised a few dollars for the waterfront redevelopment, but that's pretty general. That's not going to deliver votes. What it's going to do is keep (Toronto mayor) Mel Lastman quiet. As far as building a courthouse in a particular riding or some riding-specific money, it just doesn't happen. Those days are gone, as far as Toronto and Ontario are concerned. If they tried to deliver based on riding-by-riding representation, they would get absolutely hammered by the people in this region.

Reflections on Leaving the Government Back Bench

It was kind of strange to get booted. I was one of only 40 Liberal MPs in 1984 that was elected. Together with Brian Tobin, Sheila Copps and Jean Chrétien, we helped rebuild the party. And I remember Brian Mulroney saying the Liberal Party was dead. I received a fax a few days after I voted against the budget from Jean Chrétien saying that I was no longer a part of the caucus. It hurt, but in politics the highs are incredibly high and the lows are incredibly low. And justice ultimately is done. One of the lows was the day I received the fax kicking me out of the caucus, but the high was on June 2, 1997, when I beat the Liberal Party. I beat Jean Chrétien when the people of this riding said, "John, what you did was right. You're our representative, we want you to represent us in Canada." I was the only independent elected in Canada and that was one of the incredible highs in my career.

Since then I've been on a continual high because I've been able to go where the spirit takes me and where my constituents want me to go. I feel that I've been part of a very unique democratic exercise here in the riding of York South–Weston and people seem to like it. This time around I hope to carry on. People of this riding like what I've been doing. I have a track record. It's not as if I'm coming from left field.

Chapter 2
The New Democratic Party

BILL BLAIKIE

Bill Blaikie was first elected to the House of Commons in 1979 and has been re-elected six times. He has served as the NDP social policy and health critic, the NDP member on the Special Parliamentary Task Force on Federal-Provincial Fiscal Arrangements and as chair of the federal NDP caucus from 1983 to 1984 and from 1993 to 1996. From 1993 to 2001 he was the NDP international trade critic, and has been House leader since 1995. He is also the critic on intergovernmental affairs and has taken on new responsibilities as the NDP justice critic.

TOPICS:
A History and Present View of MP Political Frustration
Committees and House Votes: The "Party Line" Must End
Committees and the Media
The Power of the Prime Minister
Powers Outside Parliament
The Media
The McGrath Committee

The Changing Role of MPs
Guardians of the Public Purse
Why Won't Parliamentary Reform Happen?

A History and Present View of MP Political Frustration
There is a long-running frustration for members of Parliament that goes back to the 1980s and before. Members of Parliament do not have the power that the people who elect them think they have, or think they should have. There have been various attempts at parliamentary reform, to try to give individual members of Parliament more power as individuals, and collectively as members of committees.

We need to transfer some of the power now concentrated in the Prime Minister's Office to ordinary members on both sides of the House. Members need to be free of the various structures that prevent them from having the kind of say that constituents would like them to have. We also need to enable the committees to function more independently. We are mainly talking about freeing up government backbenchers because opposition MPs are already free to criticize the government. We want government backbenchers to be less constrained by the kind of party discipline that has made the Canadian parliamentary system so rigid.

At the moment I am involved in a special committee of the House, comprised of the House leaders, called the "modernization committee." It may well produce some good results but the very name "modernization" points to the fact that government is more interested in process and efficiency and less in the redistribution of power in Parliament. So I don't really expect that what will come out of it will address the heart of the matter.

The real goal of parliamentary reform, or at least anything that is worthy of the name, should be to address the lack of power on the part of the members. It should seek to redistribute power within Parliament. I am confident that the modernization committee, which operates by unanimous consent, will make some valuable recommendations. However, I don't think it will be able to address those substantial issues of redistribution of power.

Committees and House Votes: The "Party Line" Must End
Committees are charged with examining legislation. They should have the power to amend the legislation and not just sit there taking orders

from the minister, or for that matter, having the minister take his or her orders from the bureaucracy. If the majority of members of a committee, including the Liberals, thought there were problems in a piece of legislation, they should agree to make appropriate changes. Instead we have a situation where the government says, "No, that is not a problem and we will not fix it. And it will be passed exactly as is, thank you very much."

It would be a breath of fresh air if, in the case of public uproar, legislation could be defeated because members of Parliament say, "No, my constituents don't like that. And I don't like that. And I'm not voting for it." I think people would drop dead in the streets. They'd be so surprised. That is what people understand as a democracy: at some point members of Parliament can actually hold the government to account.

If the government always wins, if the government always gets its way, it starts to look like an elected dictatorship. That is how a lot of people feel about our current system. It is like a dictatorship in which one gets to choose another dictator every four years.

Committees and the Media
When I got to Parliament in 1979, there was considerably more scrutiny in terms of the committee having an opportunity to question the Cabinet ministers. The ministers spent more time there than they do now and committees were covered more. There was always someone from the Canadian Press sitting in committee. I think in some ways TV coverage has been hard on that kind of scrutiny because real scrutiny doesn't lend itself to a 30-second clip. Reporting a prolonged dialogue between a member and a Cabinet minister is more suitable for print media. There was more of that 20 years ago than there is today.

The kinds of problems that I am talking about have been around for a long time. Trudeau centralized a lot of power in the Prime Minister's Office and members of Cabinet began to have less power to do things on their own. They had to consult with Cabinet committees and endure endless processes. One could no longer, for example, as minister of immigration, just make a decision. One had to clear it through various Cabinets and that's how things started to bog down. The consequences are that one feels like just a kind of prop keeping the show going, or like the clothes on the emperor. We are all democratic clothes on the emperor.

The Power of the Prime Minister

Power has been leaking out of Parliament for years in various ways and we MPs are really fighting over the scraps. The fact is, the prime minister has most of what is left.

The prime minister has an awful lot of power. He makes all the appointments and everything runs through the Prime Minister's Office. It is just human nature for people on the government side, in particular, to look over their shoulder and guard against making a move that would end their career. What we are looking for is to create a new parliamentary culture. Working with the existing rules can only take you so far. Procedurally you can lead members through the waters of freedom but you can't make them drink, can you? However, you can try changing the rules to change the parliamentary culture so that more of this kind of freedom occurs. Or could occur.

The reward system certainly works properly in the view of Prime Minister Chrétien. He came up through this system himself. He played the game and played it well. If you can't play it as well as he does, then that's your problem. I don't think it's a very healthy game. We need reform inside the House of Commons to redistribute power.

So this sense of powerlessness that members of Parliament have is related not just to the fact that they themselves have so little power, but also to the fact that Parliament itself has too little power because of the way it has been abdicated. This is the larger democratic issue that parliamentary reform needs to tackle if it is really going to get to the root of the frustration members and the public feel about politics.

Powers Outside Parliament

We need reform outside the House of Commons because all the power that used to be in Parliament is no longer there. There is the power of free trade agreements, the bureaucracy, the courts and the first ministers' conferences.

Take a look at my caucus colleague Judy Wasylycia-Leis from Winnipeg North Centre. She is not a government backbencher so she is not taking orders from the prime minister. She has the freedom that opposition members of Parliament have. But all of us, no matter who we are in the opposition, are constrained by the fact that Parliament has limited control because of things like trade agreements.

For example, Judy is the health critic and she would like to have a different policy with respect to the availability of generic drugs. That's not a matter for Parliament anymore; that's a matter for the World Trade Organization. So we are all faced with those kinds of restraints. We are also faced with the fact that our colleagues, the people we are talking to, the people that we are debating with, are not free agents because of the political party system, so it doesn't matter whether you persuade them. You can persuade them all you like. If you can't persuade the people who tell them what to do, you haven't persuaded anybody.

The Media

To add to the problems, the wrong things in Parliament fascinate the media. If someone does constructive work, that is pretty boring stuff compared to what's happening in the leadership races of the various political parties. When people call each other names in the House of Commons and are nasty to each other, the media are always there end-lessly rewarding the wrong behaviour. It's just another problem that we as members of Parliament have.

The McGrath Committee

The role of Parliament hasn't changed. It was weak in the 1980s, it was weak in the 1990s and it's weak now in this new century. What we were trying to do with the McGrath Committee in the mid-1980s was strengthen the independence of individual backbenchers and strengthen the power of the House against the Cabinet, the executive and the prime minister. We were trying to strengthen the role of individual members by strengthening committees, giving more independence to members collectively and individually. We've had very little progress in that. A few things have happened. There are more private members' bills that come to a vote and are sometimes passed, but by and large the committees are as much under the thumb of the government as they ever were. In fact, in some cases it's worse.

The Changing Role of MPs

Some members are more interested in the accountability and spending side, others are more interested in the policy side and some are interested in the advocacy side, in other words, going to bat for various disadvantaged groups or individuals.

I think there's more on the advocacy side now and less on the accountability and policy side. There is more playing of the ombudsman because people search for meaning in their lives and if the meaning is removed over here, it has to pop up somewhere else. The other way people search for meaning in their political lives, unfortunately, is through publicity. So publicity becomes an end in itself. Rather than publicity that comes from doing a particularly good job on an issue, publicity becomes an end in itself around here and the media are always happy to play that game. Unfortunately the media most often rewards the wrong kind of behaviours.

Guardians of the Public Purse

One of the roles of a member of Parliament is to act as a guardian of the public purse. It's the spending and taxing aspect of the job. It's also a question of policy. What is the government spending? Is it spending it wisely or not? There is also the policy aspect. What is the government doing to address various problems?

Before my time, in 1969, the House of Commons did hold the government to account for spending. That's when they used to decide to refer all the main spending estimates to the committees and put a deadline on when those estimates would be reported out of committee.

But now, when committees are under the thumb of government, then the spending of government is very hard to examine in a truly investigative way because it's the committees to which the spending estimates are referred.

It's extremely difficult to use committees in the way that they ought to be used, to really give the government a hard time in the sense of scrutinizing government activity both on the expenditure side and on the policy side.

Why Won't Parliamentary Reform Happen?

People who have power like to keep it. That's what stands in the way of all kinds of reform. It stands in the way of economic reform, social reform and parliamentary reform. Very seldom do you see people who exert power over other people willing to give it up. That kind of power could disappear tomorrow if the Liberal back bench (or the government back bench) was willing to take chances and live courageously. But that's not happening.

JUDY WASYLYCIA-LEIS

Judy Wasylycia-Leis has served as deputy chair of the NDP caucus since she was first elected to the House of Commons in 1997. She is currently NDP spokesperson for citizenship and immigration, health, status of women and seniors. Prior to elected office in Ottawa, she worked as executive assistant to federal NDP leader Ed Broadbent and was co-ordinator of the premier's secretariat and of the executive council policy group for Manitoba premier Howard Pawley. She also worked as the co-ordinator of the Women's Directorate in the Manitoba government. She was first elected to the Manitoba legislature in 1986 as the MLA for the constituency of St. Johns. In April 1986 she was appointed to Cabinet, where she served as minister of culture, heritage and recreation. In 1988 she became the NDP critic for family services and the status of women. After the 1990 election she served as the NDP health critic and NDP deputy leader.

TOPICS:
Politics in Her Blood
Her Role as a Back-Bench Minority Opposition MP

The NDP Voice in Parliament: "The Fourth Party"
Using Private Members' Bills to Promote Change
"Trained Seals" on the Liberal Back Bench
And They Call It Democracy
The Committee System
The Need for Parliamentary Reform
A Paternalistic Government
The Concerns of Her Constituency
Do People Vote for Her or Her Party?
Is It Worth It?

Politics in Her Blood

Politics consumes my life. I started my political life as a parliamentary intern, working as the women's organizer for the federal NDP. I worked for Ed Broadbent (former NDP leader) and for Howard Pawley, the NDP premier of Manitoba, in the 1980s. I ran for the Manitoba legislature three times back then and was elected in 1986. I became a provincial Cabinet minister in 1988 and I was re-elected as third-party opposition in 1990. Then I started into federal politics.

The hardest part of the job is juggling family responsibilities in Winnipeg with a crazy schedule of commuting to Ottawa every week. I don't know if many people appreciate just how many demands there are on our time. It means no time for me as a person. My whole life is devoted to the political work in Ottawa and my constituency, and through all of this, still trying to be a good mom.

When the House of Commons is sitting I'm back home every weekend, returning Thursday or Friday and then back to Ottawa on Sunday night. I used to take a direct flight Monday morning, but Air Canada cut back and now I fly Sunday night, which cuts into my family time. If I'm flying, I'm worrying — get this done, get my suitcase packed, make these calls, get over there, do that. It's too bad.

I have two children, both quite young. My older boy has a major disability and requires care and attention around the clock. That poses an extra challenge for me and my husband, who really has the lion's share of the work when I'm in Ottawa. We manage because I have a wonderful husband and good care and support in the neighbourhood. If I have to leave Parliament for a week because my child is in the hospital, then so be it, people understand. It hasn't been easy, but that is how life is.

It's a good thing that I've been a politician all the time I've been married. We've been married 28 years, so it's just been part of our lives. I imagine if this were new, it would be very difficult for any relationship. But thank God, Ron, my husband, has understood it.

Her Role as a Back-Bench Minority Opposition MP
I am in politics because I believe government has a role to play in ensuring that the wealth of the nation is shared and that everybody is able to participate in conditions of equality. I see my job as fighting for investment in programs that will create some security in people's lives and give them a chance of equal participation in society.

I see my job in government as two-fold. I have to keep fighting for systemic change, for the federal government to be involved in housing programs, social service supports and health initiatives. But at the same time I have to convince them that those programs won't succeed unless they work hand in hand with communities like Winnipeg North Centre and their organizations.

I can be effective whether in government or in opposition: what's required is that an MP be prepared to acknowledge and support the community's efforts and work.

Half of an MP's role is to empower people. If I can give people a voice so that their concerns are recognized and translated into action, I will have done my job. The other half is to demand that government be involved in the redistribution of wealth so that there is equality between communities and so that places like Winnipeg North Centre are not abandoned and left to fare on their own.

I think people have noticed that I have been busy over the last three and a half years. I think they see me as a very loud voice in Parliament and they value that. I take nothing for granted because the political situation is so volatile. Good incumbents and traditional strongholds don't mean anything if there is a move in an entirely different direction. I was a victim of that when I ran federally in 1993, when a good strong seat like this one went Liberal because people voted to get rid of the PC Party.

As an opposition member, I have more chances to stand up and fight for my constituents. I can question the government and present ideas at the committee level. I can hold the government to account for its failure to represent people in my riding. There are frustrations, the pace of change is slow, but I know that I can eventually get through to the government and make a difference.

I got re-elected with a bigger majority than ever because I am seen as a fighter and a scrapper, and that's what I'll continue to be. I'm going to be a louder voice than ever because the Speaker is far away from us and it is going to be hard to get noticed.

The NDP Voice in Parliament: "The Fourth Party"

We are the fourth party in a hierarchy of five, with only 13 members. We get few opportunities to ask questions and debate the issues. The more members we have, the more effective we can be. I am definitely feeling stretched to the limit because I have four critic areas and two very active committees.

Despite our small numbers, NDP MPs do two vital things. First, we give voice to people whose voices would not otherwise be heard, and thereby validate their concerns and empower them to keep acting and changing society. Second, we can influence the government and slow down their agenda — which is moving so fast in a right-wing corporate global direction — and we can actually make a few changes.

I wish I had more chances to hold the government to account. We have five parties in Parliament and share time on a prorated basis. We just have to use every opportunity we can.

I keep reminding myself that if we had not been there, many issues in Parliament would not have been on the agenda. When the banks talked about merging and becoming monster banks, you can be sure Paul Martin would not have halted the proposal had the NDP not objected. We may not change the banks' minds overnight, but we can get changes to legislation, try to force the banks to give some commitment back to the community, and we can advocate alternatives like credit unions. It's a combination of working within Parliament for legislative change and working within communities to generate new ideas.

We have fought to get the government to reinvest in housing. Despite all the rhetoric, in *Red Book III* there isn't a single mention of restoring the money needed for co-operative or social housing. I have spent three and a half years as virtually the only voice in Parliament on health care. Until the eve of an election this government did not take the issue seriously.

In my riding today, an NDP voice in Parliament is about the best bang for your buck. The issues we push are not part of the government agenda nor are they Liberal priorities. Without the NDP pressuring government, we will see no movement at all. We have been able to force the government — kicking and screaming — to take a few steps in the right direction. We have seen some health-care money restored and some progress on education — no comprehensive plan, but at least something.

We have also been able to forestall a pretty right-wing agenda when it comes to global trade, the export of water and environmental protection. Our presence has been critical for allowing the full range of issues to get on the agenda and for people's voices from Winnipeg North Centre to be heard in Parliament. If the NDP didn't have a critical mass in Parliament, those issues would not be raised. I know from talking to colleagues who were in Parliament before 1997, when we didn't have official party status and we couldn't speak in the House, that we had very few opportunities to get our message out.

Using Private Members' Bills to Promote Change

We can also express our constituents' will in private members' bills, motions and petitions. The last thing we want is for people to feel so helpless and cynical that they say, "What's the point?" We have our own agenda, we have our own priorities and we intend to pursue justice and equality in that context; if people see the government acting on that level, they will see that there is in fact a purpose to participating in the democratic process.

The more an issue is presented to the government, the more it gets noticed. When people send letters and faxes and e-mails, government has to pay attention because they are an indication of public opinion. Private members' motions may not have a hope in heck of ever becoming law, but they matter because they can actually inspire the government to steal the ideas and incorporate them into their own legislation. We may get no credit for the end result, but what's important is planting the seeds that eventually bear fruit.

I never give up, I never despair. I do get discouraged. There are days when I feel like I am not making a difference. There are days when the pace of change is glacial. I wonder if it's worth all this juggling, my family being back in Winnipeg and me being here. But every day there's evidence I'm making a difference in someone's life.

"Trained Seals" on the Liberal Back Bench

My frustration as an opposition backbencher is surely nothing compared to the frustration of a Liberal backbencher — a voting machine following the dictates of the prime minister and his office. I am in a better position to represent my riding than if I were a trained seal on the Liberal back bench. I have more freedom in the opposition. But in many ways our jobs are similar and we all have to find ways to influence an agenda that is pretty much set.

I have watched Liberals begin their term in Parliament saying, "I'm going to fight to eradicate poverty, fight for the compensation of hepatitis C victims and fight for the homeless," but in the end their hands are tied because of government policy and a very tight voting structure.

I have talked to Liberal backbenchers who are frustrated because they get instructions on how to act, how to vote, what to say, where to go. Jean Chrétien cracks the whip. He doesn't allow for dissension within ranks or different views, and he certainly doesn't make room for an agenda that speaks to the needs of working people and families.

I see how little influence Liberal backbenchers have had in speaking up for the kinds of issues that are of primary concern in my riding. It doesn't matter whether an MP is on the government or the opposition side, but the way our system is now structured and the way the prime minister dictates the agenda, there is not much a Liberal backbencher can do for an area like Winnipeg North Centre.

And They Call It Democracy

I have noticed a big change in the democratic process over the last several years. I see MPs and Parliament being increasingly disregarded, and I think there has been a deliberate attempt to circumvent democratic institutions.

My biggest concerns are decisions made in the Prime Minister's Office and decisions made at the level of the unelected World Trade Organization which are never brought before Parliament. The global corporate forces have such a powerful agenda that this prime minister and this government are prepared to sacrifice democracy and bypass Parliamentary representation.

I saw a whole number of critical bills come before Parliament, and just when the debate was getting interesting, just when people started to provide input and have an impact on the issues, the prime minister brought in closure. He shut down the debate and forced the bill through Parliament. If it is in our country's interest to get people more involved in politics and more concerned about losing our democratic values, then the prime minister is not helping the cause.

The Committee System

I feel good about being part of the committee process, proposing amendments and getting them on the record. Some amendments actually get approved, yet one of my biggest disappointments in Parliament is the committee system. I was told that this would be the one place to get beyond partisanship and to develop good public policy for Canadians. It doesn't work that way. The party lines are clearly drawn and the government cracks the whip. Our powers are very limited

For the last three and a half years I have been frustrated with the health committee because it has been totally controlled by the government and we're unable to set an agenda based on the concerns of the people. We have a minister of health who comes in and tells us what our priorities are. Do you think the health-care crisis is on the agenda? Do you think the future of medicare is on the agenda? Not a chance. This is a good indication of how dysfunctional Parliament has become. I think there is now enough dissatisfaction that we can demand changes. MPs from all parties are now talking about this. It affects us all.

The Need for Parliamentary Reform

Voters understand that Parliament is dysfunctional. They understand it when they tell the government that their number-one issue is health care and it's nowhere to be seen or heard on the agenda. They understand it in basic democratic terms. If the vast majority of Canadians feels this way, why is health care missing from the budget-making process and the legislative agenda?

As people see the gap between their concerns and the government's agenda, they will demand change at the parliamentary level. One way to achieve it is to grant the committees more power to set the agenda. Talk to Canadians in their workplaces, homes and coffee shops, and allow time and space for feedback from constituents, instead of making a decision behind the scenes and laying it on the line.

In order to restore the people's confidence in the public process, critical parliamentary changes have to be made. MPs and committees of the House need to have a greater role. Parliament is not functioning the way it should. The system has become so dictatorial and autocratic, so many decisions are made outside of Parliament, that people are looking for easy, simplistic solutions like the Reform Party's referenda and recall of MPs, instead of addressing the root of the problem and reforming Parliament. If we actually forced Parliament to give more power to committees, it would make a difference.

A Paternalistic Government

As an MP I have to overcome the paternalistic "we know what's best for you" approach. I have to convince government that communities themselves know what's good for them. They have ideas about what will work, and the role of government is to support those initiatives, not to neglect communities or to dictate to them. This requires fundamental change, and that's not easy. We are trying to turn around the whole decision-making process. Government is used to deciding what is best.

The way to go is to follow the self-help model of community development: empower those who want to make a difference. Solutions have to come from communities themselves. They have to identify their problems, put supports in place to help individuals and express their uniqueness. Government involvement alone is not enough to sustain a diverse community like this one. If initiatives do not come from the ground up and we do not work hand in hand with organizations like the North End Community Renewal Corporation, then we will not succeed. Governments don't create community. Community comes from associations and individuals and organizations working together to find solutions to some very serious problems.

The Concerns of Her Constituency

My riding is unique. In Winnipeg North Centre we have deep-rooted problems of poverty and homelessness, people on social assistance, people dealing with enormous difficulties and barriers. We have a very large Aboriginal population, a very culturally diverse area, an area that has a long history of self-sufficiency, which has been lost over a period of time as businesses and people have moved out. We are in a process now of trying to renew the community, and that will not come from a handout from government. There's an expression — if you give a family a fish, it'll feed them for a day. Teach a family to fish, you'll feed them for a lifetime.

This area is absolute proof that the Liberal government has missed the boat when it comes to people's priorities: food banks tripling in the last 10 years, the price of homes dropping astronomically, housing stock deteriorating all around us. These are prime examples of what happens when a government abandons its responsibility for providing a social safety net. We are suffering. People have been hit hard. They don't have the support even to get by on a day-to-day basis, never mind dream the big dreams and think about the wonderful opportunities that await us all.

I am hearing from people about the fundamentals of life — access to health care, education and housing. I sense a great deal of anxiety about the future. Will health care be there when I need it? What is the world coming to — all this technological change — what does this new economy mean for me? Will my kids have access to jobs and training opportunities? How can I plan for the future given the uncertainty? And I think they are looking for government and their representatives to say to them that it doesn't have to be like this.

Do People Vote For Her or Her Party?

I am not torn between my identity as an MP and as a lifelong New Democrat because the policies and philosophy of the NDP are in sync with the issues and concerns of the people of Winnipeg North Centre. Some people say that we are trying to create public opinion when we focus on health care and education and housing, but in fact we *are* the public opinion. These are the number-one issues in this constituency. There is absolute confidence in our approach.

The voters here vote for the NDP, for a set of ideas, values and a direction that will help this area. But they also count on a representative who is outspoken and active. I don't think that I would be able to hold on to this seat unless I was clearly a part of the community and vigorously pursuing their issues.

If I feel that a policy has not been developed to the fullest, I may sometimes disagree with a majority decision of our caucus, but I am a team player and I work for change within the party. Usually the party evolves to meet the changing needs of a community like this one.

Is It Worth It?

It's a rare accomplishment, but I actually succeeded in getting a motion passed by Parliament. I had a private member's motion that called for warning labels on all alcoholic beverage containers to tell pregnant women not to drink because of the risk of fetal alcohol syndrome.

How did I succeed? I started working on it four years ago. First I introduced the motion, then worked with community groups back in Winnipeg. I sought support from the other parties in Parliament, then put out notices and got the community to back it 100 percent. After all that work MPs felt that it was a good idea and they had to support it. It got almost unanimous support in Parliament. It gives me a sense of accomplishment to have actually effected some change in this place.

I am in politics to give a voice to people who are struggling daily and who feel unsupported while trying to be all things to all people.

One of the greatest joys in the job has been knowing that from my example other people, especially women, see that it is possible to get involved themselves. Although there is enormous pressure to be a perfect role model and to try to be a superwoman, people understand that if I can do it so can they. It is challenging and difficult, but also rewarding. I am lucky in many ways and feel it is an enormous privilege to have this position.

ALEXA MCDONOUGH

A lexa McDonough earned a Bachelor of Arts degree from Dalhousie University in Halifax in 1965 and a master's degree at the Maritime School of Social Work in 1967. She became the first woman to lead a recognized political party in Canada upon her election as leader of Nova Scotia's New Democrats in 1980. She was re-elected to the House of Assembly in 1984, 1988 and 1993 and was elected leader of the New Democratic Party of Canada in October 1995. In 1997 she led the fight to re-establish official party status for the New Democratic Party in Parliament. She became the member of Parliament for Halifax in 1997 and was re-elected in the November 2000 general election.

TOPICS:
The Challenge for the NDP
Fixing Parliament
On MPs in General
On Judy Wasylycia-Leis

The Challenge for the NDP

For a small party like ours, with 13 members, it is very difficult to hold a government as arrogant as the Liberals to account. They are very arrogant about their massive majority. It is very difficult for us to hold the government to account when there are two other larger opposition parties, the Alliance and the Bloc, who share a pretty destructive objective. One wants to make sure that Canada doesn't work, that Confederation doesn't work, and that the federal government therefore isn't allowed to work. The other one wants to make sure that politics doesn't work. They are busy de-marketing politics, which leaves you wondering about their idea of democracy. But I have to say that despite all of these frustrations, I am privileged to have a caucus of 13 members, with people like Judy Wasylycia-Leis, who are not worn down and not defeated by the magnitude of the task. All it does is make us fiercer and perhaps all the more dogged and determined because of how big the task is.

There is no question that we face lots of limitations. We have far fewer opportunities to participate in Question Period and in parliamentary committees. But I think we use those opportunities well. We try to use them strategically. We have to be creative about how we get our messages out. We don't necessarily have the entire press gallery lined up to give us visibility and provide exposure for our point of view. But, as we often remind people, "Democratic" is our middle name for good reason. We believe seriously that we have to be connected to the grassroots. We have to be very clear about who we are here to represent. That means we just have to work doubly hard to keep in contact with people out there, in the real world, on the ground. A lot of times being on Parliament Hill doesn't feel much like the real world.

The federal New Democratic Party is now very much engaged in a major rethink. We need to do that. The reality is that at 13 seats we don't have the numbers. We don't have the influence. We don't have the resources that we know we need to get the job done. That job is to hold the government to account and to press for alternatives. Some of the best work of the New Democratic Party has come from persuading the government of the day that they were not responding to people's real needs and aspirations, and bringing enough political pressure to bear to force them to do so. So there is no question that we need to put everything on the table. We have to get out and really generate a great big lively debate about our future course. Policy, organization structures, strategies, tactics — all of these things are up for review. I feel very confident that what can come out of it is a much-invigorated social democratic party. We are going to do better in the future.

Fixing Parliament

I don't suppose there has ever been a time when Parliament has worked to everybody's satisfaction. No question about that. We do have many reasons why we need parliamentary reform. When a government that is so arrogant to begin with has such a massive majority, it's a huge problem. It's a problem to have a prime minister with such unfettered powers, almost unprecedented in other parliamentary arenas. It's a problem to not have more independence of committees. It's a problem that many Canadians feel that the vote they cast doesn't actually show up in the composition of Parliament. They don't hear their voice in Parliament because we have a first-past-the-post electoral system. Consequently people either tend to feel that they vote for the winning side and get represented or, increasingly and alarmingly, great numbers of people are not voting at all. We need a system of proportional representation, where every vote counts and every vote influences what the composition of Parliament will be.

I think all of these parliamentary and electoral reforms are very important. We have been trying to encourage discussion about them and gain support for them. But I think we also have to be realistic. They are not bread-and-butter issues for people. They are not the kind of issues that people around the breakfast table, when they are trying to figure out how to get through the day, are really focused on or really excited about. People are trying to get by, feed their families, educate their kids and get health care for their aging parents. So it's a special challenge to figure out how to get some leverage and some momentum behind those kinds of reforms, but I think they are nonetheless important.

On MPs in General

There are lots of jokes these days about how members of Parliament and politicians in general are trusted even less than whoever is thought to be at the bottom of the totem pole. I think it's a bum rap but I also understand it. Some of it starts with politicians who get elected to government saying they will do something, and then do the opposite and appear to be virtually unaccountable. I think many people are really fed up with governments that are unaccountable and with politicians who act cynically. The result from that, not surprisingly, is a lot of cynicism from the public. I think generally speaking you will find that most members of Parliament and most provincial members as well — I can say this from my experience provincially — go into public office because they think they can make a difference. And most of them work pretty hard.

On Judy Wasylycia-Leis

Judy WL, as we all know her affectionately, is a sparkplug. She's a bulldog. She is an energizer. She is also stubborn as a mule, and the government is discovering that. She never gives up. Her kind of persistence and dogged determination becomes so important, particularly for a small opposition party.

Her day is one great big juggling act. She has a heavy load from the point of view of her critic responsibilities, health being a top priority for Canadians and for this party. She has a long history of working on behalf of women. She was a women's organizer for the NDP 25 years ago when we first met, and she is very dogged now about her responsibilities as a status of women critic. She plays a key role as an officer of the caucus: she is deputy chair and a member of the executive team. She also plays a big role at the grassroots of the party, both in the context of her own riding in Manitoba and linking up people across the country. And all of these things are on top of her principal responsibility and commitment, which is to the voters of her riding who sent her here to Ottawa to represent them. As if that is not enough, she is very devoted to her young family back in Winnipeg. They can catch her on the phone several times a day and have a quick chat.

I'm sure some people say to her what they say to all of us, "How do you juggle all this? Doesn't being a member of Parliament make extraordinary, unreasonable demands?" But I think it's fair to say that Judy Wasylycia-Leis would be just as busy juggling in just as many crazy ways if she were doing another job. This is the job she took on with her eyes wide open, having originally been a parliamentary intern here, a staffer with a previous federal leader, an organizer with the federal party and a Cabinet minister in the Manitoba NDP government. She clearly had a very good understanding of what she was getting into and still jumped in with both feet, thank goodness.

LORNE NYSTROM

L orne Nystrom became the youngest member of Parliament in Canada's history at age 22. Re-elected eight times, he has served in Parliament for 29 years. His long career includes responsibilities as NDP deputy House leader, NDP critic for finance, employment, food and agriculture, trade, regional development and the Constitution, as well as chairing NDP task forces on employment and parliamentary reform. He is also the only member of the Privy Council from any of the four opposition parties. From 1993–1997 he ran a successful consulting firm involved in the political development of newly democratized countries. Mr. Nystrom speaks for various organizations in Canada and internationally. He is an advocate of the democratic reform of Parliament and of Canada's electoral system. He has recently released *Just Making Change*, a book which simplifies financial issues for the reading public.

TOPICS:
Electoral Change
Accountability and the Vote
Obstacles in Proportional Representation

Electoral Change

I am very involved in the movement toward electoral change. We have a national organization and Web site called Fair Vote Canada. I'm going across the country discussing and promoting the idea of proportional representation (PR). I also introduced a private member's bill to look at various forms of proportional representation that might be relevant to our federation. The bill calls for an all-party committee to look at proportional representation and, if they come to a consensus, bring it back to Parliament. If Parliament agrees with their consensus, then we would have a national referendum on a new PR system, as opposed to our current first-past-the-post system.

The reason we need electoral change is our current electoral system really distorts the results. The Parliament that people elect doesn't in any way reflect how people vote. We have a majority government now that was elected by a minority of the people. We had an election in Prince Edward Island about a year or so ago where the opposition got over 40 percent of the vote, but they only got one seat, while the government got 26. There was an election in British Columbia not so long ago where the opposition got more than 40 percent of the vote, but only got three seats, while the government got 76 seats. People are becoming cynical about the electoral system because it doesn't reflect how they vote. Too many people are wasting their votes or feel their votes don't count. If you had a mix of proportional representation in our system, then every vote would count and we'd not only have equality between citizens but the Parliaments we elect would better reflect how people feel.

Accountability and the Vote

One of the only mechanisms of accountability is the vote, which happens once every four years. Back in 1993 the Conservative Party came out of the election with only two seats nationwide. The Bloc Québécois had 54 seats and were the official Opposition, even though the Conservatives had a lot more votes than the Bloc Québécois. In the next Parliament the Alliance, or the Reform as they were called in those days, and the Conservatives each had about 19 percent of the votes, but the Conservatives got 20 seats and the Reform got 60 seats. In that same election campaign, the NDP and Bloc both had 11 percent of the votes, yet the NDP got 21 seats and the Bloc got 44.

Historically, we have had many, many provincial governments that were elected with fewer votes than the main opposition party. For example, Lucien Bouchard received fewer votes than Jean Charest did, but he won a majority government and the Liberal Party formed the Opposition. The same thing happened the last time the NDP won in British Columbia. All these distortions in the system indicate that we need a reformed voting system in this country. Most other countries in the world have a different system. We are one of only three countries in the world with a population of more than eight million people that uses the pure first-past-the-post system. It's only the United States, India and us. Even Britain has started to make a change. They have a blend of PR in the Northern Ireland Parliament, the Scottish Parliament and the Welsh Parliament. All MPs to Brussels in the European Union were elected through PR, and they're looking at the possibility of doing the same thing in Westminster in the next two or three years.

Back in March I was the host of a forum, I think probably the first forum in Ottawa, or certainly Parliament Hill, on proportionate representation. We had 70 or 80 people who came from across the country. It was interesting because while I sponsored the forum, it was co-chaired by Walter Robinson, the head of the Canadian Taxpayers Federation, a very conservative individual, and by Judy Rebick, who is a left-wing feminist, author and broadcaster. This issue cuts right across the political spectrum. It's not ideological in terms of political left and right. It's really a question of the outsiders looking in and trying to create a voting system that's more democratic, more inclusive, and empowers people. A voting system that has a blend of proportional representation. It's an idea that's accepted in almost every country in the world and we are just lagging so far behind.

Proportional representation improves accountability because it's an elected Parliament where everybody's vote is equal, everybody's vote counts and nobody's vote is wasted. It would also change voting patterns because many, many Canadians now vote for the lesser of two evils, and in doing so, I mean, you still get evil. If Canadians voted for their first choice, we'd have a different Parliament and we'd have different voting patterns across the country. In the system we have now people will often vote for Party A because they don't like Party B. They really want to vote for Party C, but think Party C can't win. You get all this strategic voting in the country. If everybody's vote had equal weight and everybody's vote counted for that four-year period of time, then the governments would be a lot more accountable. They'd all seem more accountable as well because you'd have more and more minority governments, forcing politicians to work together. When they're forced to work together, they have to be more accountable, otherwise you're going to have the whole thing fall apart.

So far they're just talking about reforming the House itself, they're not even touching the Senate. The existing Senate is, according to all the polls, supported by five percent of the people; 85 percent of the people either want to reform it, re-elect it or abolish it.

Obstacles in Proportional Representation

The obstacles to proportional representation in Canada are the politicians because the present system elected us and it's worked very well for those of us here. No incumbent prime minister, whether it's Jean Chrétien or someone else, is likely to bring in a PR system. The last time the politicians voted on PR was in 1923, a long time ago. My motion to consider this system was deemed votable last fall, but just before the vote was to be held Mr. Chrétien called the election, so there was no vote. We have to get this idea out amongst the people of Canada and have it as a sort of a popular idea. It has to be an issue amongst the public. Opposition parties have to buy into it. The NDP have, for the first time in a couple of years, voted at our national convention and passed the motion endorsing PR in principle. The Alliance Party is very close to doing the same thing. Joe Clark and the Conservatives are starting to think about it, the Bloc is thinking about it and we have some renegade Liberals thinking about it. Eventually, if there's public pressure, there'll be enough of a buildup so when we have a new government in power, or we have a minority Parliament or even a new prime minister with an existing party in a minority situation, there may be a change.

NDP Mini Caucus Meeting

During the course of production, Judy Wasylycia-Leis allowed our cameras in to tape an NDP caucus meeting. The following dialogue clearly shows the level of frustration many MPs face.

Chaired By: Judy Wasylycia-Leis
Attended By: Lorne Nystrom, Bill Blaikie, Wendy Lill, Dick Proctor, Peter Stoffer

Key Areas Covered: Lack of MP Power, Committee Criticism, Public Perception of MPs, Need to Engage Public

Reference Biographies:

Wendy Lill was elected as the member of Parliament for Dartmouth in 1997 and 2000. She is the NDP critic on culture and communications, and the spokesperson for the party on issues related to human rights and persons with disabilities. She has been nominated four times for the

Governor General's Literary Award for Drama. She is the past president of Integration Action Group, a provincial advocacy group for children with special needs; vice president (eastern) of the Playwrights Union of Canada; co-founder of the Eastern Front Theatre Company; and a member of the Writers' Federation of Nova Scotia.

DICK PROCTOR is the MP for Palliser (Saskatchewan) and has served in the House of Commons since 1997. He is the chair of the New Democratic Party caucus and critic for agriculture and agri-food, Canadian Wheat Board, Western Diversification, co-operatives and sports. He has a degree in journalism from Carleton University, and worked for newspapers in Toronto and Edmonton as well as for CBC Television. He has worked for two public sector trade unions and spent three years working in Mexico as a project planner on behalf of the Canadian Labour Congress.

PETER STOFFER was first elected MP in 1997 for the riding of Sackville–Musquodoboit Valley–Eastern Shore. Prior to election he worked with Canadian Airlines as the chief emergency warden, the health and safety representative and as a customer service leader. Peter has received a Community Service Award and an Award of Merit for Environmental Work from the Nova Scotia Department of the Environment. He was a guest of His Royal Highness Prince Philip at a dinner to recognize his fundraising work for the World Wildlife Fund of Canada. Peter is the federal NDP critic for fisheries and oceans, defence, veterans affairs, ACOA (Atlantic Canada Opportunities Agency) and regional and rural development.

NDP Caucus Meeting Transcript:

JUDY WASYLYCIA-LEIS:
Thanks a lot for agreeing to come together on short notice to discuss an issue that we've talked a lot about in the past, and Lorne has worked on a great deal in the past. That's parliamentary reform. We made a commitment in the election to address this. MPs from all parties are talking about it. There was a feeble reference in the Speech from the Throne to put a little more money toward research, which doesn't address the concerns we all have. What's the point of research if you can't do research

on what's important? We have to decide, as a caucus, what we want to focus on, in terms of parliamentary reform. For me the greatest frustration has been the committee system because I was told this would be a real opportunity to raise issues, but I feel that it's just a make-work project, and I don't have any ability to influence the agenda. I think the number of times closure has been used in the last little while is a problem. There is also the whole sense that we don't have much power as MPs and that so many decisions are being made in the PMO and outside of Parliament, whether it's free trade agreements or just the executive running the show. I think we have some big issues, and we need to figure out our strategy going into this session. Bill, you are probably the best person to give us some perspective on all of this.

BILL BLAIKIE:
You mentioned things being decided outside the House. Things are even announced outside the House. I'm told that Don Boudria announced this morning at the Press Club breakfast that an electronic voting system is going to be put in the House of Commons. This is the Liberal idea of reform. It may be a form of modernization, but it's not reform in the sense of trying to give more power to members, either individually or collectively on committees, and they just don't seem willing to put their own members who sit on committees beyond the reach of the party whip and empower them to work with opposition members. That's the key thing. You have to make it so that the government members on the committees can't be yanked if they start to have independent thoughts or critical faculties.

PETER STOFFER:
Which is what happened with Baker in the fisheries.[1]

BILL BLAIKIE:
That's right. They put in the goon squad and yank all the people who have now come to know something about the issue, and therefore know that the government policy is wrong, and then they put in a bunch of guys who don't know anything about fisheries. So this is the key: put people beyond the reach of the party whip. Not even the Alliance proposals call for that because they want to be able to yank their own members.

JUDY WASYLYCIA-LEIS:
What would that take? A rules change?

BILL BLAIKIE:
It would take what the McGrath Committee recommended in 1985, which is that if you're appointed to a committee, you're appointed to it for the life of the session or for the life of a Parliament, and if you are absent, the only way you can be replaced is if you appoint your own replacement. The whip doesn't appoint your replacement. So if you are pursuing a particular line of thought which is critical of the government, or perhaps a departure from your own party, you can appoint someone who will continue your line of thought and you're not subject to having the whip say, "All right, that person is being far too independent or knowledgeable. Let's yank him." That would be a key reform, if you ask me.

JUDY WASYLYCIA-LEIS:
What about electing the chair?

BILL BLAIKIE:
As long as there is a government majority, the chair would probably still be somebody from the government, unless there was somebody on the opposition side who really commanded the respect of everyone. If you had a truly free election, you could end up with some chairs being from the opposition. We did have that for a little while with the legislative committee. Another thing that flowed from the McGrath Committee, which has since been shelved, was to set up special legislative committees for legislation and leave the standing committees to do investigative and more reflective kind of work. The chairs of the legislative committees were chosen from a panel of chairs that included people from all parties. So we had NDP members, like Neil Young, who came to be known as a very good chair. That was scrapped, not because it didn't work in itself, but because there got to be so many committees. Legislative committees were meeting at the same time as standing committees; people had to be at two meetings at the same time, and it kind of collapsed.

DICK PROCTOR:
I must say, listening to Don Boudria's response to Joe Clark's speech last night, I'm very pessimistic that we're going to be in for any major

dose of parliamentary reform. I thought that Clark made an extremely evenhanded speech. He talked about what has happened in Parliament over the last three decades. He wasn't finger-pointing at the Liberals. He mentioned that Conservative governments had done this as well. And Boudria's response was entirely partisan, to get up and lambaste him in a very nasty, aggressive way for ills that the Conservatives had brought on to stall parliamentary reform. It seems to me that if that's the tenor and the tone, we're in for a long, slow ride to any meaningful reform.

LORNE NYSTROM:

I think, Judy, there are two things: there's electoral reform, and then parliamentary reform. On the electoral side we have to look at things like proportional representation. Every country in the world of more than three million people, except for us, India and the United States, has some semblance of proportional representation at this time.

Next look at the abolition of the unelected, undemocratic Senate. You can bring some of the checks and balances that the Senate is supposed to provide into the House by stronger committees, by giving committees the right to do more of your timetabling and to initiate legislation. If there is free election of chairs, it will occasionally result in an opposition chair, and if there is a free vote for the chair, you might get a better government chair. This is what we now have with the Speaker of the House. So we could call the precedent that we have in the House for electing a Speaker and elect the chairs of the committees.

The other big thing on the Parliament side is to take away some of the power of the executive and the prime minister. There is no democracy in the world that I know of where the prime minister or the president has so much power to make appointments — the head of the police, the head of the court, the whole court as a matter of fact, the head of the military, the head of every important federal institution in the country. In my opinion the prime minister should in many cases only nominate a person, and the relevant parliamentary committee should ratify or reject that decision. That way you force the prime minister or the minister to be more careful about who they suggest to head the CBC, or whatever it may be. In the case of the Supreme Court, there must also be some provincial input.

We need more than just electronic voting, which might expedite democracy or speed up the efficiency of democracy, but doesn't really reform the system.

JUDY WASYLYCIA-LEIS:

I really wonder then what we should focus on. What should our priority be in this whole pursuit of parliamentary reform, and what opportunities do we even have to advance the agenda?

BILL BLAIKIE:

The Standing Committee on House Affairs and Procedure is committed to a major reform of the standing orders — or rather a major review. Whether they're committed to a major reform, that might have been just wishful thinking on my part. But that is certainly one venue where we could make those kinds of arguments and I'm sure other people will as well. The task will be to make sure that this happens in a balanced way. Parliamentary reform should always come in a package. There are things that the government would like to see changed. There are things that the opposition would like to see changed. The problem is that since the mid-1980s the only kind of parliamentary reform we've had is what the government wanted fixed. Not only do they fix things that bother them, they also tend to take back aspects of previous packages that they now find irritating, and the opposition doesn't have that power. Parliamentary reform is a kind of risky business because you can give up things as part of a package and then find that five years down the road, the government takes back its part of the bargain and you don't have the power to do the same. I've seen that happen. Nevertheless, this review will be taking place, and we will be looking for that kind of balance. For instance, if the government wants to do away with this marathon voting, fair enough. It is kind of ridiculous. But then we need to have some means by which the power of the government to introduce and enforce time allocation and closure can be moderated. One of the things you can look at is giving the Speaker more power to say, "I'm sorry. We haven't had a good debate on that, Mr. Government House Leader. You can't do that yet." At Westminster and other parliaments there is precedence for a more activist and powerful Speaker.

JUDY WASYLYCIA-LEIS:

What would our priorities be? The committee system, the number of times that closure is used when we're debating a bill, the power in the PMO in terms of appointments to key bodies in this country — are those the three issues that we're focusing on? Obviously we have quite a different position from the Alliance, which focuses constantly on free votes, and as far as I'm concerned, that issue detracts from the real issues at hand, and I think we ought to be clear about what is meaningful reform.

LORNE NYSTROM:

I think the priority should be first of all to strengthen the parliamentary committee in order to restore a really meaningful role to a member of Parliament and give the committee more independence to initiate legislation. Also, have a free election of the chair, and just have more power than we have today, similar to some other parliamentary democracies.

The second thing is to take away some of the power that now resides with the PMO and the PCO. They have far too much power in this country to make all the determinations. They select the Cabinet ministers, the parliamentary secretaries, the committee chairs, the Supreme Court justices, the head of the military, all federal institutions, and one goes on and on and on. It's not really a democracy.

In terms of free votes, I think I'd like to see not more free votes, but fewer confidence votes so that when you get to some really important issues, that shouldn't be at the feet of the government.

JUDY WASYLYCIA-LEIS:

Right.

LORNE NYSTROM:

Back-bench MPs could vote against the government without the government falling. I think that would really improve the process as well, and we don't have that today. Almost everything is confidence unless you deem it not to be confidence.

One other point, Judy. We also have to separate the parliamentary reform from the electoral reform. In the last campaign, for example, we had over a million people disenfranchised because there was no enumeration house to house. I think we should look at proportional representation. Even Britain is bringing in PR, in the Scottish and Welsh Parliaments. So those are issues we have to look at on the electoral side, along with the Senate itself, which certainly should be abolished. It's not elected, not democratic and not accountable. Instead, bring some of the original roles of the Senate into the House of Commons, a reformed House of Commons, to provide more checks and balances for the ordinary member. I think that would be an exciting agenda. Some democracy, some power to the people makes the role of Parliament much more meaningful.

PETER STOFFER:

Judy, if I may add, the reason we're doing all this is to tell the people of Canada that their actions, their voices, their vote counts. We've got to make sure that we're not doing this just for ourselves. Our jobs could be easier, or at least more relevant. We need to make sure that we're doing these things for the people of Canada, to get back into democracy. Our committee on the fish, the first East Coast report, is a classic example. We spent $183,000 of taxpayer money, and one of the first times ever, produced a unanimous report. Five political parties, as diverse as Reform, the Bloc, Alliance, and everyone put all that together, put it in the House of Commons for a vote. And the same Liberals who signed the report stood up and voted against it.

BILL BLAIKIE:

To strengthen the committees is one thing. But there was a committee strong in and of itself that empowered itself and made a unanimous report, and when it got to the House, it was killed. The point is, if you can't change the culture of the House, you can change the culture of the committees all you like. But if committee reports are only going to be killed at the next level in the House, you've still got a problem. There you have the party-discipline thing. These people actually vote against what they have signed.

PETER STOFFER:

We have to make sure that we act according to the wishes of our people as well. Deborah Grey has just focused attention on all of us by getting back into the pension plan after years fighting against it and destroying many good political careers along the way, calling them porkers and saying, "How dare they rob the Canadian taxpayer," and "Not me, I'm not going to take it." And all of a sudden she has an epiphany and says, "Oh, maybe I need it now." And she went right back into it. That reflects upon all of us and needs to change as well.

JUDY WASYLYCIA-LEIS:

It's a good point. We're talking a lot about rule changes. Rule changes reluctantly pulled from the government may not necessarily give us a lot more freedom and liberation as MPs. There is a range of things that we have to do. I know you, Wendy, have talked a lot about just trying to be true to the mission you set up for yourself when you got elected.

WENDY LILL:

It would be interesting to think about what kind of parliamentary reforms could in fact clean up the image of parliamentarians in the public eye because we are battling a hostile media wash about what we're doing here. We all know that we're here for pretty noble reasons. I really look around the whole place and I think that it can be said that people are there to actually represent their communities. But we are all painted with the same brush. There is a sense that we're all self-serving and not effective in any fashion. It's a real hit on democracy. Are there simple ways that we could improve that image?

BILL BLAIKIE:

It's interesting you should say that, Wendy, because one of the ironies for me is that now you have the Alliance members, formerly Reform members, and they want more power and Parliament to have more power. They want to have it with more respect. And these are the people who spent 10 years running the place down. Ten years of making a political career out of exaggerating and misleading the Canadian public with respect to the lives of Canadian members of Parliament and the House of Commons. Now they are coming here and after a while saying, "Gee, how come people run. How come this place doesn't work? How come people don't have respect for this place?" Well, surprise, surprise! You're the ones who made a career out of running the place down. And now you're unhappy about it. They now realize, I think, the value of a lot of things that they once pretended to despise, or perhaps really despised. But there hasn't been any kind of mea culpa. You have the

Deborah Grey thing, and a lot of other things where they've realized, well, maybe that wasn't such a bad idea after all. Some of these things were good ideas all along. But we have come through a decade in which this institution has been repeatedly and deliberately attacked for political reasons. Despicable political reasons.

DICK PROCTOR:
And it's not just the Alliance. I mean, Don Boudria here reverted to his best rat pack days yesterday in attacking what I thought was an incredibly honest speech by Joe Clark, saying, "Look, all governments have made a lot of mistakes within the last three decades. Let's fix it up, let's do something about it." It was an evenhanded speech. He wasn't finger-pointing. That's not the way Boudria responded. I'm sure it'll be Boudria bringing in time allocation and closure, and the electronic voting bill isn't going to solve the problems or make voting more responsible or make Canadians understand and appreciate what we're trying to do here.

LORNE NYSTROM:
I think the changes will be basically window-dressing, Judy. A government with so much power concentrated in their hands is not likely to change things. So I think what we have to do is to mobilize public opinion and put pressure on government. We have to commit the opposition parties. There will be a change of government someday. If we can commit more and more politicians, that's how we will really change this place and democratize it. Chrétien, if he wanted to, could leave a bit of a legacy by democratizing the place, but he's not likely to do that. Maybe the next person will. But only if this becomes a big issue with the public.

JUDY WASYLYCIA-LEIS:
We're in a difficult position in Parliament as a small group in what has become like a sports arena, with scores being kept in terms of who has the punchiest line and the greatest antic. That much is a function of the power of the media. Our dilemma is, do we play the game to get attention? Or do we try to have a new approach to politics and hope that has an impact? Or does the fact that the Question Period is televised and so much media focus is on performance make that impossible? It would be

interesting to see in this context what we can do to change it. You, Bill, were here before TV.

BILL BLAIKIE:

Lorne actually goes back to before television. *(Laughter)* I think that televising does have a big downside to it because of the way the media use the television clips. They tend to reward the wrong kind of behaviour. I don't want to be accused of being a sort of fan of B. F. Skinner, but there is a kind of Skinnerian thing. If you reward the wrong behaviour all the time by putting it on the national news, that's the kind of behaviour you'll get because publicity becomes a substitute for substance or for real accomplishment. Now, that's not true of all members, but some members, and some parties more than others, will respond to that kind of culture. We have a great deal of that.

LORNE NYSTROM:

I remember one of the consequences of television coming in was members were forced to be more image conscious. It affected almost everybody in terms of the kinds of clothes you bought and wore, the kind of tie you had and things of that sort, in order to project a better image and look better on television. That wasn't really thought of so much before, when you just had scrums. I remember, for example, one Conservative member who sat in the back. He had the most beautiful ultra-suede jacket you could possibly find, but it was the same colour as the curtains of the House of Commons. I remember they showed this poor PC member from B.C. — they showed him on the national news a few days after television came in. All you could see was the face and a mouth. The wonderful, beautiful jacket — he couldn't wear it anymore in the House of Commons because he was in the back bench and it blended in with the curtain.

DICK PROCTOR:

The other thing about television in the House of Commons is that we have more media, more journalists around here than we've ever had before, but they're exclusively focused on Question Period. They don't for the most part come to our committees to hear what's going on. I don't disagree with the earlier comment about a lot of committees being make-work, but occasionally there are good things that come out of committees that we participate in that we feel good about. I know there are darn few reporters in the agriculture committee on a regular basis to understand what's going on. I think that the focus on Question Period is all wrong. It would help if the journalists spread out and took more action, but CTV and CBC and Global all cover the same clip, and do it religiously.

BILL BLAIKIE:

Because of the way the media uses the television clips they get (from Question Period), they tend to reward the wrong kind of behaviour. If you've got to reward the wrong behaviour all the time by putting that kind of behaviour on the national news, that's the kind of behaviour you'll get because publicity becomes a substitute for substance or for real accomplishment.

An example of this goes back to 1985. There was a PCB spill around Kenora, Ontario, and I was the NDP environment critic. The spill happened on the weekend, and so we're all back here on Monday, eager to ask questions of the government on this issue. The minister of the environment at the time was Suzanne Blais-Grenier, and on the Monday I asked a couple of questions in Question Period about what the department was doing. I was information-seeking, constructive, not sort of trying to blame her or anything like that. That night on the news, nothing. People started to call my office: "How come the NDP doesn't care about the PCB spill? You guys never raised it. Oh, you did? Well, I never saw it."

So on the Tuesday, a bit more stubborn, I ask a second series of constructive questions. Again, nothing on the news and more calls from citizens: "I thought you guys cared about the environment. This lake's filling up with PCBs and you guys don't care."

Well, on Wednesday morning we sat there, Jim Fulton (NDP MP from Skeena in B.C.) and I, and we said, "All right, we're going to fix this. You go in, you do this. I'll go in, I'll wave my hands around, raise hell, call for the resignation of the minister." So we went in and we scripted it and raised hell in Question Period. That night, I'm all over the news and everybody's saying, "Great job, Bill."

Now, the problem is, I thought I was doing a better job on the Monday and Tuesday.

Lorne Nystrom:

So that's television and that's image and that's acting.

Judy Wasylycia-Leis:

So what should we do to handle this dilemma? Do we, in order to get media attention, bring props into the House, do we engage in gimmicks, do we do anything to get attention?

Bill Blaikie:

I don't think we should. The Alliance have been very good at that, but I think they debased the place doing it. I just tend to be on the stubborn side on this.

Lorne Nystrom:

But we have done that from time to time. I remember Jim Fulton, for example, putting a dead fish on the prime minister's desk. I remember during the Crow debate[2] farmers came down here with petitions signed on great big pieces of plywood, four feet by six feet, and they couldn't find anybody to volunteer to present these big petitions, so I volunteered and probably you, Bill, and Jim Fulton for sure helped carry them in. The whole place went wild. The Speaker had to close the House for a few minutes. And I remember old Tory MPs coming over and giving me hell about degrading the place. So from time to time we've been guilty as well. We sure made the national news, though. Everybody heard about the Crow because of that particular stunt. Now whether we do that or not, Judy, that's a debate, and I hope we don't have to do that kind of thing. But occasionally we have.

Peter Stoffer:

We know the media operates on the principle of action, controversy and motion. Darrel Stinson took his coat off — remember that? — and said, "Who are you calling a racist?" That's being played on the news, time and time and time again.[3] But have Parliament and the media ever got together to discuss this and say, "Look, you guys are Canadians as well. You know how we act and you see us on a regular basis; is there any way the media can change their portrayal of us?" Has that discussion ever taken place?

BILL BLAIKIE:

Some attempts have been made to have that kind of discussion, but by and large the media are the most un-self-critical institution in the country. They have nobody criticizing them. Everybody else has somebody criticizing them. The media have nobody criticizing them, except politicians from time to time, and the media always get the last word on the politician and so you do it at your peril. When we had special committees on parliamentary reform, we tried to deal with this. We had witnesses from the media, but they're very, very touchy. They just think that they're beyond the reach of human reflection.

LORNE NYSTROM:

I remember when television first came into the House there was a debate over what the camera could focus on in terms of the kind of image you want to portray, using a very tight shot or a wider shot. Often you would think the House is full, Judy, because you have four or five MPs behind Dick or Peter — whoever is speaking — and the House may have only have 18, 19 people in it. So we try to a certain extent to control the image in the House. That's only the formal part of it, and more colourful stuff may be missed. But that might be a good thing.

JUDY WASYLYCIA-LEIS:

Let's come back to where we started. I think our biggest concern as members of the NDP caucus is for all of us as elected MPs to have a greater say in the decisions that affect this country. In the area of decisions about spending we seem to have completely lost all power. We don't even get to the Estimates in any meaningful way, let alone question the government on its spending priorities. If we want to ensure that public opinion is reflected in the legislature, I think we want to have a hand in crafting good legislation. And yet closure is brought in time and time again. How do we, just to come back to that main point, how do we ensure that we can move this place, reclaim Parliament, recover our strong, effective national legislature so that we can each do those kinds of tasks and responsibilities that we committed to when we got elected.

PETER STOFFER:

Voters who don't vote say, "Well, my vote doesn't mean anything, I don't have a say. I feel left out of the process." But there have been some successes. I thought one of the greatest successes we've ever had was when Bill got in those two amendments on the Aboriginal issue, on Bill C-20. I saw Bill's speech. I watched him and it was incredible, it was forceful, it was direct, and I'm sure Stéphane Dion was scared.

BILL BLAIKIE:
I don't think he was all that scared.

PETER STOFFER:
But because Bill was forceful in his concern, and had well-thought-out arguments, the government bent and it was passed. But those successes are few and far between.

BILL BLAIKIE:
But the real dynamic there wasn't specific to the Clarity Bill. It happens whenever the government feels that it needs and wants your support. Therefore they have to take you seriously. Therefore they have to say, "Well, look, what would make this bill such that you could vote for it?" They do that often on back-to-work legislation because they know they have to get it through. So we've got a certain amount of bargaining power. What we need to do is create a Parliament in which we have that kind of bargaining power more often, on a regular kind of basis. And you do that by freeing the place up from party discipline to a degree, so the government backbenchers can have that kind of bargaining power or can have it in combination with opposition members. With proportional representation you don't have cheap majorities that come with less than 50 percent of the vote. So when they're talking to you, they're talking to somebody they might need tomorrow. In this context they're talking to people they'll never need, except in very, very rare political circumstances. So they can afford to just ignore you all the time. We need to create a Parliament in which that dynamic that applies rarely applies regularly.

LORNE NYSTROM:
Which is why minority Parliaments have always been the most useful. The best Parliaments we've had were the Pearson one between 1962 and 1968, when health care came in and the Canada Pension Plan and the like because there was constantly a minority, and also the Trudeau

Parliament between 1972 and 1974 that brought in Petro-Canada, the farm investor program and the indexing of wages and pensions, things of that sort. At the time there was always give and take in Parliament.

BILL BLAIKIE:
The early 1980s was another time, even though they had a majority. They felt they needed the NDP because of the illegitimacy of their constitutional proposals. When they need you for legitimacy, you can bargain with them.

LORNE NYSTROM:
That was the third point. It was the early 1980s, the Meech Lake days and also the mid-1980s bill going to Charlottetown because they were looking for a majority in the country to get the constitutional package through. We had provincial governments and good ties with the Aboriginal people and so on. But that's no problem. It should always work.

DICK PROCTOR:
But the reality is that you two are both talking about minority governments of the 1960s, the 1970s, etc. We are in a whole different ball of wax. We're five parties, all with official party status for two successive Parliaments now, and a big Liberal majority for the third time. We're not addressing Judy's question about how do we come to grips with it, given the reality. We're talking about creating a better yesterday. We have to be figuring out how to do it in the environment we're in.

JUDY WASYLYCIA-LEIS:
Great point.

BILL BLAIKIE:
We need to look at how we could create that same dynamic in a different circumstance, a majority five-party Parliament. That's the point I was trying to make. They have to need you.

JUDY WASYLYCIA-LEIS:
They don't need us. Parliamentary reform, if it happens at all, will happen over a long period of time. Is there anything we can do, right now, as we begin this legislative session, to actually have a bit more power and

feel like we're actually initiating and making a difference? Are there other tactics we can use in committee? Are there things we can do with private members' business? Anything that will help set the public agenda?

LORNE NYSTROM:
I think one thing we have to do is use parliamentary items outside of Question Period a lot more. We now only get two questions a day.

JUDY WASYLYCIA-LEIS:
Right.

LORNE NYSTROM:
So we have to use more private members' initiatives, maybe more speaking in the House, more petitions, more points-of-order that are more political. I think the other thing too, Judy, is more extra-parliamentary stuff. We pick two or three causes and go out there and do the extra-parliamentary stuff maybe a bit more than we used to.

NOTES

1. George Baker was a Liberal MP for 28 years and chairman of the Standing Committee on Fisheries and Oceans. Baker was bounced in a Cabinet shuffle and many believed it was as a result of his open criticisms and a negative report, presented in the fall of 1998, on the Fisheries and Oceans Department.

2. The Crow debate centred on the question of who pays for the movement of Prairie grain. In 1897 Ottawa and CP Rail agreed to a deal whereby in exchange for a $3.4-million subsidy to build the railway from Lethbridge, Alta., to Nelson, B.C., through Crow's Nest Pass, CP Rail agreed to a fixed rate of moving grain from the Prairies to Thunder Bay. The rates were to last forever but became the subject of complaint in the 1960s and 1970s due to increasing transport costs. Ottawa stepped in with the Western Grain Transportation Act in 1984, which committed the government to further subsidizing the farmers in the transport of grain, thus creating the Crow

Benefit. The basic argument was that paying the Crow Benefit discouraged diversification and farmers were more likely to export grain that qualified for the subsidy than process it locally.

3. Darrel Stinson was a Reform (Alliance) MP from B.C. In February 1997 Mr. Stinson was speaking to Bill C-53, which creates early-release provisions for inmates in provincial jails. He was expressing his concern for citizens, particularly the elderly, who "are afraid to go out at night and get a loaf of bread." During the debate Stinson complained about being called a "cold-hearted redneck" for his views and an "extremist." The name-calling went one step further when Liberal MP John Cannis called him a "racist." Stinson lost his temper and physically threatened Cannis by taking off his jacket and charging across the House of Commons floor yelling, "Do you have the fortitude or the gonads to stand up and come across here and say that to me, you son of a bitch!" Stinson was restrained by other members and then returned to his seat.

Chapter 3
The Liberal Party

REG ALCOCK

Reg Alcock has served three terms in the House of Commons as the member of Parliament for Winnipeg South. He has served as parliamentary secretary to the minister of intergovernmental affairs. During his tenure he played a pivotal role in the passing of the government Bill C-20, commonly known as the Clarity Bill. He has served on many committees, including acting as chair of the House of Commons Standing Committee on Human Resource Development and the Status of Persons with Disabilities. He has been a member of the Standing Committee on Justice and Human Rights, chair of the Manitoba Liberal caucus and a member of the Standing Committee on Citizenship and Immigration. He was a Liberal member of the Manitoba Legislative Assembly from 1988 to 1993. Known as the most technologically progressive member of the House of Commons, Mr. Alcock is acknowledged as an authority on how new information and communications tools will affect government operations. He is part of the Harvard University policy group that studies the impact of information technology and communication tools on the public sector and government.

TOPICS:
Life as a Liberal Backbencher
Frustrations with the Process
The Reform of Parliament
Parliament Reclaiming Its Authority
Committee Work
The Role of the Media
Technology and Accountability
How E-Government Would Change Things
An E-Government Conference
The Value of Experience
Getting Constituents Involved

Life as a Liberal Backbencher

The House of Commons is not an easy place. There's an element of toughness about the House that I think will always be there. It's tough to drive things through the House; it's tough to build a consensus. There is a loss of authority which has meant that some of the big instruments of a government, the executive, the departments, no longer use the instruments of the citizens, or no longer see a relevance there.

What the House doesn't do is work in a way that's consistent with the real world, and as a result it's afraid to exercise the authority. That's a huge problem that we've got to solve, and it makes the job in the House tough. But I think I'm better able to accomplish it from the inside, pushing on it. I am the tool right now, for better or worse, through which citizens exercise their voice in the affairs of the country. The central job I have is to ensure that the structures that provide voice and rights to people are strong and healthy.

Opposition, competition keeps you sharp. We don't have any competition. What is happening across the floor is largely a joke, so the government becomes soft and complacent and doesn't take the opposition seriously. There is a sense on the part of the Alliance that people are going to push a button and I'll do exactly what the last person in my office tells me to do. There's more unanimity in the voting among the Reform-Alliance group than there is among the Liberals.

Politics is a team sport. Here, if I fully understand 30 percent of the votes I make, I'm doing well. This is a very, very complex business, so we organize ourselves into groups. I have developed expertise in certain areas and I call upon the group to support me and I deliver support. That's what being in a party or a parliamentary system is all about. We sign on to a certain set of principles when we run for a party.

I didn't have a strong expectation that I would be in Cabinet in the short term, although you would always like to be there. Right now, in a sense, the interesting thing is that I can focus on the issue I want to drive in a way that I couldn't if I had to manage a particular portfolio. Would I like to be there? Yes, I could have more influence in pushing this file. I would drive this file from Cabinet, and that would be great.

I chose to be a Liberal. I did it because I share a certain value set that gets represented by that party, as did the Reform-Alliance guys and the NDP. So the fact that we vote together shouldn't come as a huge surprise. Now, it's true that there is whipping on three votes a year that are truly confidence votes. There are other votes where the government can say, "Here's the confidence vote. If it fails we will have an election." But there are only three real confidence votes. The rest of the time you vote because you're with the group: "You dance with the one who brought you."

Frustrations with the Process

I served in the provincial house. I was both a bureaucrat and a politician in the provincial legislature and we had a fair bit of access to what was going on. The provincial house plays a very direct role in overseeing the expenditures of government. In Ottawa the system is so much bigger and it has become so ritualized that I think the House has lost a lot of its relevance. You can still do things if you're smart and you work hard. But the level of accountability that should exist is gone. The government has become so large and so complex. It's difficult to understand how it functions. It's too easy for you to be led astray by extraneous issues.

I have referred to MPs as eunuchs. Actually everyone is — certainly in terms of the House and its authorities. That was a remark that was specific to a ruling on the application of the Access to Information Act. I argued that if we didn't have the information, if we were denied it by processes, if we were kept out of it, then basically we couldn't function. If information is power and we don't have it, how do you do your job? But even take that up to one other level — when you've got a beast as big as this thing, there isn't anybody in the system who can grapple with it.

The Reform of Parliament

There's an old saying that for every complex problem there's a simple answer. That's wrong. The more you get into things, the more you can understand the texture of it. I chair this roundtable, and we have some of the most senior analysts and mandarins in Ottawa — retired deputy ministers and such who are very experienced. I was listening to two of them talking and making interventions at the roundtable. One said, "Well, of course, the House of Commons is irrelevant." It's easy to make fun of politicians because nobody likes politicians, right? But take out the word "politician" and put the word "citizen" in. To say that it's irrelevant is such a shocking thing that surely we have to fix it. That's my argument with Prime Minister Jean Chrétien. Yet I also think Chrétien is the guy to lead it, despite all of the battles he gets into.

This is a change that has to happen on behalf of all of us, but it is going to threaten the system. It's going to threaten the bureaucrats. It's going to threaten those people who hold power right now. It is a process wherein those who have power give it up. People just don't do that easily. There are very few examples; I can name two. Czech Republic president Vaclav Havel and Jose Figueras in Costa Rica. Other than that, it's hard to identify political leaders who have voluntarily given up power.

I think we're at the point in time where we have to reconceptualize how democracy works. What is the answer to that? I don't know but it's not working well right now. It's time we confronted that and stopped trying to deal with it incrementally because we're not even on the verge of an incremental change.

The McGrath process used a special House committee to do it the last time. All parties are represented and there is proper debate on the setting of the agenda and the searching for the scope of reforms. You can take this into the restructuring of government — proportional voting, the role of the Senate and the role of the Queen. I'm part of the party, so we've already begun a process internally; I myself and some of the members who are interested in this are forming a committee. We're starting to formalize a caucus process and starting a discussion to define what exactly we mean. I'm leading a process that is looking at how we can restructure some of the activities in the House and reduce the level of control of the PCO and PMO. Changing the rules is not unimportant, and we'll address some of the immediate concerns. But it's tinkering;

the big reform is going to be to help the institution figure out its role in a vastly changed society.

We've got a committee looking at changing the rules of the House. As I got into the issue and tried to understand what was happening with Parliament, it occurred to me that Parliament is one of the few institutions that has not evolved. There are those who say John A. Macdonald would be quite happy with the way power and authority are distributed here. Part of the way Parliament lost authority was because of the need of the external world to have decisions. If Parliament can't figure out how to integrate itself better with citizens in the community and to start to operate in real time with citizens, then it's always going to be out of step.

I used to see this as the desire by certain forces to centralize authority away from the House. I saw it as the action of clerks who, over the last number of years, would try to remove decision making because the House can be a messy place. But what occurred to me is that it's a much more generic thing than that. It is this issue of speed. One of my friends was telling me the other day that if the Supreme Court announces a decision on Thursday, he might see it in his court on Monday or Tuesday. Everybody and everything is moving at a different pace. We no longer have time for the contemplative, sober-second-thought kind of activities. But Parliament hasn't challenged itself in terms of how it reforms itself to play in that faster world.

What's a structural change in government? One is the issue of privatization. I led the ports when we did the transportation reforms. The argument was that this port would be better if it could be out in the private sector so it could innovate faster and be more responsive to local community. These were very positive reasons for doing it. But if you think about that for a second, you turn it around, what's that say about government?

I wrote a little op-ed piece called "Let Them Eat Skink" about the little lizards that drop their tails. The government is kind of like that. When it's under pressure it cuts off a piece and sort of throws it off so people can get interested in that. Then it crawls off in the bushes unchanged.

Parliament Reclaiming Its Authority
When the nobles took a hold of King John, wrestled him down and said, "You're going to pay attention to us," that was the start of the first House

of Commons. A bunch of nobles took him by the throat and said, "You have to do this." This was to exert control over the king for taxation and the spending of taxes. We don't take any time at all on that now. All these things go on without any kind of overview, and it's wrong.

Actually the House has enormous authority, but at certain key points that authority is controlled by one person. We need to separate that to allow the House to function as a body and to demand accountability from the government. Why won't it happen quickly? Well, because it's good to be the king. I don't mean to be too flippant about this, but people suggest that the prime minister should instruct us to do parliamentary reform and I keep saying to the prime minister and my colleagues, "No." The House exercises the rights and responsibilities of citizens — they tell us. The House needs to assert that responsibility, not go begging, cap in hand, to the prime minister for it. My challenge to him, publicly and privately, is to get into it with us — but as an equal.

The elite control Ottawa. Senior mandarins and senior folks in some of the interest groups that circle around Ottawa exert an enormous amount of control and I think a very unhealthy amount of control. An awful lot of control has been centralized in the higher levels of the bureaucracy and in the Prime Minister's Office.

Committee Work

There are some rule changes that would change some of the illusions now present. One is to break the prerogative around how members get appointed to committees. Committees actually have enormous power and if members got onto a committee and stayed on a committee for the life of the Parliament, they would have huge authority.

Committee work is a big issue around here. We have 170 members, so there are people to fill those spots. I've tried to avoid taking up too many committee responsibilities but I've had really good experiences on committees. I think it depends on the committee; it depends on the budget; and it depends on the other 30 members who are on the committee. It depends on the experience of the chair and the minister. If you get experienced members and a confident minister, you can do a lot of good stuff. But if you have a committee that becomes highly partisan, you're not really discussing any issues, you're just fighting all the time. And this seems to be what occurred on the health committee in the last House. Then it becomes a waste of time.

Part of my interest in reform comes out of the desire to see committees assuming responsibilities that they currently have. They have the authority. For example, the finance committee is extremely effective. It's in part because Finance Minister Paul Martin is very strong and very confident. He believes in group process, so he sends it out to do his work. It's a process that he respects and he interacts with, and I think the members there feel that they make a real contribution to the building of the budget. A minister who is less confident will rely on control to drive something through the House. I think that's a sign of weakness.

Ministers represent their departments — that's their role. So you would expect an adversarial relationship, in a sense of challenging, questioning and searching for the right answer. If the situation becomes politicized, the whips can drive it so that the government members defend the minister instead of being part of the process.

The Role of the Media

There once was a much greater individual authority in the House and in the way committees functioned. Television changed that. Television, when it first came on the scene, was a hot medium. It needed an image, and focused on leaders right across the industrialized world. This concentration of power over a period of 30 or 40 years slowly moved to the centre. But now we have the world of the 100-, soon to be 200-, soon to be 500-channel universe.

Television is a medium that likes simple stories, so it is easier to focus on a leader than it is to focus on a whole group of people. So the story of the Canadian Parliament is the story about Pierre Trudeau and Robert Stanfield, not a story about anybody else. Over time that has empowered the leaders in such a way that other things began to happen. In order to control that message, to make sure that it was clear, they began to take more and more control of the policy levers. You see the creation of the Privy Council Office in 1972 that began to centralize all the activities in the various departments. They went through a filter in the PCO. Trudeau set it up with (Clerk of the Privy Council Office) Michael Pitfield.

When you step outside of the 30-second sound byte, what you step into is a world of great complexity. You have the 10-second-clip nonsense but that's trivial. That's a waste of people's energy. Our information world has sort of fragmented in such a way that people are going to be able to sit and think about these things.

Technology and Accountability

I've come to parliamentary reform through the electronic government door, if you like. I think Senate reform, proportional voting and all those things are important, but those are not the issues that drive me right now. It's the issue of the power balance between the executive and the House of Commons. By this I mean the way that decisions get made, the way departments get held to account, the power balances between the departments and the House and re-establishing the right of citizens to hold a government to account through their representatives.

One thing that computers are very good for is handling large, complex amounts of information and allowing you to extract knowledge and understanding from it. But to do that you have to have the information organized in a different way. You move from a government that is accountable in a bunch of vertically organized departments to a government that is essentially a network. That changes everything. It changes who's accountable in the network. Where does accountability lie now? We've got to think about that.

I spent 14 years involved with a research group at Harvard that works on the issue of how the new information technologies affect the structure of organizations in government. I think we're on the verge of a very radical change in government. Rather than being driven by the ability to further the communication to involve more people in the process, it will change the nature of the information flow, and change the nature of the information that you have at your fingertips in order to hold government to account. These tools give us an opportunity to change the paradigm.

The decisions we don't like are often the decisions that are made in the darkness. When you expose them to the light they don't get made. It's this openness of information that is a very important tool for a free and democratic society. The Internet changes everything that people talk about. The problem is, it hasn't changed government yet. It's coming, but it hasn't done it yet.

It's taken me several years to convince the structures around here that I know something about this. First off, they sort of rejected some of my analysis, but I think now they've come to the point where they realize it has some strength. We have talked about moving into the age of the knowledge economy. We have to get our instruments in tune with that.

How E-Government Would Change Things

E-government is government that is maximally transparent, openly comprehensible and maximally accountable to its citizens. Take the HRD (Human Resources Development) thing we've just been through. Assume we had electronic file management from the beginning. You could know, if you wished, on a real-time basis exactly where you were at with that spending. You could answer those things within one news cycle. Who got what, when and where? All of the accountabilities. All those things are just automatic with these systems and then you can look at the beast.

E-government is fast and efficient in the delivery of services, at a substantially lower cost. About 50 percent of the public servants will be retiring in the next five years, which is an incredible opportunity to retool. Handling information digitally reduces the cost of paper, the time, energy, trouble and assistance that are built around with accountability mechanisms.

Government spends as much money trying to hold itself accountable as it does delivering services. Hold that information differently and you reduce that cost enormously. I think public expenditure is 40 percent of our GDP (gross domestic product). If the government moves a little faster, if it's a little more efficient, our productivity goes up. But most importantly our comprehension of what government is and isn't goes up. That to me is the big win for citizens because if you understand something, you can manage it.

I think it will help members of Parliament, citizens and everyone understand what government really is. It will take off the table a whole bunch of debates about whether this or that was appropriate or inappropriate. Was it corrupt or was it not? You don't have that when you've got a fully transparent system. It'll make the system inherently less corruptible.

We move from having accountability once every four years to where I, as an MP, act as much more of a guide, an assistant, a leader of the people within my community, a clarifier of their values. I think that's how the MP's role will evolve. Life is complex and people are very busy. As an MP I get paid full time to think about these things. My singularity as a decider will be reduced because people will have access to the same information. A lot of things will come off the table and my God-like authority will diminish substantially. But where I'll gain authority is where I think that real legitimacy lies — in constantly renewing people's respect for my individual leadership.

The first challenge is going to be to get Canadians on side with this so they understand. This is a huge, huge issue that has to do with the rights of citizens and the way power is exercised in this community, so it takes a lot of thought and negotiation. You've got to bring everybody in. The executive has to play a role. The lobby community and the NGOs (non-governmental organizations) that circle around this place need to be part of the discussion. Citizens need to be part of this too.

Having the university there, I have a constituency that is quite computer literate. Have they thought specifically about these issues? No, but I have, a lot. It holds great hope for us, but it's going to threaten a whole range of entrenched interests — public service interests, political interests and all that coterie of elite that revolve around this place.

An E-Government Conference

There is a natural division between the House and government. People think of government as being the House of Commons. It's not the government. There is a wall between. Public servants don't easily open up to politicians. The recent E-Government Conference was trying to create an environment in which public servants and politicians could talk about the change that this technology drives. I think for the first time we're beginning to work on it together. The deputy ministers around here are far more responsive.

We've had a sense for some time that there was an appetite for the conversation we've had in the last few days. There are a group of public servants at all levels, politicians at all levels, citizens at all levels who are beginning to understand the enormous power of these tools.

I spent a lot of time having a conversation with Paul Martin about the importance of these tools and Paul Martin is one of those rare individuals who is not afraid to admit that he doesn't know something and then struggle to figure it out. So he's been thinking hard about this. Some leaders say, "Well, that's important. You go do it." The real leaders have to take it inside. They have to feel it and believe it. That's what Paul Martin has done over these last few years. But we went to Paul because of his area of responsibility. Financial markets were among the first to become horizontal. He's had to live in that world and that's why we brought him here to talk about that. He did a brilliant job. Treasury Board President Lucienne Robillard is the person who's responsible for the government on-line, so we went to her and asked her. I thought Mel Capp (Privy Council Office) was the most courageous of all in the sense that he has the biggest price to pay for being too much in the public eye. There are not a lot of rewards for public servants in any of this. But he is an incredibly bright man and he understands the importance of this debate. Now, he was pulling us back a bit, but he was here because he knows that this debate is an important debate. And we didn't have anybody say no. Everybody we asked, when we gave them the rationale, came.

The Value of Experience
There is value to experience. If you look at the British House of Commons, over half the members have been there 10 years or more. Here it's 10 percent. We need to build expertise in order to exert control over those who basically manage the country.

As I got more experienced, and the same is true for all of my colleagues in opposition and in government, I began to notice that there is a problem. After Prime Minister Trudeau left, Paul Tellier and (Brian) Mulroney came in, in 1984. Mulroney had the largest majority in the history of the country and the largest number of brand-new, inexperienced MPs.

When I first got here I didn't understand all this. It took me some time to develop the depth and the strength to challenge the existing system. Well, you could imagine what it was like when the whole House was like that. Paul Tellier, who was the clerk of the Privy Council, was able to push PCO control through the roof. Not to slam Mulroney, but he was a novice. The one thing Chrétien knows is how government works. My argument to him is, "Boss, OK, you've got the skill, now you've got to help us do it."

In 1993 when there was another big whack of new members, we didn't even talk about this. Now, all of a sudden it's on the agenda. One of the reasons is, we've got a more experienced House. A whole pile of people are here who are in their third term, many in their fourth. Now, you've got people who have some experience and some sense as to how to make this place dance. We'll get the change but when you're brand new and you're trying to figure out where the bathrooms are, it's real hard to grapple with reform.

Getting Constituents Involved

There is a sense that there's a great deal of apathy in politics. I don't believe that's true. I think what there has been is a lot of bad strategy about how you talk to people. I've worked hard since I got elected. I did it when I was in the provincial house and I'm doing it here by giving people ways to become part of the process. I get the largest amount of handwritten mail of any MP in Ottawa, not because I'm terribly magical but because I work at it. When the House is sitting and issues are active, I'll get anywhere from 400 to 800 letters every week.

I'm very proud of the fact that so many people get involved, but more importantly, rather than judging my success back home, it drives my agenda in Ottawa. Quite often I'll walk into caucus with a handful of these letters and say to the prime minister, "In my riding I've got …" and I'll sort of read from them. Because people read the papers, they follow the news and they know what the issues are. So if we're debating a particular issue in Ottawa, you can be certain I'm going to receive a flood of mail on it from people in my riding. It helps me understand how their opinion fits with the direction it is going.

I represent 60,000 voters and 100,000 people. There's a huge diversity of opinions. I send about 60,000 to 80,000 pieces of direct mail out every month to people in my riding. I have a circulation that goes to my advisory network where they get stuff on events that are taking place in the government on a regular basis. Everybody in my riding gets something from me once a month.

We've organized an urban caucus and I'm on a task force that's looking at re-establishing the relationship between the federal government and cities. Manitoba is a bit of an anomaly in the West. The Liberals historically have had a difficult time holding seats in Western Canada, and yet we've got this little island here of six seats that seems to be fairly secure. Certainly the Alliance is interested in trying to consolidate the West and come after us. The NDP has some strength here, and there's a provincial New Democrat government.

It's a riding that has had Liberal representation more often than not. I think it was only held a couple of times by the Conservatives since the war. Lloyd Axworthy represented the area before me, James Richardson before that and Margaret Konantz before that. There is a tradition here and there's an awful lot of people that know me and who I worked with before. It's a riding that is heavily focused on the new economy, on education, so a lot of the things that we're talking about are viewed quite positively.

GEORGE BAKER

George Baker was first elected to the House of Commons in 1974. He served for 27 years without interruption as the MP for Gander–Grand Falls. From August 1999 to October 2000 he served as minister of veterans affairs and secretary of state (Atlantic Canada Opportunities Agency). Mr. Baker has also served as parliamentary secretary to the ministers of fisheries and oceans, transportation, environment and national revenue. Prime Minister Jean Chrétien named him to Canada's Senate in March 2002.

TOPICS:
The Diminishing Power of an MP
Party Discipline and Sanctions
Committees
The Fisheries Committee Report (An Example of How
Committees Work)
How Parliament Used to Be the Guardian of the Public Purse
Political Short-Term Interests

Question Period Is Not Our System's Accountability Mechanism
The Need for Parliamentary Change in Question Period
The Only Potential Avenue for Parliamentary Reform

The Diminishing Power of an MP

In my 28 years in the House of Commons I've watched power being drained from the member of Parliament. Years ago it was very common to see an MP actually hold up proceedings, using various means.

Over the years, in the Canadian Parliament, there has been a recognition that a political party is elected to govern, and the function of the official Opposition is the accountability of the government. In other legislatures the accountability of the government is the function of not only the official Opposition, but also the other opposition parties *and the backbenchers of the governing party*. In Great Britain, Australia or any Scandinavian country, that's how the legislatures evolved.

In Canada Parliament is almost a mirror image of what the British House was like 30 years ago. That doesn't mean that the Canadian House of Commons is less efficient. In some ways it's more efficient. But the power of a single member of Parliament has eroded considerably over the years. There was a time when any MP could actually make the government accountable in a procedural way. Today, under our standing orders, an MP can't hold up Parliament or stop the proceedings.

In Canada the party in charge can stifle and control the input and power of an individual member of Parliament. Should the MP have the power to hold up an entire bill indefinitely? Should you have a system whereby a committee can investigate whatever it wants, whenever it wants, with no control from the party in power?

The principle is that the government is elected to govern and the opposition doesn't have the right to hold up the government's business. Government has become complex and you must have some facility to pass laws and make changes. So the government has to be allowed to govern. But this has meant an MP's power has eroded in stages. Rule changes have eroded the MP's power to the point that if you're not on the whip's list, or you're out of favour with that party, you can't even speak, let alone ask a question in Question Period. Under present procedures in the House of Commons, all that an MP can do is refuse unanimous consent on every occasion that he or she wishes. That's just about the only thing left.

Thirty years ago, as an MP, you could stand up and the Speaker of the House would recognize you. All of the MPs would be popping up like jackrabbits, and the Speaker would select someone to ask a question. Today you go into the House and the Speaker calls a name. The person says, "Oh, is that my name?" because it's on the list.

It means an MP has to be in good standing with the party, the leader and the whip to get on Question Period and to speak in the House of Commons. Where did we get the custom that every question is decided upon by the whip of each political party? Where does that leave the individual MP? It's a very structured system that needs to be re-examined.

Party Discipline and Sanctions

The MPs know that their entire effectiveness as members is held in the hands of the party leader and the whip. Their power can be thwarted if they're out of sync with their leader or their party.

There are whole lists of sanctions that can be brought to bear against a maverick MP in our political party system. For example, MPs must be in good standing to get on the committees that they want to join. The opposition parties and the government can choose on which committees backbenchers or private members can sit.

There's an election for the chair of the committee, but these matters are really decided beforehand by the executive. If you aren't in favour of the government of the day, then you aren't going to be the chair of the committee. Also, a member must be in good standing to go on trips that examine policies overseas.

The government caucus serves a worthwhile function. It's one place where an MP can be frank and open with his leadership. But we have a serious problem in the caucus of any opposition party, in that the backbencher in opposition can't speak to a Cabinet minister or prime minister and say, "You're not doing a good job on this."

Committees

The power taken away from the ordinary member of Parliament was supposed to be compensated for in the committees. But that's not how the system has evolved.

In other parliamentary systems, the committee has a lot of power and can originate its own terms of reference. This means that it can investigate whatever it wants to.

The news media don't attend Question Period in the British House of Commons; they attend the committee meetings. It's a completely different ball game.

If a committee wanted, for example, to investigate medications for cancer patients, it could do so in Great Britain and Australia, but it couldn't move forward in Canada. We take our direction from the House of Commons. We can't do anything that the government doesn't want. That's the way the system is set up.

In 1968 the committees were empowered to bring experts in to better sink their teeth into issues, move forward and make suggestions. Now they're encumbered by "terms of reference" determined by the leaders in their party.

The Fisheries Committee Report (An Example of How Committees Work)

I was in the centre of a controversy over a report from the fisheries committee. I was chairman of the committee and we were allowed to hold public hearings about fishing areas in Canada. We interviewed the fishermen rather than the bureaucrats or the so-called experts in the system.

In our report we condemned every government that had been in power since about 1965. We singled out certain years, regardless of the political party in power at the time. We said in the report that they had done an absolutely disastrous job of managing the fisheries.

Practically every stock we had was disappearing. Canada allowed 17 foreign nations to fish off the East Coast, the Nose and Tail of the Grand Banks and the Flemish Cap. How can you have proper management of the fishery if 17 nations have to sit down and determine quotas? We've lived with this system for years, and it's still in place.

It was a unanimous report from the all-party members of the committee. I stand by that report today. We recommended that the limit be extended out to 350 miles of jurisdiction over the ocean floor, basically to kick out all of those foreign nations.

Common sense tells you that if you appear to be out of step with your party, you'll be sanctioned. Some people say that I was removed as chairman of the committee, but I wasn't fired. Committee chairmen were re-appointed with each new session of that Parliament. Well, who selects the chairmen? Each political party selects the members of the committee and, of course, the person in favour with their own political party at the time would get the chairman position.

Now, if I were in a position of power within the Liberal Party, would I have re-appointed me as chairman of that committee? Why would I do something stupid like that?

The moment came to recommend new members of the committee, and they were changed. The chairman, my position, was given to someone else. I wouldn't say that it was intentional, but that's the way it appeared. That's the system.

How Parliament Used to Be the Guardian of the Public Purse

I've watched the power shift from the House of Commons to the executive and the Cabinet. MPs no longer debate money bills either. No longer is the executive held accountable for estimates or even the money vote.

About 20 years ago the government was defeated on a money bill with a vote of no confidence. A precedent was set when the House changed our procedures to prevent that. You can't have a government where bills are defeated.

The auditor general says that the role of MPs is to be the guardians of the public purse. If they can't hold the government accountable for very basic things like money bills or estimates, how can they fulfill that role?

Political Short-Term Interests

We have a system in which change needs to be made by the very people who have a vested interest in not making change: the politicians. They know that the average period between elections is three years. We're elected to get re-elected. Every one of us is planning for the next election right after each election. That's our system.

Question Period Is Not Our System's Accountability Mechanism

The argument could be made that the government is not held accountable for substantive things because under our system Question Period is the only opportunity to deal with them. The critics of our committee system, compared to other nations, have a very legitimate point. The opposition parties and their leaders should be held accountable for what they aren't pursuing in the only forum that they have to make the government accountable, Question Period.

Our Question Period becomes a political game of trying to embarrass the government. The questions are limited to 25 seconds, with 34 seconds for an answer. It's the short term all over again. It's not the long term.

It could be that political gamesmanship is responsible for the depletion of the fishery. When was the last time that you heard a question in the House of Commons concerning the destruction of our fish stocks? Not this year, not last year, not the year before, not the year before that. The very nature of our system means that these important subjects aren't really dealt with.

How can it be the best when a situation like the fish-stock depletion is allowed to happen? There are so many subjects that mean a lot to Canadians and not all are brought up.

The Need for Parliamentary Change in Question Period
Is there a need for parliamentary reform in Canada? It depends on whom you talk to. A parliamentarian from Australia or Great Britain might say, "These guys in Canada are crazy," because the opposition has all of the power.

The greatest power of sanctions in the House of Commons lies with the leader of the official Opposition because that's the prize position for asking questions. The opposition monopolizes Question Period. They can embarrass the government. In other systems you can't because you have to give 48 hours' notice of your questions.

For an ordinary government backbencher in Canada, Question Period is where the action takes place. But the party whip determines who gets to ask questions. The Speaker is given a list to follow. Where does that leave the government backbenchers? They can't ask any questions.

Under other systems there is no such list, no such control. In other systems an ordinary member of Parliament, a backbencher, has power, more power than a Canadian MP has. These systems have evolved into democracies for the ordinary backbenchers.

In Canada the parties have the power, not the individuals. Does our parliamentary system need change? You have to balance one against the other.

The Only Potential Avenue for Parliamentary Reform
The Speech from the Throne said, "The procedures of the House will be re-examined ... because individual members of Parliament should have more say, more power."

That means that the MPs, particularly the backbenchers, will be able to hold the government accountable for its actions, no matter the case.

There will be mechanisms, agreed to by the different political parties and a group of people outside the chamber, to accomplish this.

There may be interesting reform soon. There should be.

Reform of the Canadian Parliament is going to take the route of the other legislatures under British parliamentary systems. In those cases it's not the politicians that have brought in meaningful changes, nor their parties — the changes have always been brought in by an outside body of people.

If you want to change procedures, you need to have people from the outside making the recommendations. Set up an outside committee made up of academics, political scientists, members of the press gallery and members of the general public who will recommend changes to procedure, as they do in Great Britain and Australia. In those systems they make recommendations to a House of Commons standing committee. Invariably those changes are accepted.

The major difference between our system and others is that we don't have independent academics, media or members of the public determining and recommending changes to our parliamentary procedures.

Over the years I've heard it said that "in all of those other systems, the independent body only makes recommendations. Therefore, it has no real effect because it can't bring about change." The answer is that in each of those systems the political parties follow the recommendations. It would be embarrassing for them if they didn't.

The Canadian House will likely take that route. They will take it out of the hands of the politicians because nothing will ever get done that way.

If you leave it in the hands of politicians, you won't get change. The opposition parties have to agree. They want to hold the government accountable. They want to have their day in the sun. They're not going to give away the rights that they have now.

The government isn't going to give up power, nor is the opposition. So we have to establish a body of non-politicians, people unaffiliated with the parties, to make recommendations. That's the only way that substantial change will happen. That's how it worked in all of the other legislatures, and that's the way it will end up here in Canada.

Brian Tobin

B rian Tobin began his political career as an aide to Newfoundland provincial Liberal leader Bill Rowe in 1977. He later became assistant to federal Liberal Cabinet minister Don Jamieson. He was first elected in 1980 as MP for Humber–St. Barbe–Baie Verte in Newfoundland, where he served as the parliamentary secretary to two fisheries ministers. In 1993 when the Chrétien government swept to power, Tobin was named federal fisheries minister, where he served until he jumped back into provincial politics near the end of 1995. He was elected premier of Newfoundland on February 22, 1996. In the fall of 2000 Mr. Tobin resigned early into his second term as premier of Newfoundland and was named the federal government's minister of industry. He was elected again as a Liberal MP in the November 2000 election for the riding of Bonavista–Trinity–Conception. He was re-appointed minister of industry and served in that position until resigning from the federal Cabinet on January 17, 2002, citing personal reasons.

TOPICS:
Reflections on a Political Life
The Role of Industry Minister
Facilitating His Riding's Growth
Leadership Conspiracy Theory
The Myth of Concentrated Power Behind Closed Doors
Types of Accountability
Media's Role in Accountability
The Opposition's Role
Transparency Has Its Limits
A New Deal for Atlantic Canada
Challenging the Economic Basket Case Image of Atlantic Canada
Myths and Realities of Atlantic Canada
His Rural Newfoundland Riding
Addressing Regional Concerns
The Structure of Confederation
Parliamentary Reform in Action
How Technology Could Transform Newfoundland
Change Is Never Easy

Reflections on a Political Life

I have been a member of Cabinet. I have been a premier. I have formed Cabinets and selected Cabinets. For me what matters, and this is going to sound rather trite, but it's people. People. I suppose it's fair to say it's the Irish background, it's the Newfoundland and Labrador background. Some people live to make a lot of money. Some people live to make great art. Some people live to design large buildings and to build them. Others spend a lifetime trying to write a perfect poem. But every one of them has value in our community.

I love what I do. I love meeting with people; I love being part of the public dialogue and debate in this country. I'm at a stage of my life where, after nearly 21 years, it would be a lot easier to go out and work nine to five, spend half the week on the golf course, and trade on all of the knowledge, experience and contacts of 21 years in public life. It would probably pay a lot more, too.

Being premier of Newfoundland and Labrador for five years, I woke up many mornings realizing that the whole planet didn't wait with bated breath for the next utterance from the House of Commons. There's a world out here of children, families, animals, trees, environment, activity, commerce, entrepreneurship, hopes, dreams and fears. Sometimes nobody knows about those debates but those of us who are members of the House, and those who cover it. Sometimes the heat and noise and light which we focus on breathlessly is entertainment just in that chamber. It doesn't really impact the lives of people in the larger community.

Don Jamieson was a federal Cabinet minister for Newfoundland and Labrador, and was Canada's minister of foreign affairs, amongst other portfolios. He said when he retired that the greatest regret that a politician could have is to have spent a career in public life and never have really taken a chance, really left a mark. What drives me is the desire to make a contribution. Taking on causes that have long been ignored. I think about the fish fight and the European Union. Showing up in Montreal days before a referendum campaign, trying to organize a public, coast-to-coast response to that referendum campaign. That was a risk. Leaving the premier's office to run in an election campaign is a risk, but in my mind it's the right risk for the right reason.

I've had a career that has been defined somewhat by doing the unorthodox and taking chances, for example, in the approach to the turbot dispute to take direct action against the Spanish fishing vessels on the high seas. I don't want to be a daredevil of Canadian politics, but if the issue's important enough for the country, you've got to be prepared to fail for the right cause. That's good public policy.

The Role of Industry Minister

I prefer not to talk about what members of Parliament can do versus what ministers of industry can do. That's an unfair way to characterize the role of MPs. I've been on both sides of the House, and I like to think that I made a contribution on both sides of the House.

My mandate is to work on behalf of all the people of Canada, in the area affected by the portfolio of Industry Canada. That includes all of the mature and well-established sectors of the Canadian economy, but in particular all of the new parts of the economy, the IT sector, the information technology sector, the science and technology sector.

This is a $4.2-billion department, with 17,000 employees and 15 or 16 different agencies and four or five different ministries all reporting through Industry Canada. So it's a very big piece of work. I knew that to be effective here at Industry Canada, I'd have to do my homework, get out and talk to as many industry partners as possible and sit through a great many hours of briefings.

Facilitating His Riding's Growth

I have a mandate as a member of Parliament to try and facilitate economic growth and investment in my own riding and my own province as well. I try to get back to Newfoundland and Labrador at least three times a month, back to my constituency, Bonavista–Trinity–Conception. We've been able to get a fair amount of activity. We're going to have seven or eight major projects getting under way this year, and put millions of dollars' worth of new capital infrastructure in place in harbours. We're about to roll out 30-odd million dollars' worth of infrastructure investments for the whole province. A lot of that is going to the constituency of Bonavista–Trinity–Conception to get proper water systems in place.

Clearly I'm going to make sure that my area is well represented, and clearly I'm going to make sure that my constituency has a fair opportunity to participate in the kind of programming the government offers. I bring forward proposals from my constituents, from private sector players, from communities, from economic development groups, tourism development groups within my riding, to Jane Stewart, or my colleague, Wilbur Thibeault, and the folks at Atlantic Canada Opportunities Agency, ACOA.

But I wouldn't want to suggest that there's going to be a special allocation for my riding as opposed to other ridings. I think Percy Barrett (local MHA) did what a local member of the House of Assembly would do during an election campaign in trying to point out that he believed that I would have an opportunity to be effective as a representative. I think Percy made the comment as much in jest as anything else.

The Business Development Bank is the source of questions in the House, about its role in Shawinigan and various investments. It reports to Parliament through me. I'm the minister who responds on behalf of the Business Development Bank in Parliament. It was a role I was very happy to play. This was essentially an attack on the prime minister, by some of the opposition parties' politicians, notably Mr. Clark. The RCMP have investigated and closed the book. The ethics conflict commissioner investigated and closed the book. Important public business was lost while there was an attempt to try and make a scandal out of something that didn't resemble one at all. Important time in Parliament was wasted.

Frankly we've now moved on to other business. Questions are no longer being asked about this, or are being asked very infrequently.

Leadership Conspiracy Theory

The opposition may say that all the power is in the Prime Minister's Office. It's one or two unelected, faceless, unaccountable people in a dark backroom running the country. That's a great conspiracy theory, but it isn't the truth.

This prime minister is successful because this prime minister delegates. Anybody who believes that Paul Martin is not playing a substantial and important role in shaping the fiscal and monetary policy of Canada is dreaming in Technicolor. Anybody who believes that we're standing still over here at Industry Canada is dreaming in Technicolor. Anybody who believes that Allan Rock is not having a substantial impact, and I know this full well from the vantage point of being a premier, is dreaming in Technicolor.

I have the same opportunity as anybody else in Cabinet or caucus to be heard. When I was leader of a government in Newfoundland and Labrador, I treated all of my colleagues with an equal measure of respect and attention. I expect Jean Chrétien will do the same.

A leader who fails to challenge and to draw from those around that leader is bound to fail. The mark of leadership is the capacity to keep the troops together in the tent, to acknowledge and encourage differences of opinion and then to build consensus. Jean Chrétien recognizes that he can't do it all alone. He's got a lot of bright, energetic and ambitious people around him.

The Myth of Concentrated Power Behind Closed Doors

There is a bias that there's some powerful handful of people, off in one of the buildings here, that runs the whole country and the rest of us don't have a chance to participate. Anybody who believes that Cabinet operates completely disconnected from the power and the responsibility of caucus is making a very big mistake. Let me tell you, we don't do it alone. Ministers have an ability to speak inside, to be part of the decision-making process.

There is a greater disbursement of political power in this country today than ever before. I was here 20 years ago when Trudeau was the prime minister. It is less caucus-driven today than it was 20 years ago.

The House of Commons and members of Parliament have more influence. When I came in 1980 the committee structure was a lot less influential than it is today.

Types of Accountability

This is the most accountable democracy in the world. I'm accountable in a variety of ways. I talk to the media once every day and on Parliament Hill. I'm accountable in Parliament every day in Question Period. I'm accountable to citizens. I'm accountable to the parliamentary committee, the Standing Committee on Industry of the House of Commons, which has members from every single party. It is free and open and able to review every program and every expenditure of the Department of Industry.

In the British parliamentary system the prime minister and ministers are given notice of the day they're going to have to ask questions, and they're given in advance the questions that they have to answer. In our system we go to that House, we walk in the door, we have no idea what questions are going to be asked, but we're expected to answer on the spot as best we can. It's a very transparent and accountable system. The test of the auditor general, the test of the standing committee, the test daily of Question Periods, if there's an urgent or emerging issue that we have to respond to, it's pretty thorough. Beyond that, of course, there are opportunities to talk to members of the press, who will ask questions and demand answers.

Media's Role in Accountability

Governments should be challenged by the media and by the opposition. We live in a day when there are two news networks that operate 24 hours a day. All news, all the time. We live in a day when there are more newspapers and reporters on Parliament Hill than ever before. We live in day where I go to my computer, push one of my Web sites and come up with complete coverage of what's happening all across this country. We live in a time when the average citizen has access to information in more ways, faster and more accurately than ever before.

We've never had such a broadly based capacity to know what's happening to us as citizens, to participate in that process if we choose to, and to find ways to make ourselves heard. Now, does all of that suggest in any way, shape or form that we shouldn't be tough-minded in holding governments accountable? Not at all. But, my gosh, the democracy of today is far more open and transparent than the democracy of yesterday.

You have news organizations, newspapers and radio. You have Internet access, which is instantaneous. You have 24-hour news channels. You have an Access to Information Act, which allows you to find out who wrote to me and how I responded. None of those instruments existed 50, 60, 70 years ago. Parliamentarians came to Ottawa in a train, and once or twice a year they went back. Other than that, they operated here behind closed doors. No Access to Information Act. No instantaneous coverage of Question Period, no press scrums with live coverage by Newsworld and Newsnet.

Can government be more open and more transparent? I would say yes. But the system has become far more open, far more responsive to what's happening out on Main Street. In my mind, it's primarily because of technology. Technology, lights, camera, sound communicate pictures and images and messages, including the voices of people who live all across Canada, right back to the policy makers.

The Opposition's Role

I've spent almost as much time as an Opposition member as I have as a government member, and I was never constrained from being able to vigorously engage in debate and to access good information and to put it to use on the floor of the House of Commons.

A good opposition MP is able to gather a great deal of information and to use that information in standing committees, to use that information in Question Period, to use that information taking advantage of the free press and giving their views, their comments. So if opposition members are having difficulty, I'd suggest they've got to work a little harder, be more focused. If you spend your time divided amongst yourselves, as we've seen with the Alliance recently, going through this never-ending leadership crisis, it's very difficult to be focused on doing good research, asking good questions and holding the government accountable.

Transparency Has Its Limits

We've got a new government in British Columbia that's going to experiment with transparent and open Cabinet sessions. It's important to have vigorous debate, and that means sometimes you have to have closed doors. Quite frankly, you get good, vigorous, strong, sometimes quite diametrically opposed views being expressed in a Cabinet meeting or in a caucus meeting when members know that what they say behind closed doors stays behind closed doors.

If we invited all citizens to participate in every decision, I think we'd have a pretty fractious decision-making process. That's why we seek mandates at election time. That's why we have Parliament — because that's the open forum to challenge and test the ideas of government. That's why we have parliamentary committees. That's why we have a free press in this country. All of those things are there to give transparency to the decision-making process. When you live in an age that functions at the speed of the Internet, we need an effective and timely decision-making process.

About corporate confidentiality, if a corporation accesses export financing, which every country in the world offers to its companies, and that corporation then has to open its books to the public or make itself transparent in a way that no other corporation would have to, then consider the competitive implications of that. Lost confidentiality, the advantage to your competitors of getting access to certain kinds of information. I don't think we can expect that of our corporations. We need to know who's being assisted, what amount of assistance is being provided, whether the funds are being repaid. These are legitimate pieces of information. But to get information that would breach corporate confidentiality, I don't think anybody truly expects that.

It's our money that we provide to public servants, by way of their salaries. It's our money that we provide to pensioners, by way of their pensions. It's our money that we provide to provincial governments. Nevertheless, the notion of confidentiality is still basic. We don't publish a list of every pensioner in the City of Toronto and say, "Here's what they received from the federal government." It's our money, but it's also their privacy, their personal privacy, that's at stake.

A New Deal for Atlantic Canada

One of the structural problems is that we have to have an equalization formula, specifically a claw-back formula. Provinces like Nova Scotia and Newfoundland and Labrador, newly ascendant in the oil and gas industry, should have an opportunity to keep a little more of the royalties that are coming in so that we can actually catch up with the rest of this country in terms of quality of life, infrastructure and services.

Newfoundland and Labrador have oil and gas; it has hydropower, it has minerals, it has fish and it has tremendous natural resources. And it has one of the poorest economies in North America because we keep making bad deals. People who own the resource are entitled to a fair share of the rent on that resource. I am confident there will be a Voisey's Bay deal and it will involve benefits for the province of Newfoundland and Labrador, beyond giving permission to put a hole in the ground and take the oil out of the ground. I have no doubt about that.

Atlantic Canada cannot break free of its circumstance, change fundamentally its circumstance, until there is in a sense a new deal. That's what I'm going to Ottawa to participate in. Our objective in Canada shouldn't be to maintain Atlantic Canada as a quaint region, slightly underdeveloped, very nice people. Our objective should be to help Atlantic Canada help itself to become a full player in the federation.

As a premier I learned that borrowing the most and taxing the most doesn't create prosperity. If it did, Newfoundland would long ago have been the most prosperous part of Canada. I learned that old-style subsidies, while they're tempting as short-term fixes, are part of the problem. We need to talk about restructuring the basic economy of rural Canada and of Atlantic Canada and, for that matter, of the North.

This province of Newfoundland and Labrador is turning a corner, and I don't think there's any turning back. *The Globe and Mail* a few days ago had a big headline saying, "Newfoundland and Alberta to lead Canada again over the next two or three years." The most important thing that's happened is that we've had confidence reborn in the people of this province. We've had a revolution between our own ears. We believe in ourselves again. If we're given that kind of good neighbourly conduct, then Atlantic Canada will finally break the bonds of dependency.

Challenging the Economic Basket Case Image of Atlantic Canada

The Atlantic Provinces Economic Council has done a province-by-province comparison study to look at the levels of business subsidies all across Canada. It turns out the lowest level of business subsidy in Canada is in New Brunswick. The next lowest level is in Newfoundland. The third lowest level is in Nova Scotia. So the perception, fed by a right-wing, mindless agenda, which we've seen mostly propagated by the *National Post*, that Atlantic Canada is an economic basket case where businesses survive only with subsidies is not true.

We have to stop seeing government assistance for Atlantic Canada in the context of propping up Atlantic Canada. Atlantic Canada doesn't want to be propped up. One of the problems Atlantic Canada has is that most people from outside the region have no idea of the changes taking place. Halifax today has an unemployment rate of 6.5 percent. Moncton, 5.5 percent. St. John's, Newfoundland, 9 percent. But if you ask most people in downtown Mississauga what the unemployment rate is in those three centres, they'd say 15, 20 percent. Most of the growth in those centres is associated with IT, information technology.

Myths and Realities of Atlantic Canada

How do you tackle the stereotype, this notion that anybody who comes from Atlantic Canada is an old-fashioned politician interested in subsidies? It's the same as somebody in Atlantic Canada having the notion that somebody in Toronto has no vision for the whole country, no concern for the whole country because they're ensconced in the big city. That isn't correct, any more than it is correct to say that everybody out West is on a farm, looking for a subsidy to maintain their way of life.

Characteristics of Newfoundlanders are ingenuity, perseverance, dogged determination, love of life, great sense of humour, great passion for everything that we do, never done in half measures. Done to excess perhaps, sometimes. That's part of the passion of this place. Poetry, literature, music, colour, coastlines, the environment, all of those things that enrich the soul even more than the pocketbook.

You know, people refer to Newfoundlanders as people who won't leave home. There's another stereotype. The reality is, no group of people in Canada have been more ready to move and pursue work. Maybe in this country we're spending too much time talking at each other. Instead of responding and listening and having an exchange, we're all sending out messages in each of the regions. That's something we all have to work on. We've got to find a way to listen to each other and not just talk at each other.

His Rural Newfoundland Riding

This is a large rural riding. It covers three bays, Bonavista, Trinity and Conception. Some parts of the riding have been devastated since 1992.

They had plants that employed up to 1,000 people. Those plants haven't come back and the fishery hasn't come back. It would be the equivalent of Ontario losing the entire auto industry at one stroke.

The issues here are jobs, health care, regional development and what role Atlantic Canada will have within this country. Atlantic Canada wants to be a full partner in that. Another issue is what kind of Canada we'll have — Canada that continues to value caring and sharing, or a different kind of Canada where you build fences and it's every family for themselves.

Addressing Regional Concerns

Ministers are very aware, and the prime minister's very aware, of what is being said in the various regional caucuses across the country, what's being said in the national caucus and what's happening in the standing committees of the House of Commons. I pay particular attention to the Standing Committee on Industry. While Cabinet ultimately gets to make the call, every member of Cabinet has got their finger on the pulse of a great many institutions. Parliamentary institutions, caucus institutions, other sectors of the economy all come to bear on judgments.

C. D. Howe's old desk is in my office. He would sit at this desk and he'd determine, virtually by himself, the economic policy of Canada. Two or three times a year he'd get on a train and go visit the major centres of Canada and tell them what he had decided. Today, three and four times a week I'm somewhere in this country. What am I doing? I'm being accountable. I'm answering questions. I'm being responsive.

The Structure of Confederation

Governance has become much more complex. If there were to be a legitimate complaint about government, it's that governments, rather than saying, "We've got a plan and we're going to stick with the plan," try to be responsive to every pressure. In trying to be responsive, government is losing coherence in the presentation of government policy.

If I were to tell you that the House is going to be a different place, I'd be telling you something I know not to be true. The House is the House. The House of Commons was designed a long time ago. It is an adversarial forum where you put people for nine, 10 months a year, two sword lengths apart, and have them go at each other, as governments and as critics, trying to position for the next election campaign. It's a very adversarial system. Has it got its flaws? Yes. Has it got its ugly moments? Yes, indeed. But of all of the democratic systems that we know about in the world, it's one that works very well, flaws and all.

One of the problems with government is that you have three different orders of government that often aren't working in partnership. What I bring to the table is an ability to get all of the cylinders firing together toward a common and productive outcome.

Parliamentary Reform in Action

Can we democratize the system further? Can we have more free votes? The answer is yes. We can continue down the road to reform to make members more accountable to their constituents and to make the government more accountable to Parliament.

The premiers got together with Prime Minister Chrétien and hammered out the Social Union. First of all, the Social Union has been a matter of debate in Parliament and a matter of public debate for a long time. Secondly, there were ministers appointed by every province who worked for probably 18 months, negotiating with each other, having meetings, inviting public comment. Really, what was presented to the prime minister and to the premiers was the work of ministers on behalf of governments.

How Technology Could Transform Newfoundland

Distance used to be a great divider between those who had opportunity and those who didn't. In the new digital age, the great challenge is that digital divide — in other words, access to the Internet on a high-speed basis.

Now what holds us back? What holds us back is infrastructure. What infrastructure? High-speed broadband Internet service. If you can't get on the highway, you can't participate. Nobody that I know of in Newfoundland or Labrador, Atlantic Canada, or Canada's North, or parts of the West or Northern Ontario, is interested in simply maintaining an economy on the basis of seasonal industries or short-term assistance only.

The Liberal Party is committed to providing a high-speed broadband service to every community in this country by 2004. The new economy impacts not just the large centres of Toronto, Montreal, Vancouver and so on. Atlantic Canada can be effective, too, in applying for TPC, Technology Partnerships Canada, funding or applying for funding for our centres of excellence, our universities, under CFI, the Canada Foundation for Innovation.

We're about to roll out a $700-million Atlantic fund for innovation. One example of the work that's being done is in the community of Clarenville. There are players coming to Clarenville from all across the province and from across the country for a conference in June. Small business players are riding in to talk about how to attract call centres, for example, to equip the college with high-speed broadband services and to attract IT sector players.

Change Is Never Easy

There is hurt with respect to the old economy. It isn't a question of someone deciding that some sectors shouldn't continue. The marketplace has made that determination already, in some places. The question for us is, do we take the few resources we have and try to sustain things that are not productive? Or do we get in there and by smart investments give people the opportunity to participate in global commerce and still live in regions of this country beyond our big cities?

I don't think you tell a 55-year-old fisherman who's hurting that the Government of Canada is going to abandon him or abandon his family. I'm not of the school that says that people are just collateral damage in the game of capital. They're citizens, and they're entitled to the support and the empathy and the assistance of governments. But they're also entitled to the truth. I think about the 55-year-old fisherman's son and his grandson. I think about maintaining a fishery, a fishery that's enabled by technology, a fishery that's changed by technology, a fishery that moves up the value chain so that we run the plant 10 months a year instead of 10 weeks a year.

DENNIS MILLS

D ennis Mills was first elected as a Liberal MP in the 1988 election. He was re-elected in 1993, 1997 and 2000. From December 1993 to February 1996 he served as parliamentary secretary to the minister of industry. He is chairman of the Subcommittee on the Study of Sport in Canada; he is also a member of the heritage committee. Mr. Mills has published two books: *Developing an Agenda for the 21st Century* and a proposal for tax reform, *A Life Less Taxing*. Prior to entering federal politics Mr. Mills was owner of Chairman Mills, a special-events management company, and worked with Magna International as corporate vice president.

TOPICS:
The Effectiveness of MPs
If the Executive Is Too Powerful
A Hope for Change from the Prime Minister?
Media Coverage of Parliament

The Effectiveness of MPs

The issue of making the role of a member of Parliament more meaningful so that members could provide better service to their constituents and the public came to a head in the summer of 2000. There was a meeting in the Railway Committee Room led by Peter Dobell, the director of the Parliamentary Centre, who was talking about parliamentary reform. Clifford Lincoln, a Liberal MP from Montreal, stood up and said, "The whole place needs to be blown to smithereens, and we have to start all over." I got up and made some interventions. I said that essentially lobbyists are listened to on Parliament Hill more than members of Parliament. I thought that there should be a review of the whole Lobbyist Registration Act.

The pendulum had swung to a point where MPs were essentially nothing more than voting machines. It was frustrating because that attitude is not what the life of an MP is all about.

Now members from the government side and the opposition side have come together, and I think that it's going to be a central issue of Parliament.

If the Executive Is Too Powerful

Traditionally, the executive of any government is the central power. It has a huge amount of influence on the agenda, style and momentum of the government. I am not debating that. What we are talking about here is a sense of balance.

In the House of Commons we are all elected to reflect the needs and wishes of our constituents. If an executive becomes insensitive to those needs, then it doesn't create a positive dynamic.

A Hope for Change from the Prime Minister?

The prime minister has also come full circle on this issue, stating that not only are we going to reform the House of Commons, but we're also going to make the role of MPs more meaningful. In his first press conference after the 2000 election, he challenged MPs to be more creative and show more initiative.

He has carried that idea forward not only in the Speech from the Throne, but also in the House of Commons, when he singled out Paul Szabo, an MP from Mississauga who has taken the initiative over the last few years to deal with fetal alcohol syndrome. Paul has taken that issue out of the mothballs, moved it from the back burner to the front burner, and it's now a national policy. The fact that the prime minister actually cited a specific person as an example speaks volumes of his intention to celebrate and honour other MPs who wish to energize the House and show creativity.

This is a near-miraculous development in the prime minister's commitment to renewing this institution. I'm hopeful that we're going to have a resurgence of MPs' ability to provide better service to their constituents.

Media Coverage of Parliament

There's a lot of fantastic work by committee members that very rarely sees the light of day. By and large the media do not cover those committees' meetings, so they miss a lot of issues of vital interest to the people of Canada, and the public doesn't get an accurate reflection of the passion, quality and commitment of many members of Parliament.

I think that the media are primarily responsible for Parliament becoming a dumbed-down organization. I call this hall right outside the House of Commons "Hooker Alley." It's where dozens and dozens of journalists hang out after Question Period and look for quotes and clips from members and ministers.

The reality is that, as 99 percent of members of Parliament would tell you, Question Period is orchestrated. It's not a genuine event. The questions are anticipated. They're generated from the morning newspapers or clips on morning television, so the real dynamic of MPs on either side of the House responding spontaneously to things doesn't happen.

There are a lot of journalists on the Hill who take the time to write in-depth, substantive pieces. But a number of journalists just hang around in Hooker Alley day in and day out, looking for the 15- or 30-second clip. And I don't think that it represents the essence of what's happening here.

ALAN TONKS

Alan Tonks is the Liberal MP for York South–Weston in west Toronto. He was elected to Parliament in November 2000. Prior to his election to federal politics Mr. Tonks had a 30-year career in municipal politics in the Greater Toronto Area. His former duties included mayor of the City of York from 1982 to 1988 and chairman of the Municipality of Metropolitan Toronto from 1988–1997. From 1997 to 2000 Mr. Tonks served as the chairman of the Greater Toronto Services Board, a body created by the province to help the 30 municipalities in the Greater Toronto Area work co-operatively.

TOPICS:
A Lifetime in Politics
A New Role in the Federal Government
The Job of a Government-Member MP
A Government MP is to the Constituency's Advantage
The Culture and Power of Parliament
Party Loyalty
Taking Constituents' Concerns to the Government

A Lifetime in Politics

My message is I'm Alan Tonks. I used to be the mayor of York. I used to be the Metro chairman. I am the chairman of the Greater Toronto Area. I want to take that experience to Ottawa. I think a candidate is stronger with a good team and I've always found that the strength of a team will do a better job at servicing the public than an individual crying in the wilderness.

Traditionally this has been a Liberal riding and traditionally that has been enough. It will be a great challenge for me to consolidate support and bring it behind me solely as a Liberal. That probably would not be possible. But as a Liberal and a former mayor and former Metro chairman and a former leader in the Greater Toronto Area, it may be the combination that will enable me to outpace all of the combinations that exist out there.

A New Role in the Federal Government

This is my first time in Parliament. As you leave here on a cold night, you look up at those Parliament buildings and feel proud to be representing the people in your constituency. This is the mother of Parliaments and a tradition of the British parliamentary system and I feel really proud to be here. I have to admit that the rhythm of the job is like a long-distance race. You have got to be pumping all the time. I'm enjoying it very much, though. I've been in civic politics for 30 years. I've seen how you can effect change at the municipal level. At the federal level, it's not as quick. Whatever you work on, it just takes longer.

Every bit of this job is challenging. I find the work within the committee that I selected, the HRDC, human resources development committee, to be particularly challenging. Some people think that power is concentrated at the top, and to some extent it is. But community programs that focus on everything from apprenticeships and post-secondary education to children's initiatives to employment insurance are important. Those are the issues, really, that protect my people in my area and it's absolutely a challenge to serve their needs and interests. It always is. It doesn't change by the size of the arena because you still have that, serving your constituents, right at the centre of why you're here. So it's every bit as challenging as anything I ever had before. Besides, as mayor and Metro chairman I knew the network of people I needed to deal with. Here I'm building it up and that's very important because all politics is, is networks and people that will help you do the job.

102

It's not as though I'm working for the smaller pieces of legislation and not the grand themes. It's actually just the opposite. That's what people think they see because they see Question Period. They think that that's the nature of the House. The real nature of the House is the tough sledding that's going on. For example, take two subcommittees: status of persons with disabilities, chaired by Carolyn Bennett, and the national children's agenda, chaired by John Godfrey. If you saw the concrete stuff that's coming out and those initiatives, you'd know that that's where the real action is. That's where the real relevant stuff is going on — the stuff that affects the people in the country. You see the partisan nature of the House in action but the real work in the House goes to the committees. I'm in the agreement service group development skill committee where we talk about community programs. It takes time to work through that and often what you see isn't what you get. That's where the real work is going on. For example, you work on amendments to the employment insurance plan through the committee system and then see the results in the House. By the time it gets there, there really isn't anything huge to disagree with. So it gets caught up and you see the partisan nature and that's all you see.

The Job of a Government-Member MP

When you talk about the health-care system, or when you talk about what Mike next door is telling you, your ability to translate that into strong policies within the government caucus is a fundamental part of your job. There's an individual job to criticize, for the media, to be a good constituency person. But a huge part of the job is to develop policies in health care and in everything from social services to environmental initiatives; things that are going to make your community strong. This community has huge needs that can only be met by strong governmental support and that's the role that a member has to play.

A Government MP Is to the Constituency's Advantage

Being a part of the government side will bring more influence and more support to York South–Weston. In fact, it will build strong cities across the country. I am a Liberal and my values are Liberal. I've always been Liberal and this constituency has voted Liberal because they believed in those values, and I represent them.

I think my constituents see my role very clearly as representing their views but I don't think that they elected me to go into the Cabinet. I do think they expect me to be able to plug into where the power is to implement programs that are in their interest and that's my role. Getting into Cabinet is not your sole motivation to run for Parliament. Your motivation is to support the program that best serves the needs of your community.

My promise is to develop from my experience. I can use my relationships. I've never burnt bridges; I build bridges. After nearly 30 years in politics you develop a simpatico relationship with your colleagues. They will listen to your insights that come through your community. I offer the opportunity to change governmental policies where they may not be as focused as they should, in, for example, infrastructure funding for cities, transit subsidies, that kind of thing. I can convince the government to change direction from the inside, whereas I think that a lone voice on the outside has a hollow ring to it.

I can play a stronger role within the caucus, within the government — more so than someone who is on the outside looking in. I can be the voice for this constituency, not only to bring better government and services to the constituency, but also to do that for cities across the country.

When you're part of a team and you're on the field occupying that field against the strategies and tactics of an opposition, you can accomplish more because the team will help you. You define the strategies, the vision and the goals that you want from your community and then you bring the full force of government to achieve those goals. In that sense, with the team behind me, I can do a better job than someone who doesn't have a team.

The Culture and Power of Parliament
The frustration is the appearance that the prime minister and the Prime Minister's Office are exercising power. The frustration is that there are issues that transcend differences. I come from a municipal background where you must serve all of the community. The danger in the House is that we're never really able to bring all of the sides together, to convince people that we are developing a national consensus on our ideals and values which make the country strong. I kind of like to get back to basics. Let's not just give the appearance that we have to disagree on

every single issue. There are elements of policy that we can all agree on that are going to make the country stronger, regardless of party.

I haven't been in the House as long as some backbenchers who feel the frustration regarding too much power in the Prime Minister's Office. My initial reaction is that it isn't the structure of the parliamentary system, the committee system and the subcommittees, but the House rules and procedures that are as much at fault as the culture itself. The feeling is that people are here for the right reasons and that they should give that message out. They really feel frustrated because that isn't the message that's going out to the country, and I feel that same frustration.

I think we should start to work on relationships, not necessarily the structures. We should work on our networking and trying to cross the floor on some key issues, for example, the issue of cities. I think developing a national consensus on the role of cities is important and we can develop more cross-party agreement on that.

The agreement was that an ethics counsellor would be responsible to the prime minister, who's responsible to the House. It's a matter of accountability. I had no problems with the accountability of the prime minister and I still don't. I think that that's been grossly exaggerated. My colleagues elected me. We're accountable through the prime minister for our program to our constituencies. Part of today's team on the field is to have a Cabinet system and we believe in that. So I'll serve in any capacity to put forward the agenda of the people of my area.

Party Loyalty

The parliamentary system is running on a program that your party stands for. So I've had no problems with that at all.

My granddad told me, and he was a Conservative, "You choose your party and you stay with that party. If it's wrong, you change the party, but you don't change parties." You have to bring in every power that you have. At the end of the day, because we have a democracy and the majority must rule in every sense, then you support that party position. You don't undermine it; you get on with the next issue because it isn't that the party is always totally wrong or totally right.

Taking Constituents' Concerns to the Government

We have been building the riding association. Judy Sgro, who had a great campaign here last time, went to York West, so there was no organization here. I always feel accountable to the people who have stayed loyal to the party, who have been out there pounding doors and trying to carry a message. So the first thing I'm going to do is bring all those people together in the association. I'm going to try and reach out into the community to find the major position and issues they'd like me to focus on in Ottawa, and I'm going to take that to Ottawa.

The issues they have highlighted in terms of their concerns for the constituency are housing, deteriorating apartment buildings, the deteriorating business strips as a result of de-industrialization, and the congestion on the roads linking this area. Also included are the lack of social services and backup for the community and the issues of an aging population as it relates to the health-care system. I'm going to try and articulate those issues as clearly as I can in caucus to get some changes in terms of government policy, hopefully arguing convincingly about those issues so that the prime minister and members of caucus will listen.

DON BOUDRIA

Don Boudria has represented the Ontario riding of Glengarry–Prescott–Russell in the House of Commons since 1984, and is currently government House leader. Between 1984 and 1993 he held several Opposition critic portfolios, including agriculture, supply and services, public works and Canada Post. He was first appointed to Cabinet as minister for international co-operation and minister responsible for La Francophonie on October 4, 1996. He was appointed minister of state and leader of the government in the House of Commons in 1997. From 1981 to 1984 he represented the riding of Prescott–Russell in the Ontario legislature. Before entering politics he worked as a federal employee.

TOPICS:
Parliamentary Reform
What Should Be Done
Comparing Parliaments
Modernization

The Committee Report
What Isn't in the Report
Electoral Reform
The Committee's Approach
Parliamentary Committees
Proportional Representation
Keeping Government in Check
The Centralization of Power

Parliamentary Reform

After the 1997 election we had five parties in the House of Commons for the first time. We had to revise most of the rules in order to permit the parties in fourth and fifth place even to have a right to say anything in the House of Commons. It was just not provided for in the old rules because no one had ever conceived of five parties in a Westminster-style Parliament, as we've always had in Canada.

The job of House leader is more challenging with five parties. When I was made leader of the government in the House of Commons in 1997, I could never refer back to precedents to see what we did the last time we had five parties because it had never happened before. It wasn't insurmountable, but certainly different and more challenging.

Every change in the number of parties in the House of Commons changes the way that the House behaves. If the House were reduced today from five parties to two, that would probably trigger a number of necessary changes again. It's a living organism. It's not static. One has to adjust constantly to the conditions. During the entire last session there were probably one or two changes per month.

Ten years ago if any of us had predicted that there would be as official Opposition a regional party from the West or a separatist party from Quebec, we probably wouldn't have believed it. Yet that condition exists now in the House of Commons.

Two Parliaments from now, who knows what the configuration of the political parties will be? We can't predict that. We just have to adjust accordingly as time goes by. Reform is an evolving thing.

So it isn't as if somebody woke up three weeks ago and discovered parliamentary reform. It occurs all the time, except when Parliament is shut down or during an election campaign.

In the 1993 to 1997 Parliament changes were made. Changes like permitting the review of the budget and hearing witnesses before it was produced; permitting committees to produce their own legislation rather than having it come out of the House; and having the future years' expenditures incorporated into the Estimates process, rather than only the current year's. All of these reforms have gone forward all along.

Changing times make parliamentary reform happen frequently. There's hardly a month that goes by without some rule being changed. Just today we changed a rule in the House of Commons about the number of committees.

Reform wasn't an issue during the election. It does become an issue during the election of Speaker because that galvanizes it. The candidates who speak on issues involving the functioning of Parliament automatically trigger a debate in that regard.

But no one would be shocked to hear that during door-to-door canvassing in the last election campaign, I wasn't asked about parliamentary reform. Can you imagine knocking on doors and hearing someone say, "I'll vote for you if you change report stage"?

That's not what Canadians say. They say, "What are you going to do about child poverty? What are you going to do about high taxes? How is your policy going to influence our health care?" and whatever else they want to raise.

The number of members on the finance committee, or how we deal with the report stage of bills, or whether or not a bill can be sent to committee before or after second reading: those weren't the issues raised door to door at all. There's no groundswell demanding reform.

There's always room for modernizing how we do business in Parliament. And I for one am interested in discussing this with House leaders of other political parties. The week that Parliament came back we had no fewer than three meetings about changing various rules. It's not uncommon that we would have that happen every week that Parliament is sitting.

What Should Be Done

We on the government side certainly want Parliament to function properly, to have good debate and by and large to be fair. The opposition generally wants that too, but people get into their various positions and negotiations aren't always easy. But we've succeeded many times in the past, and I'm optimistic that we'll be able to change a number of rules again and make Parliament work even better.

One of the great accomplishments in recent years has been parliamentary scrutiny of legislation in committees. We do that better than the U.K. We do it better than most countries.

We're proposing to increase funding to the research branch of the Library of Parliament. They're the ones who put together the research papers and other documentation necessary for members to do their work in that regard.

A second goal that needs to be addressed is modernizing the voting system in the House of Commons. It's very impressive for the clerk of the House to be able to recognize 301 people at 50 yards without mixing up their names, but it's not exactly a modern way to do it. It's a horse-and-buggy system. We should have electronic voting in the House of Commons, if only to cut down voting time.

Third, a glitch occurred in the rules in the last Parliament. We have a report stage of bills in the House of Commons, and this glitch essentially meant that a member of Parliament, by changing commas to semicolons in a bill, could keep the House going 24 hours a day, for days on end. Unfortunately this has now happened, so it has to be addressed.

The glitch is new. What happened is this: on one particular deal, about two and a half years ago, the opposition decided to put forward a number of frivolous amendments. I don't say that in a disparaging way; they were frivolous by definition.

For instance, you can change a comma to a semicolon and that constitutes having a vote. And if it constitutes having a vote, then it takes 12 or 13 minutes to vote on it. So if you produce enough of them, you can stop Parliament from functioning.

Another example comes from the last clause of a bill, which says that this bill will come into force on, say, June 1, 2001. You could produce an amendment to say that it will come on July 1, August 1 and September 1. You could produce thousands of these amendments that don't do anything.

How can one person have 2,000 positions on the date that a deal should be implemented? It's ridiculous. You either want it on a certain day or you want it on a different day, but you don't want 2,000 different dates for the same piece of legislation.

In parliamentary jargon they're called "wrecking amendments." They're trivial amendments designed to do nothing but delay the process. They're a loophole in the system, stopping the government from legislating.

That was never how the report stage was supposed to work. The intent was to permit MPs who aren't on a committee to produce an amendment in the House.

For example, let's say that we're dealing with a bill on foreign affairs and you're a member of the finance committee. And when the bill goes to the foreign affairs committee, you're not there to produce an amendment. There's a provision in the rule that, even if you're not on that committee, you're not disenfranchised because you can always produce an amendment at report stage, if you're so inclined.

That provision was based on the British example and has worked well for years. But now someone has developed a way of using it to stop Parliament from functioning at all. Amendments are meant to amend a bill, not to stop Parliament from functioning.

The "voting machine" that MP Chuck Strahl described after one Question Period was in reference to keeping MPs here all night to vote on ridiculous amendments. That has nothing to do with the government. It was a procedural stunt pulled by the Opposition.

This doesn't mean that we must abandon the report stage of bills. It could be reformed in a way that would stop people from putting forth frivolous amendments, while at the same time permitting them to produce a real one. A system has to be developed to clean it up, as it were, and not throw out the baby with the bath water.

In the Throne Speech, the prime minister talked about sending more bills to committee prior to second reading. There's a rule that when a bill is sent to committee after second reading, you can't make an amendment that's beyond the scope of the bill. However, if you send it to committee before second reading, it recognizes broader amendments. It's a form of openness that will be beneficial.

So those are some of the reform concepts that have been raised in a specific way. In a more general way, both the Opposition House leader and I have just returned from the United Kingdom, where we saw how their Parliament worked.

Comparing Parliaments

In the United Kingdom they have a shorter lead-time to respond to committee reports. That's very positive. They also have a way of dealing with bills in the House of Commons that they call "programming," where they assign the bill to a committee, and the committee can do pretty well whatever it likes, so long as it's reported back to the House on a preordained day. For the opposition, they can have more freedom with witnesses. And there's something for the government: they know exactly when they'll get the bill back. Those are ideas to be considered.

In the Canadian House of Commons time limits are only used selectively. In the British House every bill is time-allocated. You start and say, "Mr. Speaker, this bill will be debated for four hours, or six hours." At the end of the day, it's finished.

In my case, I must actually produce a motion that I could only trigger on the second day, and I have to repeat at every stage of the bill. The Canadian parliamentary rules regarding ending debate are much softer than you would find in the "mother of parliaments."[1]

The proof is the final result. How many bills do we pass in a year, compared to the British House or another legislature? We don't pass any more of them, so it's not as if the government wanted to get all of its legislation through. That's not the final result.

Do the calculation. During our 36th Parliament, 111 bills were passed in three years. Go to the U.K. and do the same calculation for three years. Go to the United States House of Representatives and do the same calculation. Their numbers are much higher than ours.

Obviously we do not use closure very often. We certainly don't have the results to demonstrate that we're gung-ho about passing legislation.

The British House also has a parallel chamber where it can send less important or less controversial legislation. Would a parallel chamber have an application here? I don't know, but it's certainly a form of modernization. They based it on the Australian example, and both of them are apparently successful. It's certainly another issue to look at.

Already in this Parliament, though, I've succeeded in obtaining greater funding, together with other House leaders, for members of Parliament to hire their constituency staff. Members are always heavily taxed for that. It seems like the more staff you get, the more demand there is, and we're never able to do all of the constituency work expected of us. So we're receiving more funding for that. I hope that it's going to be helpful for all members of Parliament.

Modernization

I would like to see a Parliament that's more modern. It's not a grand vision of any kind. I don't want to take this institution, turn it upside down and shake it. This is a good institution, one of the finest in the world.

We have to act prudently to make it better: modernizing our voting system; ensuring that time in the House is spent debating, as opposed to changing commas to semicolons; and ensuring that what we do is meaningful to and for the benefit of Canadians. There are parliamentary committees that have an excellent track record but could work even better at improving the legislation produced by various government departments.

So that's a list of some of the improvements made or specifically announced and broader issues to be looked at over the next little while. It's not rocket science, but it's really what I'd like.

The Committee Report[2]

The changes proposed by the modernization committee will make Parliament work better. They'll make government more accountable. And they'll make the functioning of Parliament somewhat more modern.

For instance, in the area of accountability the officers of Parliament (the clerk, the chief electoral officer and so on) will now be appointed pursuant to a vote of the House of Commons. Before it was a hodgepodge. Some of them were named by governor in council, some by governor in council with ratification of the House, some with a debate, some without. Now all of these officers are uniform and subject to a vote of the House.

In the area of accountability, again, when the House uses time allocation, closure or other such measures in the future, there will be a mini-debate before a vote.

We're going to have another television room. On Parliament Hill there's one room for committees to be fully televised, complete with preset televisions for the polling system. Now there will be two of those rooms. I think that two rooms can accommodate virtually all of the committees that want to be televised. It's going to be a good investment and an improvement.

We're also going to make the chamber more user-friendly for many of the debates. For the evening debates, emergency debates, take-note debates and so on, we're going to try the British format, the dispatch box format. We're going to use only part of the chamber, near the clerk's table, so that MPs will be closer to one another. There's no point, outside of Question Period, in having them basically sit 100 yards from each other (the chamber's almost the size of a football field) and shouting. If they're face to face, particularly when they're smaller groups, it makes for greater dialogue between MPs and more constructive debate.

We're going to make greater use of ministerial statements in the House. We had gradually removed ourselves from those over recent years. On the opposition side they'll now have to give the government greater notice of their Opposition Day Motions.

For instance, if we were to debate a subject chosen by the opposition, it used to be that they could tell us at 6:00 the night before. And if they told us at that time that we would debate big industry, and the minister of industry was in Yellowknife making an announcement, what would happen? You just can't get the officials back by the appropriate time.

Now they'll have to say so at the beginning of the day before. The Speaker will arrive in his place and be served notice by the opposition that tomorrow we'll be debating such and such. So that's the process that will take place.

What Isn't in the Report

Not everything is in the report. For instance, I wanted electronic voting for the chamber. That wasn't a possibility. Everything operated on unanimity in the committee, which we didn't get for that feature. But still, overall things are good.

The report doesn't deal with internal caucus discipline of individual political parties, but that's something for each party to discuss. Should there be more free votes? There are certainly a lot more free votes now than there ever were before, and I've been around here for several decades. We have free votes on every single private member's item.

And they're not the be-all and end-all, either. We weren't elected as independent MPs. We were elected as partisan MPs. I was elected as a Liberal. John Reynolds, the Opposition House leader, was elected as a member of the Alliance. Michel Gauthier is a member of the Bloc, Peter MacKay is a member of the Conservatives and so on. Each was elected as part of a team.

I was elected as part of the Liberal group, with the platform of the *Red Book*. We're expected to come here and espouse the views that we expressed during the election campaign, not to say, "Look, I'm not bound by any of this stuff. We said it to get elected, but now I can do what I like." That's just not how it works.

If the people wanted 301 independent MPs, why did they elect zero? In the election, 1,500 independent candidates ran and none of them won. A few thousand partisan candidates ran and they're the kind that got elected.

So people expect their MPs to speak as part of a group, to espouse and defend the views that they stated during the election campaigns and that are presented by the political parties from time to time.

Electoral Reform

Electoral reform wasn't part of the modernization committee's work. It was never raised and it didn't form part of the mandate.

But on the issue of electoral reform (I'm the minister responsible for Canada's election laws), the way that it's done in Canada is that after every election, the chief electoral officer tables a report of the recommendations to make the election laws work better. The report is sent to the parliamentary committee on procedure, privilege and election. That committee hears witnesses, listens to all of the political parties, makes recommendations and brings them back to the House for legislation. Then I as the minister responsible (if I still am, the next time that happens) produce the legislation and introduce it in the House of Commons.

Generally our electoral system works well. The last election demonstrated the benefit of people being able to vote from home and with handwritten ballots. If you had to vote at the beginning of the election campaign, and the candidate hadn't even been chosen in your particular riding, you could just print the name of the political party on a pre-designated piece of paper and put that in the ballot box. Then your vote would count anyway.

There was greater access for people who were outside the country when voting, and more access through mobile phones. All of these changes were intended to make the electoral system work better.

The Committee's Approach

The system isn't flawed. It's a good system that works well. But it does need improvement from time to time. Improvements should be made in a thoughtful way, usually through changes to the rules. And these changes should be made with the co-operation of all parties in the House of

Commons, to retain the balance between the governing side and the opposition so that you don't run roughshod over the rights of the minority.

That's the approach we used in this report. We even constructed the committee in such a way that only those items where there was unanimity could be reported to the House.

We've heard several contributing officers of Parliament say that the report doesn't address the fundamental power structure and the processes where the government can control committees. The government can basically dictate the direction of policy.

But the government is elected to govern. Turn the proposition upside down and see if it works: the government is elected to govern, but it doesn't? Surely that wouldn't make much sense.

Parliamentary Committees

The parliamentary committees do excellent work in Canada. They witness about 90 percent of the legislation introduced in the House of Commons. We go through bills clause by clause. Sometimes dozens and dozens of amendments are produced to improve the legislation at report stage, or in committee, so that the bill comes back to the House improved.

I went to the U.K. last January with Chuck Strahl, who was then the Opposition House leader. The quality of work by Canadian parliamentary committees is envied by other countries.

In countries such as the U.K. they'll routinely adopt bills in committee without listening to one witness. Nobody comes. Occasionally the minister will come, testify and then that's it. They go through the bill clause by clause, send it back to the House and let the House of Lords tinker with amendments to improve the language of the bill.

Our system works better. I really compliment the MPs who work on parliamentary committees. They do very good work.

Proportional Representation

I'm one of those who believe that single-member districts, which we have now, are a very good system. I'm not in favour of proportional representation; the underlying assumption is inherently flawed.

In the riding where I was elected some people voted for Don Boudria. Some people voted Liberal. Some people voted for the *Red Book*. And some people voted for Jean Chrétien. I don't know how many there were of each. All I know is that the sum of them elected me.

116

What proportional representation purports to say is that 100 percent of the people who voted for me voted Liberal. They only wanted to vote Liberal and there was no other consideration. And anyone who voted against me in my riding voted Alliance. Therefore, all of those votes belong to a party and none of them to a candidate. So the party should have a proportion of that, as votes assigned to them, even though that may not have been the intention of the voters.

The inherent flaw of proportional representation is that it gives seats to people who didn't win, on the premise that all votes belong to the political parties. At an internal party convention that doesn't apply. It isn't a consideration.

That it makes losers win is something that people should think about. For a politician to assume that everyone wants to vote for his or her party and no one wants to vote for an MP is bordering on arrogance.

If one alleges that MPs aren't sufficiently independent now because ties to the political parties are too strong, then how can one at the same time advocate proportional representation, where the only role of the MP is to represent the party? The MP then has the seat by virtue of not having constituents.

By virtue of having been defeated in the previous election, the MP's only elected because of the relative proportion of people that got on the list. So by definition list MPs will have no constituents and will be responsible only to the officials of their parties.

If the allegation is that party discipline is too strong now, how does creating proportional representation achieve any objective of diminishing it? It's oxymoronic. It just can't work.

There's a balance in the system. The MP is elected. He or she knows that some people voted for the party, some for the party's policy and some for the party's leader. An MP knows that he or she is elected by the aggregate of these and must always bear all of them in mind.

Keeping Government in Check

We live in a system known as responsible government. That means that the governments are in power so long as they retain the confidence of the majority of the House of Commons.

If the majority of MPs decide to vote non-confidence in the government, then the government is no longer the government. It ceases to exist. And the leader of the government, the prime minister, is forced to attend to the sovereign, the governor general, to ask for dissolution and call an election.

Ministers hold the executive power, while MPs hold the legislative power. Of course, ministers are also MPs, so they share some of that; but the reverse isn't true.

MPs have the ultimate tool. They can choose to defeat the government, should it be hopelessly bad. MPs can collectively vote non-confidence in the government. Their vote turfs the rascals out. It defeats the government and causes an election.

I'm reminded of the United States's example of Richard Nixon and Watergate. When members of both Houses ceased to want Richard Nixon to be the president of the United States, they still had him. After months and months of acrimony, they still had him.

In the House of Commons, if someone wants to vote non-confidence in the executive, it takes about eight minutes, not months. That's the beauty of our parliamentary system.

But again, the system has that balance in it. By defeating the government, you're defeating yourself. So in the next election you go to the people, having defeated the government to which you belonged.

In the case of a minority government, that would be a little bit easier. In the case of a majority government, it would seldom happen, unless the people felt that the government in power was dishonest or unworthy of having power at all, and that having it there any longer would be inappropriate.

The legislative arm has the authority to do that now. This is a very blunt instrument. It should be used sparingly. The fact that it's used at all illustrates its inherent value.

The Centralization of Power

I've been around here for a long time. This year I'll be celebrating the 35th anniversary of my arrival, not as an MP, obviously, because I was only a staffer here at the beginning.

I don't think that power is more centralized than it once was. I can't detect that at all. Going back to the Pearson government and measuring it vis-à-vis today, I think that this prime minister and this government are more accountable to MPs than Mr. Pearson was.

Mr. Pearson didn't go to caucus, except perhaps every now and then. Prime Minister Jean Chrétien walks into the caucus room, sits there from beginning to end and doesn't even remove himself from the room for 30 seconds. Once a week he's there for two hours for his back bench, listening to all of that. He meets MPs every day in his office after Question Period. He's very accessible to his supporters in the House of Commons.

He attends Question Period three times more often than, say, the British prime minister, who only goes once a week. Our prime minister goes three and sometimes four days a week to the House of Commons during Question Period. The level of accountability is high. The prime minister has set that bar quite high.

A Cabinet minister has more power than a backbencher, through executive power. The minister has executive power under our Constitution, as is the case in the U.K., Australia and New Zealand. Money can only be produced by the government. It can't be produced by someone who isn't a member of the executive.

Furthermore, a tax can't be generated by anyone without executive power. It can't originate in the Senate. It has to originate in the House of Commons. That's also true in the United States. A motion of ways and means has to be introduced in the House of Commons and then adopted. The motion is permission to produce the bill to generate the tax.

So all of these executive powers belong to the government. But again, that isn't unique to Canada. That isn't even unique to British-style democracy because it's also the case in the United States. The power to nominate belongs to the executive.

Some MPs say that power has been removed from the legislature. But we've modernized the estimate process in the House of Commons. We have future years' expenditures reviewed by parliamentary committee. We've democratized the budgetary process. Every year now the finance committee travels throughout the country, making a contribution to arguably the most important issue that Parliament ever handles: the tabling of the budget by the minister of finance.

All of these tasks are occurring, and they didn't even exist 10 years ago. People can't say that MPs have less power now than they did before. They might crave or want more power. That's a normal aspiration. Everyone wants to be in Cabinet and so on. That's all OK. But it's not the same as saying that they have less power than they did 10 or 20 years ago. As a matter of fact, I would argue that MPs have a lot more influence now.

NOTES

1. Unlike the British House of Commons, Canada does not have standard or regular time allocations on debating bills; as a result, debates can go on for days, rather than hours.
2. Don Boudria was interviewed on two occasions — the first was prior to the modernization committee report and the second was after. The modernization report was tabled in the House by the Special Committee on Modernization and Improvement on the Procedures of the House of Commons in the summer of 2001. Full details are available at www.pco-bcp.gc.ca/lgc.

MARLENE CATTERALL

Marlene Catterall first joined the Liberal caucus in 1988 as the MP for Ottawa West. She won election to the House of Commons for the fourth time in 2000 and was appointed chief government whip in September 1999. Prior to entering federal politics Ms. Catterall was well known throughout the region as a City of Ottawa alderwoman (Britannia Ward), from 1977 to 1985, and as a councillor with the Regional Municipality of Ottawa-Carleton (1977–1985).

TOPICS:
The Role of a Government Whip in Parliament
Party Discipline of the Government Whip
The Fundamental Importance of Accounting for Money:
The Business of Supply
A Perceived Need to Hold the Government Accountable for Spending:
The Subcommittee on the Business of Supply
The Business of Supply Report: Process of Implementation
The Business of Supply Report: What Happened to It?

The Role of a Government Whip in Parliament

The position of government whip goes back to the British Parliament centuries ago when, literally, Parliament didn't meet very often. When Parliament was to convene, it was the whip's job to go throughout the countryside, literally whipping his horses to stop at the farm gates and at the factories and shops and bring the members of Parliament back to London. That's where the term comes from.

I have a whip. It's in a sealed glass case. If I ever have to take it out, I figure I've failed because my job is to make sure that whatever legislation comes into the House of Commons is something that by and large is satisfactory to my party's members (the Liberals). And that they're going to be there to vote for it. My main instrument, frankly, is constant phone calls: "The vote's on. Are you going to be there? If not, why not? We really need you there for this particular vote."

Part of my role is making sure that MPs in my party aren't just griping behind the scenes, that they're trying to achieve something constructive. When legislation comes to Parliament, there should be a substantial consensus among the Liberal members. If not, it will go to committee and there will be some improvements. I figure it's one of my major responsibilities, if there are some concerns about legislation, to work with the minister, to make the prime minister aware of those concerns, to work with my caucus colleagues and try and resolve those concerns before a vote is held.

Party Discipline of the Government Whip

As government whip, I have to decide who's going to sit on what committees and advise the prime minister on who should chair what committees. It's also putting people in those niches where they will be able to do the kind of work that they're interested in, where they feel they can make a real contribution. Now, there's always some work that would not be everybody's first choice and somebody's got to do that. But I also have to try to make sure that people have the opportunity to do the things that are really of interest to them.

I suppose if somebody were consistently not being a team player, not co-operating, leaving it to everybody else to carry out their responsibilities and just not being here to do what they were elected to do, I might say, "Gee, I'm not going to give that person that seat on that committee when four other people want it." Is that a disciplinary measure? Maybe, but above all I've got to be fair. And if people see that I'm being fair in giving out responsibilities and certain privileges, conferences, international conferences, committees people want to sit on, special task forces they want to set up, then I'm building teamwork and I don't have to rely on disciplinary measures.

The Fundamental Importance of Accounting for Money:
The Business of Supply

The spending priorities of a government indicate where its social, economic, cultural and environmental priorities are. Where the money goes is where the government's going, frankly. I don't think of money as the be-all and end-all of everything government does, but if you don't get the dollars accounted for, you cannot do the things you want to do.

The fundamental role of Parliament is to decide what resources the government should have, what they're able to spend them on, and to hold the government accountable for meeting what Parliament has approved. If we're not doing that, then we're not exercising full public accountability in the interests of the taxpayers, as well as in the interests of Canadian society, which is supposed to benefit from government programs and services.

The other factor that was very important is, members of Parliament are not now using the capacity they have to hold government accountable, to have more influence on spending priorities and therefore to have more influence on the policy priorities of government.

When I first came to Parliament I was appalled (I'm still not exactly delighted) by the way parliamentary committees dealt with the spending estimates. It basically becomes a shooting gallery. The opposition is there to try and find a target in the Estimates that allows them to shoot at the minister and criticize the government. After nine years on municipal council in Ottawa, I was used to a very detailed, very thorough study of budgets, what the problems were and what the long-range plans were. So I found this sort of superficial consideration of spending estimates in the federal government really quite concerning.

Some people look at the internal auditors as the enemy, there to find out your faults. I regard the auditor function as the biggest assistance government has in terms of finding out how well we are doing, how well the resources are being used and whether we're getting the results we should be getting and so on.

A Perceived Need to Hold the Government Accountable for Spending: The Subcommittee on the Business of Supply

Over the last quarter of a century there has been one committee after another struck to look at the issue of how Parliament oversees money. There is a continuing dissatisfaction with members of Parliament. That to me indicated an ongoing need for a watchdog for Parliament on the spending estimates process, and where members of Parliament fit into that equation. It was something I asked to do because it's a subject that really interests me and that I think is of great public importance.

So in the public accounts committee we decided we would create a subcommittee, called the subcommittee on the business of supply. I was the chairperson. Our focus was in large part on how to put in place the measures that will enable parliamentary committees and individual parliamentarians to have a stronger influence on public policy. So that's the fundamental principle of the business of supply report that we created out of that committee in 1996.

Our primary objective in writing the report on the business of supply was to make MPs more aware of the whole package of tools at their disposal, to influence not only the immediate budget and the immediate spending plans, but longer-term, shifting priorities of the government. A number of tools have been provided in recent years. They have the planning and priorities report in the spring, which lays out not only what the department is now doing but also what they see as the challenges for the next three years. In the fall they have the performance report, so they can hold departments and ministers accountable for having achieved the results they said they were going to achieve.

The Business of Supply Report: Process of Implementation
The business of supply, the spending estimates, how Parliament works are some things that don't preoccupy a lot of members of Parliament. I think many of my colleagues are not aware of the report, but nonetheless, behind the scenes it's moving things forward.

The incentives that we tried to bring into the business of supply document have not worked completely — yet. I think nobody is satisfied with the job that committees do on the spending estimates right now. Better information, more concise and comprehensive information, is needed. It's improving the tools that members have at their disposal. They've got to say, "Am I really interested in doing this? Do I really take seriously this accountability role?" And if they do, the tools are there to let them do the work they want to do.

So the business of supply report was never adopted by Parliament. It was received very positively within the administration because it reinforced a lot of work they were trying to do. They had been, within Treasury Board, for instance, spending a lot of effort on trying to improve reporting to Parliament. We helped move that along a little more quickly. We gave the incentive for a next step. We recommended more resources for committees so they could have more independent research, not rely so much on information from the government. A Speech from the Throne actually did that, inserted more resources into the Library of Parliament and that's the main tool that most committees use to get their research done. A number of things continue to be implemented since the business of supply report was tabled. The tax expenditure report being renewed is one example. The improved reporting to Parliament continues. The annual global report on managing for results that's now tabled in Parliament every year, that's an outcome of the work we did.

We also have a spotlight now on tax expenditures. It's easy to give businesses or individuals a tax break for one purpose or another. But $1 billion not collected is the same as $1 billion spent. For years there was no way of seeing how much money was being lost to the public purse and therefore to services that could be delivered to Canadians through those tax expenditures. That's come back so we can now look and say we're spending $1 billion on this particular tax measure. Is it achieving what it was supposed to be achieving? Is it helping us get more research and development in this country? Is it helping us improve the lives of Canadians, their social situation, the environment, the economy?

Not every detail of the report has been implemented and nobody expects that that can happen overnight, but I think there's been a significant change in the bureaucracy, in how they look at the relationship with Parliament.

If there's one recommendation that hasn't been implemented but is quite important, it's establishing a committee on the spending estimates process.

The Business of Supply Report: What Happened to It?

Because the business of supply report I co-authored never was endorsed by Parliament, John Williams, who was vice-chair of the subcommittee, is putting forward a motion that the government immediately implement the recommendations of the business of supply report. And I think "immediately" is something that we knew wasn't going to happen when we wrote the report five years ago. This is an evolutionary process. Things have to develop over a period of time. For instance, John knows as well as I do (and if he doesn't, his House leader will tell him) the difficulty of setting up an additional committee right now with five parties in Parliament. It becomes practically unachievable. All the parties now have problems having members there for all the committees that are meeting.

John's motion will be debated and voted on in Parliament as a private members' bill. Normally, as government whip I would take no role in private member's business because we've made it clear that for our members of Parliament, private members' business is free votes. However, having chaired the subcommittee that produced the report, this is what I'm going to speak on.

I'll be speaking against adopting the report.

I might have a little verbal shot at John about the facility of being in opposition and asking things to be done immediately when one knows, practically, that that's simply not possible. I give John great credit for the work he's done on this. I still feel that one of our main jobs is to get members of Parliament to use the tools they now have at their disposal and to more completely hold the government accountable for its spending, but as one of the co-authors of the report, I will be voting against it.

It's not an irony. John and I worked very well together on that committee. John started out, as I said, fairly simplistically as opposition often does, thinking that all the problems could be solved if we only had free votes and if we didn't have restraints on members changing what's in the Estimates. I think he came around to understand that there's a much more constructive and positive role for members of Parliament and a really strong role for them in influencing government spending and priorities and holding government accountable.

Free Votes in Parliament: A Team Sport

I don't think free votes are the solution to the problems that people say are plaguing Parliament. A party gets elected on a platform and is accountable to Canadians to deliver on that platform. The people who ran on that platform got elected based on the promises of the leader. All the other candidates can't suddenly turn around after the election and say, "Oops, I was wrong. I'm not a Liberal. I don't support those programs." The second point is that when a bill comes to Parliament, it's already been discussed at great length within our caucus. Members who have a problem with it have an opportunity to work out those problems with the ministers. Ministers are responsive, and if they're not, the prime minister makes sure they are so that when legislation comes to the House, it's something that we've all worked on. It's a product of the team, not just of an individual minister.

It's like a family discussion about where we are going on holidays. We can all have our opinion, but once a decision is made, we all go on the same holiday. This is a team sport and you're accountable to the public for supporting the team you were elected to. The government's responsible for fulfilling its promises to Canadians. I don't think free votes are the solution here. When it comes to private members' business, as far as I know we are the only party that has said to our members, "On private members' business you're free to vote how you want." If you look at the voting pattern, you'll notice that Liberal members do vote freely and opposition party members generally do not.

Problems with Free Votes in the U.S. System

I would tell someone who is cynical about the way government works that this is our parliamentary system of democracy. I know the Alliance Party members tend to have a more favourable view toward the American system of government. With free votes you become much more subject to pressure groups. You become subject to groups that can finance themselves well. The American example is very good. Many congressmen and many senators are totally dependent on contributions

127

to very expensive campaigns from public-interest groups. Those who've got the money to have that kind of influence have more sway than they necessarily should have compared to those who may in fact be most in need of the services of their government.

Parliamentary Committees

Committees are the heart and soul of parliamentary work. I know everybody focuses on Question Period for 45 minutes every day. But in fact the bulk of work of parliamentarians gets done in their committees. There's one attached to every department, then there are some special committees that aren't related to departments of government. But that's where members work together and if it's a good committee, members tend to put aside their partisan differences and really work on the issues that are of concern to them.

The main tool that members of Parliament have is their role on committees and the power of committees to review departmental spending estimates. In fact, shortly after the 1993 election our government introduced changes that greatly expanded the role of committees and their power to virtually examine anything that the department they are linked to is doing. The committees generally have not been doing that with respect to the Estimates, i.e., the spending and the revenue sources. One of the things the report tried to do was look at incentives that would make that a more attractive thing for members of Parliament to spend some time on.

Public Perception and the Parliamentary Committee

The public seeing what members of Parliament do in committee is a very important way of restoring public confidence in the parliamentary system. We recommended in our report on the business of supply expanded televising of committee proceedings with special focus on committees that are actually doing work on the Estimates. We recommended that there be responses from the government to committee reports and that they be given a major role when the finance committee does its consultations on the next year's budget in the fall of each year. Those are some of the incentives that we recommended.

There have been a number of changes as a result of our government's reports. More resources have gone into helping and supporting the committees. We'll be doubling the amount of television time available, full time, to committees. Committees are playing a much more active role and individual members of Parliament are playing a much more active role in the pre-budget consultations. This is something that never happened prior to this government being elected. In fact, the very first letter I wrote in 1993, after the election, was to Paul Martin, saying, "I know time is short, but I think we should have a public consultation process across the country on what's going to be in your first budget." In fact, starting in November, after the election, we did have the first ever cross-country consultations on what should be in the first budget of the Chrétien government.

Parliamentary Committees and Legislation

A piece of legislation is never a fait accompli when it comes to a committee. You just have to look at the record of how committees have dealt with legislation, have made substantial changes to legislation. Liberal as well as opposition members have put forward amendments to legislation that are accepted, and they're often the result of discussions among Liberals themselves who say, "Hey, we think legislation needs to be changed in this way or that way." But that also can happen with opposition members. I've served in opposition, too, so I can speak from both sides of the House. If you've really got something that you think makes sense, you can usually persuade the government that it makes sense and that a piece of legislation should be changed.

You sit down, you meet with the officials, you meet with the ministry, you meet with the minister's parliamentary secretary, you do your homework.

Role of the MP on Government Legislation

I think that there's no reason any member of Parliament can't feel they've got a full opportunity to influence what the government is doing. That goes for opposition or government, although I suspect you have a little edge if you're a government member. You're not always going to get your way. If I see a bill in front of me with 200 clauses, I can find three or four that I don't like. But if I essentially like what that bill is doing, then I'm going to support it. If it's an improvement, even if it's not perfection, then I'm going to support it. I don't always get my way. Nobody does. But being a member of Parliament gives you an opportunity to be involved with, to be influencing, virtually any subject that you care about. There are lots of vacuums around here, lots of issues that need work done on them. If you bring some talent to this place, find one of those issues, work on it, you can accomplish what you want to accomplish.

Power of Appointment by the Prime Minister

It is true that the power of appointment is one of the ways in which the influence is exercised. I think, though, that if you have public agencies, the government of the day obviously wants those public agencies to reflect the agenda that it is putting forward and what it's trying to implement. That only makes sense to me. We've made sure that committees can review the appointments. There are a number of appointments on which there's always consultation with the opposition parties. As whip, I can tell you that, contrary to the sense that we're always fighting with each other (and that is, I guess, what Question Period looks like), there is a tremendous amount of co-operation that goes on, on a daily basis. Co-operation between me and the whips of the other parties and between us and the House leaders of all parties. There is co-operation on what is debated in Parliament, when the votes are going to be, how long the debates are, when things go to committee, if new committees are being set up and how that happens.

When it comes to appointments, for instance, I will talk to virtually all of my colleagues. I will look at what they've done in the past and what committees they've served on. I'll look at what they've said they want to do.

We started advertising appointments. That's never been done before. So any Canadian can apply for an appointment and be considered on their merits. Free votes, even on private members' business? That's never been done in this country before, by any party. That sounds to me like a great deal of progress. Consulting with the public on what should be in the next budget? Up until we were elected in 1993, this happened behind closed doors. You didn't know who the government was listening to. Now Canadians can see what other Canadians from all walks of life are saying about what their priorities are. The finance committee does a public report. They can look at that, they can compare what's in the budget and see how the two mesh. There have been great steps forward in public accountability. I became interested in politics on the theme of participatory democracy. This is my country, this is my life, this is my city, this is my community. I have a right to have a say about what happens here and that doesn't mean just by whom I elect. It means the day after you're elected, I want to be able to talk to you and influence you and organize people to lobby you. I think we've made great moves to make this a more participatory democracy.

Role of Opposition MPs: A Necessity in Democracy
When I was in opposition I didn't find it frustrating. It's much better than being in government. It's much more fun being in opposition because you have no responsibility for anything, while you do in government. But I was able, on a number of bills, to get amendments agreed to by the government. It's painstaking, careful work to demonstrate that what you're proposing makes sense, is workable, and that you can convince others that this is a good thing to do. I was also able to get a private member's bill through, so I had a very productive time in opposition. I was on the environment committee. It was maybe one of the best committees I've ever seen around this Parliament. It was one in which partisanship was totally put aside as we worked on a whole series of reports on climate change and the atmosphere, and those reports, I still think, are the hallmark of good parliamentary work.

Partisanship can be set aside. It happens all the time. It happens mostly in the committees where people tend to be on that committee because they have an interest in those issues, whatever party they're in. An Alliance member and a Liberal member will always have differences of opinion. It's that simple. Liberals will always tend to think alike. Alliance members will always tend to think alike. That's the nature of party politics. People get together because they believe in certain things, they are committed to certain values. They have certain ideas about their country and what it should be. So they work together and they will have differences of opinion with the other parties. The clash of ideas, the clash of differences is good democracy because it lets Canadians think about issues and be better informed. Canadians can, therefore, be better informed about how to influence government and, when it comes to voting, who they prefer to run the country after the next election. The committees are very good, non-partisan forums, by and large, and that's why I am a great supporter of greater televising of committee meetings and greater publicity around committee reports.

Not all committees function as well as they could. Partisanship is a part of parliamentary democracy. It's part of our political system. There's one way of getting rid of that kind of thing and that's to have a totally one-party system. It's not something I support. I think there's some work that could be done to make committees more effective. Again, I think they have to start using the tools we do have and they have to start talking among themselves about how to use their time as a committee to really accomplish what they're trying to accomplish. It involves putting aside the partisanship a little bit, and that does happen in a lot of committees.

Debate in the House still works. Members' opinions can be changed. That happens all the time in Parliament and that's why, as a party, we introduced take-note debates where we can have a whole evening on a specific issue. I think we're going to be expanding. These debates often go on quite late into the night and there aren't that many people around except those who want to speak on it. So Parliament now can sit as a committee, as a whole, so that people can sit together. They don't have to sit in their normal seats. There isn't the same formality. There can be more exchange back and forth across the aisle. This is one of the changes we've made to create that atmosphere of good debate around issues.

Centralization of Power: Power of the PM

I've heard the suggestion that there is a concentration of power that has resulted in a benign, benevolent dictatorship. I personally don't think so. It may seem that decisions are made without consultation. I've talked a great deal about the amount of discussion that goes on before something comes to Parliament. It will often go on with opposition parties as well as among the Liberal members. Things are not a surprise when they come to Parliament.

It moves the power to the people. The prime minister can say, "This is going to happen," and it will happen. How long does a leader remain a leader by doing that? You can't lead people where they're not ready to go and if you're setting off in a direction and nobody's behind you, you aren't leader for very long. I think our system works well that way. Ultimately, though, it is the prime minister who is responsible. It is a minister who is responsible and they have to make the tough decisions. Ministers have to listen to other people, they have to listen to members of Parliament, as well as listen to Canadians. But they're the ones who are accountable in the end. Now, if you want to change that whole accountability relationship and say, "I'm accountable for my own actions. I have nothing to do with what the government does or what my party does in Parliament," then you're talking about anarchy as far as I'm concerned.

Chapter 4
The Canadian Alliance Party

JOHN WILLIAMS

John Williams was elected as member of Parliament for the riding of St. Albert in 1993, and was re-elected in 1997 and in 2000. He is currently the official Opposition's chief Treasury Board critic and chairman of the public accounts committee, the only parliamentary committee that is chaired by an Opposition MP. Williams is the author of *The Waste Report*, a periodic publication on government waste that is well known for its critiques of mismanagement and lack of accountability in government. Prior to being elected Mr. Williams was a certified general accountant who had his own private practice in the city of St. Albert. In July 1999 he was named a fellow of CGA-Canada.

TOPICS:
What MPs and Parliament Are Supposed to Provide to Voters:
Accountability
How the Political Party System Has Distorted What Parliament Is
Supposed to Do
How Parliament Allows Government Spending to Get Out of Control

The Business of Supply: A Chance to Change the System and Account
for Money
Areas of Concern: How an Estimates Committee Would Allow
Parliament to Look at Spending Currently Being Ignored
Other Areas of Concern: Loan Guarantees
What Happened to the Business of Supply Report?
How the Deck Is Stacked Against Reform of Government
Spending Practices
Why Accountability Is Important but Doesn't Resonate with the Public

*What MPs and Parliament Are Supposed to Provide to Voters:
Accountability*
Accountability is what keeps people honest and focused. It keeps their
minds on the job. In the private sector it is called competition — if you
can't meet or beat the competition, you don't stay in business. But the
government doesn't have competition and that's a problem. We have to
devise other ways to hold the government accountable. We do it by
holding their activities up to the spotlight in a public forum so that all
Canadians know what the government is up to. If Canadians approve,
that's fine, but when government slips up, Canadians need to know
about that. That's when accountability kicks in.

The problem is, not enough Canadians are focused on asking,
"What is my government doing?" Parliament has lost all its authority to
hold the government to account. It has lost its control because
Parliament is not that accountability mechanism anymore. This means
the government gets away with a lot more than they should.

Government is supposed to come to Parliament and say, "Can I do
this? Will you pass this piece of legislation for me? Will you authorize
this expenditure of money for me?"

I say that accountability drives the other issues. It's a debate: more
tax, lower tax; protect the environment; don't worry about the environment. You can have these debates and in their own way they are about
accountability. Let's look at the environment, for example. Let's explain
and demonstrate how the government has failed on the environment.
The tar ponds in Sydney, Nova Scotia, for example, are an absolute disaster and people are living there. The government said, "No, we're not
even going to bother paying you to move out of there, even though it's
ridden with cancer-causing agents." The more we put the pressure on

the government and say, "This cannot be. We can't expect Canadians to live in that environment and you had better clean the place up, too," then it focuses the government and forces them to do something.

Parliamentarians think they are either part of government or on their way to becoming government. They have forgotten that they are *the accountability instruments* for government. Unfortunately Canadians haven't been taught that at school. They think that parliamentarians are the government. No, we are not the government. The prime minister and the Cabinet and the departments that they manage are the government, while all the other parliamentarians are part of the accountability processes that scrutinize the government. We, as MPs, have forgotten that. We see ourselves either as part of government or as an opposition to government.

How the Political Party System Has Distorted What Parliament Is Supposed to Do

We have forgotten that our role as parliamentarians is to examine and debate and approve government policies and initiatives. We have become politically divided, as we all know. The MPs on the government's side think they're part of government and the MPs on the opposition's side are just hoping to *be* the government someday. They get into this debate about *your* policy versus *my* policy, rather than Parliament as a whole holding the government to account and saying, "Is this legislation good? Is this expenditure justifiable or not?" That's why we have lost our accountability.

The government side will always support the government. They will not analyze what the government's trying to do. They will give the government what it wants. The opposition side basically states, "My policy is better than your policy," rather than analyzing what the government is trying to do. The opposition always loses the votes because they have fewer members, but also because we have "confidence votes." With confidence votes the government doesn't waste time selling Parliament on what it wants to do. It just cracks the old confidence whip and tells the MPs on the government's side how to vote. A confidence vote says to the MPs on the government side, "If we lose this important vote (even if it isn't really that important), we're having an election. You MPs may all lose your jobs. You don't want that, so just hold your nose and vote to give us what we want."

The job of government is to convince Parliament that what they want to do is right. As representatives of the whole country, if parliamentarians feel it is right, then likely the country would agree. Yet we, as Canadians and MPs, have forgotten that our job is to scrutinize and hold government accountable, not just vote in a partisan fashion.

Therein lies the problem — back-bench MPs don't analyze government policy, government legislation or the expenditures requested.

How Parliament Allows Government Spending to Get Out of Control

Taxes are important to Canadians. They are being spent by the ton, all $170 billion per year of them. Yet this spending goes through the House of Commons in a flash. If you don't make a special effort to notice it, you'll miss it. We approved $170 billion worth of expenditures and we didn't analyze one department or one program in depth at all.

As MPs we are given a stack of documents and that is only the summary of the spending. When you open them you see a summary. An infrastructure program, for example, that costs $2.5 billion. You can't ask an intelligent question probing what the infrastructure program is all about. You only have one line — $2.5 billion. What does that represent?

When it comes to numbers — $170 billion and stacks of budget books all over the place — MPs' eyes glaze over. The thinking is generally, "Oh, I don't understand that. I'm glad you're looking after it for me." MPs say they don't look after spending because they see me, John Williams, trying to look after it. One MP can't do it. I cannot analyze $170 billion by myself, not even as the chair of the public accounts committee with 17 members. It requires a majority in the House of Commons. It requires 151 MPs or more. The problem is, they are all off on their own tangents.

When you try to investigate some sort of spending program, the MP sitting next to you may not be interested in infrastructure programs. He may be interested in pensions for seniors. So you get no support from him to follow on your line for infrastructure investigation because he's waiting to get the microphone so he can ask about pensions. When he gets to pensions, somebody else says, "Oh no, I don't want to talk about pensions. I want to talk about the fact that our military is falling apart." So MPs are talking about defence, environment, taxes or seniors' pensions because that is their individual focus. Canadians do not get an orchestrated, concentrated, ongoing investigation on any one spending program because every MP has their own pet projects.

The process is so complex that people don't understand the process by which spending goes through the House. They say, "Let's go home. Somebody's looking after the store, hopefully." But there isn't anybody looking after the store. They vote yes and they go home. The next year we return and the government doesn't even tell us how they've spent the money.

If we are going to get the authority back into Parliament, that requires a majority of parliamentarians, which means getting some government members, too, to say, "We have got to bring the authority back into this place." That's not easy.

The Business of Supply: A Chance to Change the System and Account for Money

Understanding how government spends money is a complex issue. When I first came to Ottawa as an MP, after 1993, I kicked and screamed and made all kinds of noises about how we just voted on budgets and spending but nobody analyzed them.

This caused the subcommittee on the business of supply to be created by several other MPs and myself. The goal was to look for better ways for Parliament to oversee how money is spent. Out of that came a report on the business of supply. That's what we call the Estimates and the budgets going through the House — the business of supply.

The report we created was about 100 pages long and had 15 major recommendations, including the creation of an estimates committee to focus on spending all year round. The Public Accounts Committee, which I chair, is only a retrospective, rearguard look at what went wrong. We wanted an estimates committee to look at budgets *before they were spent.*

The report also recognized that Parliament must look at the different kinds of government spending. For example, program spending called "statutory spending," or spending that happens every year, never comes before the House of Commons for a vote. A good example is employment insurance. I think we created the program in 1947. Back when we passed the legislation, there was one little clause that said they would get the money they required. We voted in 1947 and never voted on that issue again and this is 2002. To put it in perspective, there is over $100 billion of spending on programs that is not even voted on in the House.

Our report also wanted to set up an evaluation program so that these programs are evaluated on a cycle — so Canadians can see if they are getting value for money based on four simple questions. First, we wanted to know what the program was designed to do because in many cases there isn't even a public policy attached to government programs. Currently we just spend the money and keep it circulating. Surely Canadians would hope that we should get some benefit for the money we're spending. Second, how well is the program doing? This isn't rocket science here, but the government just does not want to know the answer to how most of our programs are doing. They just spend the money. Third, are we delivering the programs efficiently? Fourth, can we achieve the same or better results for our government dollar by delivering the program in a different way in a fast-changing technological world?

The government currently does not ask these four questions.

Areas of Concern: How an Estimates Committee Would Allow Parliament to Look at Spending Currently Being Ignored

Through our proposed estimates committee we could look at statutory spending, through spending on their rent, salaries and all the management of the government. We could look at tax expenditures. Tax expenditures are these reductions in your taxes that you pay to government, like RRSP (registered retirement savings plan) deductions. It doesn't show up as revenue to the government and it doesn't show up as an expenditure for government. It's just a reduction in the taxes that people remit. Is there a benefit there? Everybody knows RRSPs are good, but how good? What does it cost the government in lost revenue? What is the benefit of people being able to support themselves in retirement? We should be asking that question. So we need to take a look at tax expenditures.

Parliament and MPs also need to take a look at Crown corporations. They're off, floating around, doing some kind of business, usually losing money in the process, and no one is really asking what's going on there.

Other Areas of Concern: Loan Guarantees

Loan guarantees, or money provided by government to private businesses or Crown corporations, show up as a buck on the government's books. Yet there might be $1 billion of a guarantee that Canadians are on the hook for. For example, that $1 shows up on one simple budget line as "Loan Guarantee, Business Development Corporation, $1" because it's not an actual expenditure. We didn't lose the money, we didn't spend any money; we're just going to backstop a loan. So an MP says, "A dollar? Why waste your time looking at a dollar? What about $100 million somewhere else? That's surely a lot more important." But that dollar might actually represent $1 billion and if the loan goes off the rails five or 10 years from now, the government may come back for $1 billion to write off the loan that went sour. By then it's too late.

We need to look at these things and that's what the business of supply report we wrote does. It recommends we set up a whole mechanism to look at this and a lot more.

What Happened to the Business of Supply Report?

Back in 1996 we had a unanimous report which all parties agreed to. Bob Marleau, the clerk of the House of Commons, now retired, said this was the best report on parliamentary reform in 50 years. Then we had the election in 1997, so it died. I resurrected it after 1997 and got it through the House affairs committee. Again, all the parties supported it and the report was tabled in the House of Commons with the requirement that the government respond, as the rules state. They have 150 days to come back and say, "Well, we like it. We don't like it. We'll change it. We'll take some of it, or none of it." They came back and said, "We'll have none of it. We're not interested." And that was about a year and a half ago. In April of 2000 they said, "That's it, we don't even want to talk about that report," so it died again.

So since the traditional committee routes did not work in getting this report heard and voted upon by Parliament, I now have another opportunity. I have put forward a private member's motion that the business of supply report be adopted in its entirety. And the motion has been deemed votable. So now we sit as the report makes it way to Parliament.

How the Deck Is Stacked Against Reform of Government Spending Practices

I will be introducing it in the House; it will be debated for three hours and voted upon. Marlene Catterall and I were co-authors of this report. Catterall is a government whip and she supported it. I look forward to

139

seeing what the government does under her direction when it comes to a vote in the House. I hope she gets back to this accountability issue that she supported so strongly on our committee. Having supported it in committee, you would think as a parliamentarian she would support it in the House. But if the Liberal government says, "We'll give that a thumbs down," and she capitulates, folds and says, "OK, we're all going to give it a thumbs down," therein clearly demonstrates why Parliament has lost its effectiveness. They can say something in committee and then they have to exercise the government's agenda, not Parliament's agenda. They change their tune and that's the end of it.

The deck is stacked against any one individual member, like myself, to bring accountability into Parliament. Parliament has allowed its authority to go to the government and therefore the deck is stacked against Parliament as well.

Why Accountability Is Important but Doesn't Resonate with the Public

Pick an issue — lowering taxes, cutting the deficit or reducing the debt. If you can take an issue and force public attention to bear on that issue, then the government will react. But the abstract notion of bringing power back to Parliament is not an issue that resonates with the public because they expect that Parliament is working reasonably well. MPs can't build a public consensus about restoring the power of Parliament. MPs would rather push issues like low taxes or the environment because that gets MPs on the 10 o'clock news. This is the kind of exposure that drives MPs.

DEBORAH GREY

Deborah Grey was the first ever Reform Party member of Parliament, elected to the House of Commons in 1989. She has since been re-elected four times. She served as Reform Party caucus chair from November 1993 to March 2000, as well as deputy opposition leader from June 1995 to March 2000. She was interim leader of the official Opposition until the election of Canadian Alliance Leader Stockwell Day in September 2000.

In July 2001 Deborah and 11 of her fellow Canadian Alliance MPs left their party and the leadership of Stockwell Day to form the Democratic Representative Caucus (DRC). Then in September 2001 she and seven of her DRC colleagues formed a coalition caucus with the Progressive Conservatives. In April of 2002 Deborah rejoined the Canadian Alliance Party under the leadership of Stephen Harper.

TOPICS:
The Life of an Opposition Frontbencher
Question Period

What You See Is What You Get
The Liberals and Medicare
Promises Delayed
Her Relationship with Her Constituents
Listening to the People
Opposition Role in Holding Government Accountable
Accountability: Her Own, Her Party's and the Government's
Breaking the Handout Habit
Media: Its Evolving Role
Think Locally, Act Federally
Priorities in Life
An Accidental Politician
Leaving a Legacy
Queen of the Independents
Spirit of the West
Inside the Reform Party
Election Reflection
Fortress Chrétien and the Chances of Reforming Parliament
Committee "Busy Work"
Deborah Grey, You Rock!

The Life of an Opposition Frontbencher
I spend a lot of time on an airplane. I travel back and forth weekly between the constituency here in Edmonton and Ottawa. I leave Sunday afternoons around 3:00 or so and get to Ottawa around midnight, and I'm busy Monday through Thursday there. I generally fly home on a Thursday night to do functions in the riding constituency office. That goes from mid-September till Christmas, when the House is usually recessed until January. We start up again February 1, until about the third week in June.

In Ottawa I get up at 6:00 and I'm in the office by 7:00. We have strategy meetings, getting ready for Question Period at 8:00 in the morning. My staff is all in by the time and I get back from that meeting, around quarter to nine. I do lots of media interviews, have committee sittings and get ready for Question Period.

I go to committee meetings or interviews or meet with lobby groups, oftentimes at supper. Then there's some quiet time in the office, most every evening after the phones have quieted down, to do some reading. I'm one who reads all my mail and then drafts responses so my staff can draft up letters the next day. Then I get up at 6:00 the next morning and do it again.

They're long days, every day — that's for sure. When I get back to the place where I stay, I try and phone my husband, Lou. He is here at home most of the time and makes a couple of trips to Ottawa a year. Lou and I spend some time on the telephone before I flop into bed. We might watch a hockey game together over the telephone, or football, or whatever.

I spend weekends at home. This last parliamentary term had about 185 weekends in it. Twenty of those weekends Lou and I were on personal time, camping or whatever we were doing. I did just a little over 20 party functions because I'm the deputy leader. All spring and summer I served as the leader of the Opposition on an interim basis. That left about 140 or so weekends at home. I don't cook, so Lou and I are out eating someplace all the time.

Question Period

The leader of the Opposition does not sit in our morning meetings and determine who's going to ask each question. We have a strategy team involved in that. It's my job in Question Period to get the prime minister off his scripted notes. That's the job I have so I'm sure lots of them would be quite delighted to see me just fade away. That's the part I love about it, I guess, living on the edge.

I'd like to think that I could ask a question in Question Period and get an answer but I've been there for almost 12 years and I've rarely seen that happen, which is a pity. Beyond just getting the factual information, it is a case again of the attitude of the government. They feel they are so superior to anyone else, that it's their God-given right to rule. Question Period is an avenue to be able to kind of draw some of those attitudes out from the prime minister and government members.

In Question Period the prime minister has briefing notes but he often relies on Don Boudria and the binder boy who sits right behind him to come up with the facts and figures and whatever their script of the day is that he's supposed to read off. He's always fairly safe if he's just reading. But you know, the prime minister gets pretty freewheeling. It's emotion rather than the facts and figures. He goes off into these long explanations about how wonderful he is and how he's been around since 1963. If he's not reading "Why I love my country," you never know what he's going to say. It's important for me to find out what the prime minister might just kind of go off on a tangent about because that's when Canadians get a chance to see him freewheeling, and lots of times they don't like what they see. I think Canadians deserve a chance to see that.

What You See Is What You Get

People recognize me. They watch me on TV, on Question Period. They know that I'm not going to horse around. I don't have time to waste giving them a line. It's never served anyone well in life and I just cannot play games. What you see is what you get.

The Liberals and Medicare

We think that part of the Liberal government has just said, "Phooey on you," to the Canadian public. They take lots and lots of tax money, then turn around after the royal flush in Ottawa, where they deal with it administratively, and send a little bit back to say thanks.

People are amazed at the gall of the Liberals. They've stripped a cool $25 billion out of the health-care system since they came in, especially in the 1994–1995 fiscal year. And now they say, "We're the great saviours of medicare. You don't want that Canadian Alliance because they're responsible for every ill and every sin in the country." We say, " That is a bald-faced lie, you pot-lickers. You stripped the money out, and now you tell us you're putting $21.5 billion back in over the next five years, and for this we're all to jump up and down and say thank you?" How magnanimous! You know, it's just unbelievable.

Let's make sure that there is stable, long-term funding for health care. That's what the Canadian Alliance is talking about. We agree with the five principles of the Canada Health Act. But, by George, I'll tell you that we want a sixth in there, and that's to make sure that there is legislated, guaranteed, long-term stable funding for the provinces so that the federal government is not going to rip the carpet out from underneath and say, "Oh, sorry. You had all this nice stuff budgeted for and too bad, we took the cash on you." They ought to be ashamed of themselves. That's the number-one issue.

Promises Delayed

Another thing I'm hearing at the doors is criminal justice. There's just unbelievable frustration. This is a concern for Canadians right across the country, but probably particularly here in Edmonton because of Anne McLellan, the justice minister. Anne said that was going to be her first priority, the number-one priority she said, when she got sworn in, in August of 1997. And here we are, it's almost 2001, and that bill, which was supposed to be the great answer for criminal youth justice, is dead.

Truth in sentencing, applying for early parole — people here are really paying a lot of attention to that. The gun-control bill specifically, a lot of people say it's urban/rural. No, it's not. It's about a government that wants to get more and more intrusive in your life and it's about property rights. People say, "Well, wait a minute here. Just how close does government come?" We have lots of people who have lived in the country, who now are living in the city, and they have tremendous collections. They're not allowed to hand those down to future generations. It's not just about guns. It's about the criminal misuse of firearms and government just spending unbelievable amounts of money going after law-abiding citizens.

Her Relationship with Her Constituents

I have constituency hours, when I'm meeting with constituents in the office. My constituents come in with federal issues. The Canada Pension Plan disability is a huge one that we deal with in our office. Even Liberals are frustrated with it. This goes beyond partisanship. The whole thing is just a nightmare and really needs to be revamped. That's one thing that we deal with. Immigration cases, people, if they're trying to have family reunification, we spend a lot of time on those issues, and income tax problems, Revenue Canada, Human Resources Development.

Sometimes people come into my riding office and say, "Well, I didn't vote for you, but I really need help on this immigration case," or something like that. I say, "Look, I'm not here just to help the people who voted for me. Sorry that your guy didn't win, but I'm your MP and I'm happy to serve you just the best way I can." I've just been amazed at the number of people who say, "Oh, thanks. You know, we appreciate that."

Through your constituency office you work with bureaucracy. People get these letters in the mail from Revenue Canada or the Immigration Department that say, "Do this or else." The Ottawa side of it is that there are some serious problems in the legislation regarding immigration. That's what you work on at this end; to say to the immigration minister, "Wait a minute here." For instance, you talk about head taxes, you talk about openness and inclusion, etc. A husband and wife came here from another country, both brilliantly educated. He was told by this Immigration Department, "Maybe you ought to change your name. It's not going to look so good when you apply for a job." Immigration Minister Elinor Caplan has the nerve to call me and three million people who supported us racist, bigots, etc. There's something seriously wrong with her attitude, and the legislation that she's bringing forward. Shame on her.

Listening to the People

By temperament I'm a visitor. I love to visit with people and talk to them. They're not nervous to come up to me. It's not, "Ooh, there's the MP," as if there's something divine, you know. We'll have a visit and they'll tell me what they think about issues. That gives me a broad cross-section. I don't just say, "I'm safe with these people who like me, so I'll go and get all their input." Not at all. I'll march right in where angels fear to tread because I want to know what people say, whether they agree with me or disagree with me vehemently.

You don't just disappear to Ottawa into the big black hole and assume all of a sudden that "I know best." That is a form of arrogance that I've watched for too many years in Ottawa. It seems to me that once a member becomes a member of the government or a Cabinet minister, all of a sudden they're not so sure they want to hear from the people. I love hearing from the people. I will never quit that.

Opposition Role in Holding Government Accountable

We have been there serving as "Her Majesty's Official Opposition" since 1997, and Reform has been there, not just when I was the only Reform member of Parliament from 1989 to 1993, but in the Parliament from 1993 to 1997. Have we made some changes here? Yes. That a Liberal would even talk about balanced budgets — it's never been in their lexicon before.

In many respects the leader of the Opposition does have a powerful position. All eyes are on him or her to hold the government accountable. You don't have the levers of power, though, to actually effect change. We just don't have enough arms to go up, or heads to stand up. Until you're there and you can write the legislation and win the votes in the House of Commons, it's still the Prime Minister's Office, although the leader of the Opposition does have a fair bit of power. I don't know if I would say it's the most powerful position on the Hill.

I think my constituents realize that a Liberal backbencher would basically be silenced. We've just recently had the election of the Speaker. The rebels were running and there were two or three Liberal backbenchers who said, "We need more power for the backbenchers." You never hear from them again. It's like they go into this crypt for the next four years.

I have a responsibility to get down there and show the other side of the coin, not just, "Oh yes, Mr. Prime Minister, everything is going just fine and we love you wasting money on some billion-dollar boondoggles." And boy, I'll tell you, it's not just the billion-dollar boondoggle. He has RCMP investigations in his riding. I mean, give me a break, it's ridiculous. These people have hired me to get down there and make a fuss about it, so I go with that inspiration. I've been sent on a mission to downtown Ottawa, and that energizes me.

People have sent me to Ottawa three times now. People say, "Deb, we know you're not just going to disappear in Ottawa and get sucked into a big black hole. We know you're going to go there and stand up and go after those guys and hold them accountable." That has been my role so far as a member of the opposition: to hold government accountable and to point out their weaknesses, but also to show a constructive alternative, to say these are some of the things that we will do when we form the government.

People just shake their heads at government. They say, "Just get down there, do what you need to do and clean it up, so that we know our tax dollars going down to Ottawa are not going to be wasted."

Accountability: Her Own, Her Party's and the Government's
My sense of accountability is certainly to my husband and to my constituents. The people will decide if they think I did a good job, even though some of my detractors would make terrible, horrible personal remarks about me and attack me. I'm accountable because I'm here, because I make myself very available to people. Ultimately I operate on a plumb line of what hangs true, whether I'm true to myself and true to the calling that God has given me to be in public life, to say, "It's all right even if I'm not popular."

The government hasn't offered me a Senate position yet. Would I be an unelected senator? No, because to whom would I be accountable, and when do you ever come up for a Senate position for doing a good job? That's what I wouldn't like about being an unelected senator. Nobody is there to hold you to account.

Breaking the Handout Habit

The prime minister says, "I'll get you a little fountain in your riding," or a golf course or whatever. That kind of stuff actually turns people's stomachs back home. I think it's unbelievable that there are still people around who say we need someone in government to be able to bring stuff back to the city and dish up the cash. Holy moly, this is the year 2000!

Since the Liberal government came in, in 1993–1994, they've taken $25 billion extra in taxes, over and above what they were. So if you figure out our little microcosm of Edmonton here, with about a million people or so, about a twenty-fifth of the population of the country, there would have been $1 billion left here in Edmonton. We can do job-creation and community-enhancement projects at the local level a whole lot better than the federal government. To say we've got to keep shipping all this money out, get an Anne McLellen or a David Kilgour who can deliver the goods and deliver the cash — leave the cash here in the first place, for heaven's sake.

My constituents expect me to make some noise, make sure government is accountable and make sure they're responsible. If anyone in Edmonton North or anywhere else in the country thinks, "Oh good, we're getting a government member, they can come and dish out the goodies," these are not goodies. These are taxpayers' dollars. As a Cabinet minister, I will assume that my position is in trust and I darn well better spend that money just as responsibly in government as I'm calling for in Opposition. My constituents would be ashamed of anything less.

There's still some of that mythology that if you have a government member, they'll be dishing out the cash to you, that voters say, "I'm going to put someone in because I'll get a road." They know that we're almost $600 billion in debt and that this country over the last generation has just become a bunch of government-program junkies. I really think voters have moved beyond that, certainly in our part of the country.

Media: Its Evolving Role

Media coverage is terribly important because I could prattle away on something, but if nobody sees it on the news, it hasn't happened. The national media filter so much of what goes on. I think that Canadians deserve a chance to see more. That's why CPAC is good. It's uncut and unfiltered, rather than trying to clean the prime minister up and edit some of the things that he's saying. People can watch uncut, unfiltered CPAC and the parliamentary channel to see the strength and the coherence, or lack thereof, of things that the prime minister says. It doesn't need to be editorialized or fluffed up.

We're not talking about manipulating the media. We're talking about the media covering events. I think that would be a really good thing for them to do. It's very important to make sure that you have coverage in the national media as well as the local media.

Think Locally, Act Federally

Obviously you need to balance between what's good locally and what's good across the country. Here in Alberta, for sure, we've been one of the "have" provinces for many years. People in my constituency would think that it was a great idea for me as a Cabinet minister to say, "Maybe we need to rethink the whole equalization thing." They also know that there are all kinds of situations where maybe sometimes I need to give up my first choice on something.

Priorities in Life

I have to have some fun every day; that's in my spirit. How do I have fun? It's meeting people; it's getting energy from people. By working with a campaign team like this, by working with a caucus who just thinks that it's marvellous that we've had this opportunity to sit in the House of Commons and change the whole political landscape in Canada. That's fun. It's a huge and awesome task, but at the same time I often laugh with my family or my husband and I say, "Why is it that God chose me to do this?" And I say, "Why me, Lord?" And you often get the voice back saying, "Why not you?" You don't want to mess with that.

I don't look five years or 10 years down the road with any grandiose plans. We know that we are Christians and we know that our lives are ordered, if you will. That's not to say that we're not going to plan for anything. I mean, I did go to university for five years, I have two university degrees.

Lou talks about leadership and if I have any grand designs on leading the party or whatever. I got married for the first time at age 41, and I am not about to just throw it away. When reporters like Anne Dawson or Tim Harper say I'm addicted to politics and I'll keep running, I say, "Look me in the eye. I married Lou in 1993. If I think that my marriage is falling apart, or I have some serious problems, or Lou is not happy with me in this role, do you think I might leave Ottawa tomorrow?" And they say, "Yeah, I think you might." And I would. Because I didn't wait this long for a man this wonderful to just say, "Sorry, sweetheart. I'm off on the political trail." It's not worth it. It's not worth it.

An Accidental Politician

I have not been politically active or aware all my life. I never, ever in a million years thought I'd get into office and be somebody. I had a neighbour dare me to run in the 1988 election, so I guess you could call me an accidental politician. But the idea of public service is something that I've always been interested in. It is my greatest desire to serve people, in whatever capacity. I was teaching school in a public school system and maybe I've learned something over the years that can help someone else.

I grew up with an alcoholic father, grew up in a single-parent family. In the 1960s in Vancouver, that just wasn't done. I've walked lots of roads and I've gone through lots of things. When I work with anyone, I can say that maybe I really do know how they feel. It's not my desire to say, "Oh, I'm Deborah Grey and you'll see me on TV." I actually don't give a sweet fig about that. What I want to do is to make a difference in somebody's life; whether it's with my husband, to just share with him and make life special for him and for me, whether it's on the national stage, or whether it's with Luba Goy on the Royal Canadian Air Farce.

Until I know in my gut that I'm supposed to move on and do something else, then, hey, I'm going to do that to the best of my ability. That desire to serve people gives me joy. To help a constituent, now that I'm elected, gives me great joy. Not to know that I was on TV that night, but that somebody got their screwy Canada Pension Plan straight or that somebody got a loved one or a family member over here.

Leaving a Legacy

My mother gave me a poster when I made Canadian history by becoming the first-ever Reformer. It was a picture of Garfield motoring across off into the sunset. His caption was, "I want to leave my paw prints in the sands of time." I thought, that's what I want to do.

The first time I ran, in 1988, and lost, I took two days off school. When I made Canadian history four months later, I got back to my home at about quarter to three in the morning. I lived in the bush. The CBC cameras came to the lake where I lived at quarter to seven in the morning and did an interview over breakfast. After I got re-elected in 1993 my school board said, "You quit or you're fired." Most of them name a school after you when you make Canadian history. It says a whole lot more about them than it does about me. Amazing.

Nellie McClung was one of the Famous Five. I don't know if you saw Frances Wright in the newspaper last week. She has managed to get the girls on the back of a $50 bill. I thought that was good. So we'll remember them once again. I won't be one of the Famous Five. I'll just be one of the old girls.

Queen of the Independents

In 1989 when I was the only Reformer in the House, I was an independent. You need 12 members of your party in the House to have official party status. Although I was a Reformer and had the whole party machinery behind me, I was considered an independent because I didn't have 12.

When David Kilgour and Alex Kindy got thrown out of the GST debate, and Lucien Bouchard got thrown out and started the Bloc Québécois, we ended up with 12 independents there. Because I was the first, they called me the "Queen of the Independents." We wanted to form our own little political band, but we never did.

I had impact. The Speaker of the House at the time, John Fraser, gave me the right to ask questions in the House. Now, granted, I didn't get many questions, but my first one was on Meech Lake. That sent Brian Mulroney just about soaring through the roof of the place. The Meech Lake Accord, the Charlottetown Accord, those were huge events, and I was one little voice there in Parliament. I was the only federal political party that spoke against Meech Lake and the Charlottetown Accord. I think it certainly had an impact — the very fact that I was talking about governments living within their means.

Spirit of the West

I think we are different out West. Unfortunately the prime minister's henchman, Warren Kinsella, who was the individual who ran the smear campaign for them, has come onboard now and said that these Westerners are just a bunch of whining losers. Frankly, I don't see that there's anything positive in that. I don't think Westerners are going to be really thrilled to see Canada One, or whatever it is that the prime minister rides around on, show up in their neck of the woods. In fact, he has spent more time in Florida, the logs say, than he has in Western Canada.

I don't think there's any need for us to whine and complain. Whether it's economic policy or social policy, we are all kids in a family. We need to be treated and considered equally and with the same amount of respect, to be able to come to the table and say we all have concerns. Quebec has concerns. So does Alberta. So does Nova Scotia and Newfoundland. I live where the natural resources are high. I don't live where there's great sea fishing. So let's come to the table, and have a government that's at least willing to acknowledge that there are amazing differences. The prime minister seems unwilling to do that because he thinks that this is the centre of the universe. He may be the centre of his universe, but not ours.

Because people out West came from back East a generation or two ago, there was an entrepreneurial spirit, that sense of adventure, that amazing desire to see more and do more and start things new. I think of Nellie McClung, one of the Famous Five; I have a saying of hers on my desk in Ottawa. It says, "Never retreat, never explain, never apologize." Just get the thing done and let them howl. If anything exemplifies and signifies Alberta, that's it. This is the birthplace of Reform and the Canadian Alliance. We are made of tough stuff, I'll tell you. You just don't even think about it, you just do it. Get the job done.

Inside the Reform Party

I don't know if my supporters would have the same demographics as the party supporters. Not because I'm the most wonderful, but because I've been around awhile. People have seen me out in the country, in a rural riding where I taught school, and now I've been in the city riding for a term. And I ride a motorcycle. Young kids think this is pretty far out. I'd say that we have good support from seniors because they've seen a lot go on over the decades. And families because of our stand on family. It's not just a bunch of grumpy old white-haired guys. Frankly, I don't pay lots of attention to demographics.

Election Reflection

I was really pleased that I had a much larger majority this time. The people in Edmonton North obviously said, "She's doing a good job for us and we're going to put her back there again." They said, "Hey, girl, go back and just lean on 'em again down there." Alberta had a good strong showing for the Alliance, and we won't be a bit shy being down here and continuing to voice our concerns.

You're certainly looking at some serious regional breakdowns in this election. I mean, the Liberals are the party in Ontario. They have more seats now in Quebec than they had before, but the Bloc still has a good healthy chunk. The Tories are relegated to the Atlantic provinces, and then we pretty well represent the West. The NDP are somewhere in the middle there, I'm not just sure but they have a "smattering hither and yon."

Fortress Chrétien and the Chances of Reforming Parliament

This is the eighth year of this Liberal reign. Anne McLellan yesterday, in the House, was chatting across the aisle with one of our guys and saying the Young Offenders Act, you know, they're going to bring it in again. They have a majority government. You know, get the thing done. Just get the thing done and let 'em howl. Gun control? She says, "Everything's going well." Well, the deadline has passed for people to register.

The federal government has centralized almost every power they can get their paws on. We have consistently said, "Give the provinces back their original jurisdictional powers. Sports, language, culture, housing, municipal affairs, labour, market training, economic development. Give those back to the provinces."

The problem with the Liberal mentality, if you will, is that they want to keep all that stuff to themselves and look really powerful. In Jean Chrétien's autobiography, *Straight from the Heart*, he says, "I really felt pretty big and powerful here." And they love that. Once you get power in your hands, you don't like to relinquish it. You need a strong federal government to look after monetary policy, fiscal policy, policing, agriculture, money markets. All those kinds of things are very important to keep in Ottawa. But you don't need to hang on like grim death to every little piece of power.

You see power centralized in Ottawa. Who has the ultimate power within Ottawa? It's more and more centralized in the Prime Minister's Office, since Pierre Trudeau's days. For the last 30 years they've been hunkering down. That's why the backbenchers are just ready to rise up on their hind feet.

But they've been talking about it for so many years, and they now think there's this revelation and revolution of parliamentary reform coming along. I don't want to burst their bubble, but it ain't gonna happen with this guy in power. He's obsessed with power. There's a movement toward hunkering down and more and more power in the Prime Minister's Office, where it's little Eddie Goldenberg who makes the decisions, not a Dan McTeague or a Tom Wappel. They're dreaming, these boys.

It makes my job harder in that there's a fortress over there in the Prime Minister's Office. That's one of the reasons the Alliance wants to form power. People across the country realize what's happening. They have Liberal backbenchers as their members of Parliament — many of them in Ontario; anyway, there are precious few out West. They know that something is sick in Ottawa.

I want to blow that place open. I'm not interested in power for power's sake. I just want to bust it open and say the people should have more access to this. Not that they're all going to come wandering in and out of the Prime Minister's Office and say, "Hi, I'm here in Ottawa and I want to change the system." But there's an attitude that they own this place, you know? It belongs to the Canadian public. That's what I'm looking forward to, busting the Prime Minister's Office wide open and getting away from that whole Trudeau model of "This is mine." It isn't his.

Committee "Busy Work"

The government knows how ineffective and inefficient things are. Liberal backbenchers go to committees and say, "We're going to do this." Every single member of Parliament, from every party, comes down here, I believe, with a true, sincere wish to really make things better in Canada. But the committees turn into busy work for Liberal backbenchers. That's what it's all about, basically: "You do a good little job on committee, and I'll make sure you get a trip to Jamaica in January, to go on some amazing study that just needs to be done at that time of year."

It's obsession with power, the lust for power, and staying in power for power's sake. Lord knows, Shakespeare's given a few comments on that. Walk into the Prime Minister's Office right now and say, "Why are you here?" The PM has been asked that, and he says, "I like this job."

No. I want a vision. This is a new century. I think what people are looking for in leadership is someone who can stand up and say, "I know what I believe, I know what I'm after, I know what my vision of the country is." He doesn't do that.

They talk about Aboriginal affairs in there, and there is a dreadful state with Aboriginal affairs right now. This is the same guy who was the minister of Indian affairs in the late 1960s, and 35 years later they're still talking about, "Gee, there are problems we'll have to look into." Is this a new vision? No. We're getting creamed on international markets with some of the trade agreements and international subsidies. The family farmers are just falling apart. And what does he say? "Lyle Vanclief, my agriculture minister here, is looking into it." It's just not happening.

Deborah Grey, You Rock!

If there are people out there who need help, let me be the facilitator, let me be the conduit to wander through all these bureaucratic jungles to help someone out; it's the best. Maybe it's because I spend so much of my life away from my husband, the guy I love more than anything else. I get to visit him on weekends and when Parliament is recessed.

I'm a schoolteacher by trade, so I spend a lot of time in schools. Yesterday I was at an elementary school, Grades 1 to 6. They had a really good Remembrance Day program. When I was on my way from the gym out to my truck it was just noon hour, all the kids were breaking, and so many kids were going, "Deborah Grey, you rock!" I couldn't believe it. These kids, they don't even know who I am. Yet there they are in that little school patrol, just giving me a thumbs up, you know? Oh, that is just great.

DR. KEITH MARTIN

Dr. Keith Martin has been the Canadian Alliance member of Parliament for Esquimalt–Juan de Fuca since 1993, and has held positions as health critic and foreign affairs critic for the party. An outspoken critic of the parliamentary process, Dr. Martin is also a medical doctor with a degree from the University of Toronto. Over the past 13 years he has worked part time as an emergency-room doctor and general practitioner in British Columbia. In 1994 and 1996 he introduced private members' bills banning land mines. These bills pushed the government to pursue the issue that resulted in the landmark 1997 UN land mine treaty.

TOPICS:
Democracy and Parliament: Who Really Decides Our Fate?
Unelected Power at the Centre
The Role of Cabinet
MPs: No Scrutiny of Budgets
Consequences of a Weak Parliament

The Opposition: We Too Must Stop Playing the Media Game
The Failings of the Committee System

Democracy and Parliament: Who Really Decides Our Fate?

The most important problem in our country today is that Parliament is run by groups of unelected, unaccountable and invisible people who surround the leadership. They rule Parliament. They tell MPs what to say and what to do. Those who don't comply are hammered from above. As a result, the public do not have a fair say in what happens. That is why when you ask people how they feel about our current political system, they say, "I don't have a voice in this. What difference does it make? I'm not heard." And in many cases they are absolutely correct. It is a real tragedy because it means that as a country we are not using all our extraordinary potential and innovative energy for the public good.

Unelected Power at the Centre

The small group of people who run Parliament are usually advisors to the leadership. They are appointed by the prime minister, who gives them power to advise him on issues. And through that they also have the power to go to Cabinet and to MPs and say, "This is what you do." Now, if you are the MP who says, "No, I'm not going to do that because I disagree with you," then you're out of a job. Those are the rules of the game. Do what you're told, don't acknowledge other information that may be contrary to what you're told, blindly follow the leader and you'll do just fine. Question the leadership, disagree with what the leadership wants to do, stand up for your constituents when it goes against the leadership's wishes, and you're toast.

To voters it means that they have a group of people they didn't elect, whom they don't know and who have power directly from the prime minister, making decisions on the big policy issues of the country and determining where the country is going. That little group tells the Cabinet what to do, what to say, where to go and how to do it.

Basically what we have done is taken the Westminster system, bastardized it and turned it into a semi-dictatorship. The voter does matter, but in fact, the only time that we can truly exercise our democratic rights as members of the public is once every four or five years, during an election. Between elections we have that unelected, unaccountable system, that pseudo-democracy, that dictatorship.

The Role of Cabinet

Most Cabinet ministers have very little power, contrary to popular belief. They themselves have been told what to say and what to do. Their deputy ministers are appointed by the Prime Minister's Office, not by themselves. So unfortunately we have a situation where Cabinet ministers, many of whom are competent and intelligent, are forced to do as they are told. Now, if a minister, no differently from a back-bench MP, were to say, "No, I'm not going to do that," they're out of a job. So as an MP you have to make a decision, I think. Do you want to fight for the right thing? Do you want to stand up and take chances? Do you want to lead from the front? Or do you want to play the game? And some would argue that if you play the game, you get to the top, you get into a position of influence. Those who get to that position of so-called influence, that Holy Grail of positions — Cabinet — often find that they are less powerful than they used to be as back-bench MPs because they have very little opportunity to innovate. Right now in Parliament, we are seeing the death of innovation.

MPs: No Scrutiny of Budgets

An example of lack of accountability is the inadequate scrutiny of how Parliament spends money. Even members within government haven't got a clue where the money is going. Money is poured in. The outcomes are not measured. The auditor general alone is doing a very good job of keeping track of where money has gone but his reports, and very eloquent, important suggestions, are always ignored. Why? Because this place has more to do with the acquisition and maintenance of power than with the pursuit of public good. And that's a huge tragedy.

Consequences of a Weak Parliament

In our country I believe we can pursue excellence because we have the people, we have the resources and we can make the structures for Canada to achieve the greatness that becomes it.

In our Parliament we have an obsolete system rooted in something hundreds of years ago in a country far away, namely England. Why don't we make a government and a parliamentary system that reflects the needs of our country? Why not create a Parliament that is nimble and that can address problems quickly? If we do that, as we must in a fast-changing 21st century, then we will be able to achieve our potential. If we don't, then we will continue to lag behind other countries, as we are now doing.

We have a situation where our country, with all its riches and potential, could be doing so much better. We are accepting far less than what we should be. I think that is the crux of the matter. Are we satisfied with mediocrity or do we want to pursue excellence?

I think Canadians intuitively know something is wrong in the House of Commons, even if they don't know exactly what it is. That is why we see fewer and fewer people voting. Sixty percent of the public voted in the last election. Only 25 percent — one in four Canadians — actually support the government of the day, and those numbers are declining. So what does that say about our system? It says that our system is becoming more irrelevant to Canadians. I think that is sad because we need this very institution of Parliament to deal with the problems of the nation and to help us achieve the potential that we have in our great country.

The Opposition: We Too Must Stop Playing the Media Game

We, as opposition, should be dealing with important issues. When we try to do so people in the media say, "Oh, that's boring." The media want to deal with the sensational rather than the substantive, and we fall in with that. In my view we should be dealing with the substantive issues more and the sensational ones less, in the hope that the media will catch up to us. At least we should keep trying. At the end of the day, if we don't put our message out to the public (and the media is the interface upon which we work), we are dead in the water. So we have to find a balance. I hope that in the future the public will demand that the media portray what is happening in Parliament more accurately, that the public will get more involved, and that the opposition will focus on more of the big issues. Right now in Parliament, we have a government that is primarily focused on keeping the opposition fractured, and to a large extent we are playing on that court. What we have to do, though, is make a new court. A new court, a new way of doing politics in our country that is fit for the 21st century. And only if we do that will we be able to achieve our potential as a nation.

Many of us in opposition and even some in government have proposed time and time again constructive solutions to change this place, to make it more democratic, to give the Canadian people the power to change things. And yet the government has chosen not to do anything. In fact, in 1992, when he and members of his Cabinet were in Opposition, the current prime minister put forth an excellent document on democratizing the House. They haven't touched that.

All of us as MPs are at fault for not changing Parliament, but ultimately it is the responsibility of the government to make changes since it has the power to do so.

The Failings of the Committee System

Committees are supposedly the place for making changes to bills. This is where the public comes in to make passionate, intelligent and effective interventions about public policy. In reality committees are make-work projects for MPs. They do reports. Those reports are done with great expense and flourish. They get a day of media attention, and then they are tossed on a shelf to collect dust with thousands of other reports.

Look at the Aboriginal affairs report: $60 million, three years, never quoted, not used at all. That's appalling in view of the terrible tragedies experienced by Aboriginal communities. We have numerous reports of health committee reports that were never implemented. Bills go to committee essentially in their final form and are rubber-stamped with minor changes. We should be following the example of England where bills come to committee in draft form so that members of Parliament can craft and mould them based on public input, but we are not seeing that at all. It's a perfect example of how Parliament is used to keep MPs busy and stupid.

The minister, through the Prime Minister's Office, basically tells committees what to do. The committees look at bills, but have no meaningful input. Public input goes into reports that are ignored. It is an issue of leadership. A leader needs to stand up and say, "I want to make our Parliament democratic. I'm going to make committees work effectively so they can mould bills to reflect what the public wants. MPs will have a useful job and not be obliged to follow like lemmings what the PMO wants, as they do now."

Individual back-bench MPs are used as voting machines and as warm bodies to sit on committees, which are basically make-work projects for MPs. MPs who try to work against this and say, "We need to change," are condemned or ultimately thrown out of their caucuses, as we have seen in the past. The penalties for not obeying blindly are quite severe in the system that we have today.

I can give examples of my personal experience in committees. I am a physician, and one of the reasons I came to Parliament was to save our publicly funded health-care system. People are dying on our waiting lists. Many people suffer in silence in the community, denied access to health care. So what have we done in the health committee over the last eight years? We have not touched the issue of how to save our public system. Rather, we proceeded to deal with cigarettes and plain packaging. We talk about Aboriginal mental health. As important as that is, why study Aboriginal mental health when a large report has just been done — $60 million — on all aspects of Aboriginal health and other issues affecting Aboriginal people? We need to act on these issues. All the interventions that we make in committee go into a big black hole, forgotten and never implemented. We recently met to discuss the Free Trade Agreement of the Americas two weeks before the meeting. A member of the public offered a very eloquent comment, saying "Why are you having this meeting two weeks before the actual Free Trade Agreement of the Americas summit? You are not meant to have constructive input into that meeting. Committees are just a show for the public to give the illusion that Parliament is working and that our concerns are being listened to." And in effect their concerns are not being listened to and that is really sad. It's a big sham.

We have many good, competent, honest, hard-working members of Parliament sitting on committees. But their good work is being deliberately tossed away and forgotten by a government that, as I said before, just wants to use committees as a make-work project for MPs.

Worse, the heartfelt submissions by members of the public to these committees are not used either, so the citizens are cut out of the loop as well. That is a real tragedy. It's a waste of human potential.

JASON KENNEY

Jason Kenney was first elected to Parliament in June of 1997 as the Reform Party MP for Calgary Southeast. He served as official Opposition critic for national revenue, and since 2000 has served as the official Opposition's finance critic. Prior to seeking election Mr. Kenney was the president and chief executive officer of the Canadian Taxpayers Federation, an 80,000-member advocacy organization that promotes fiscal responsibility and democratic reforms.

TOPICS:
Overseeing Money: A Stacked Deck Against Parliament
Overseeing Money: The Madness of Parliament
The Power of the Purse in the Hands of Bureaucrats
The Real Experts and Where Decisions Are Made

Overseeing Money: A Stacked Deck Against Parliament
I'm the principal spokesman and ombudsman for the 60 percent of Canadians who didn't vote for the government. As finance critic in the

Opposition, my job is to keep track of the fiscal and economic policies of the government. I have to deal with any legislation dealing with taxation that comes before the House.

For example, we have a 1,400-page tax code. Every now and then the government comes to Parliament with complex amendments to this Byzantine tax code that literally nobody in the country fully understands. I only have a few people on staff and I'm up against a department with thousands of employees, including expert economists and technical experts in drafting legislation and taxation.

Recently the government tabled a 500-page bill of technical amendments to the Income Tax Act and a bunch of other tax statutes. They gave us approximately 36 hours' notice to decide what our position was going to be and how we were going to vote. I have one staff member who does legislation for me, who is already working 14-hour days. We don't have the budget or the technical lawyers to get into this sort of thing. Essentially MPs, particularly on the government's side, but even opposition MPs, have to take the government at its word that legislation like this works. About a quarter of this legislation is actually fixing mistakes they've made in past legislation.

Overseeing Money: The Madness of Parliament

The bureaucrats responsible for drafting bills come to the finance minister and say, "We need to pass this legislation for these reasons." The minister doesn't read the legislation, he doesn't understand it, he just introduces it in the House. I, as the Opposition critic, do not have time to delve into it. I get a general sense of what is there, decide whether we're for it or against it and try to make some general points in the debate. That is the process. It's absolutely ridiculous. I actually asked the finance minister if I could get a briefing on this bill. He said, "Sure, if you can figure out what it's all about, let me know." This is the madness of Parliament.

Tax power, next to criminal-law power, is the single most destructive and coercive power that Parliament can wield. We can make or break people economically. We can take away the fruits of their labour. We can violate their property rights. We can do all of that through this tax legislation. There isn't a single member of Parliament who will have read this bill before it's passed, but they'll all vote on it. That is what's wrong.

The Power of the Purse in the Hands of Bureaucrats

The single most important power of Parliament is the power of the purse. In parliamentary history we spent years, literally, fighting the Crown to secure the power of the purse and protect commoners from an overly greedy monarch. Now the monarch is an executive branch of government and it has the power to bring forward legislation that raises taxes, changes tax rates and dramatically changes people's economic circumstances. Those of us who are in power, who have the responsibility of protecting the people and making sure there aren't mistakes in the legislation, don't have the time or expertise to do so. We have to trust the bureaucrats. Essentially the permanent government, the bureaucracy, drafts, writes, manages and edits this whole enormous field of tax legislation, which has a huge impact on people's daily lives.

Who are these folks? The bureaucracy are people who are good, well-intentioned, honest folks who are paid less then they probably would be in the private sector. They are in a pretty difficult position. They're given the job of managing this incredible power, this tax legislation that can make or break people economically. They work in the finance building here in Ottawa, but I don't know who they are. I might see them once or twice a year when I'm being briefed on a bill. They act in the name of the minister of finance, with the authority of the minister. We all have to trust them.

The Real Experts and Where Decisions Are Made

On tax legislation the only folks who really know what's going on are lobbyists for particular industries. A lot of the tax legislation deals with particular industries and particular sectors of the economy. If a bill deals with oil and energy industry taxation and taxation in the motion picture industry, experts in those fields will lobby the third-ranking person in the tax division of the department of finance directly. To tell you the truth, that's where the real decisions are made. They are not made in the House of Commons and certainly not in the Senate. They are made between technical experts representing particular industries and bureaucrats who are part of the permanent government. Their consensus is dropped on us.

Theoretically, all this legislation goes through with the approval of the minister who represents the government, and then with the approval of Parliament. But I can tell you, the minister doesn't understand the technical aspects of legislation any better than the layman.

Chapter 5
The Progressive Conservative Party

JOE CLARK

Joe Clark has spent most of his life in federal politics. He was first elected to the House of Commons in 1972 and was elected leader of the Progressive Conservative Party within four years. In 1979 at age 39, Mr. Clark defeated Pierre Trudeau to become the youngest prime minister in Canadian history. Mr. Clark lost the Conservative Party leadership to Brian Mulroney in 1983, but served as Canada's minister of external affairs until 1991. He then became president of the Privy Council and minister responsible for constitutional affairs.

From 1993–1998 Mr. Clark stepped outside of the political arena and became a visiting scholar in the department of Canadian studies at the University of California at Berkeley, as well as the UN secretary general's special representative for Cyprus. In November 1998 Mr. Clark returned to public life as leader of the PC Party, and became an MP again in September 2000 after winning a by-election in the riding of Kings–Hants in Nova Scotia. He was re-elected two months later in the general federal election as the member of Parliament for the riding of Calgary Centre.

TOPICS:
Need for Parliamentary Reform: Control over Spending
Need for Parliamentary Reform: Concentration of Power
Concentration of Power: The Prime Minister
Concentration of Power: The Prime Minister's Office
Parliamentary Reform: Impact of MPs
MPs' Individual Input and Influence
A Hope for Change
Consequences of a Failing Parliament

Need for Parliamentary Reform: Control over Spending
Parliament has not worked for a long time for a couple of reasons. One was a mistake all parties made about 35 or 40 years ago. We ended a system in which there could be control of spending by something called the "Committee of the Whole." Once Parliament lost its control of spending, it lost its control of the government because the only way you can control any government is through their spending power. Parliament was once able to debate spending proposals as long as it wanted. Until Parliament said "yes" the government could not spend a cent. That obviously could be abused and it was changed. Now we must bring in a system in which we restore that kind of control over spending by the Parliament.

Need for Parliamentary Reform: Concentration of Power
It is broadly agreed that we need to restore the power of Parliament. The world has changed and the capacity of governments of any stripe to control media, to control events, to control parliaments has increased remarkably. Yet the prime minister of Canada has more power in Canada than the prime minister of the U.K. has in the U.K. He certainly has more power in his country than the president of the United States has in his. That has always been the case in the system, but recent changes have made that even more emphatic and, I think, dangerous in a country like this.

It is dangerous for two reasons. Firstly, it leads to a concentration of power in a government and an increasing isolation of government. It is true that power corrupts, and now it is possible for a government of any political orientation, if it has a majority, to operate without constraint in the House of Commons. Parliament cannot hold a majority government to account.

166

Secondly, the concentration of power reduces the variety of views that affect public policy. We are a very unusual country. The House of Commons is the only national institution that genuinely represents the whole country. Every corner of Canada has a voice here. It is easy to get a very narrow view in Canada on issues. If Parliament is active, it can force a government to pay attention to a problem in the Northwest Territories or in Cape Breton. That is what Parliament should be doing. When there's too much power with the government and too little with the MPs, Parliament is diminished.

The institutional capacity of Parliament to control the government is gone, which is not the way the system was designed. That's not healthy for Canada.

Concentration of Power: The Prime Minister
The prime minister is virtually all-powerful in our system. If a prime minister leads a majority government, he controls his party, so there's not very much internal pressure. He names and fires Cabinet ministers and senior public servants. In some of the Cabinets that I have sat in, there are strong ministers who will stand up to the prime minister. I don't think you get as much of that in the Cabinet of Mr. Chrétien and I think that this tendency has gradually declined with the passage of time. What has happened here is that a number of factors have come together to make the Prime Minister's Office the centre of the system and far more powerful than the roots of the system. The system won't work that way and that simply has to change.

Concentration of Power: The Prime Minister's Office
There is an extraordinary concentration of executive power gathered around the prime minister. Theoretically the Prime Minister's Office simply consists of people who are there to help the prime minister carry out his or her functions. In fact they've become instruments of control. They want to set the agenda, which is natural enough. There is nothing wrong with them setting an agenda or bringing coherence to a government program. What is wrong, however, is that there is so little control over the PMO by anybody outside the prime minister's direct entourage. In the United States the Senate has clear powers and the Congress has clear powers. The president has an immensely powerful office in the United States, but there are also clear constitutional

limits on it. Here in Canada there are none or very few that can be made effective.

Parliamentary Reform: Impact of MPs

It is always easier to have an impact in government than it is in opposition. But we all must become genuinely committed to changes that will allow individual MPs to have a greater impact in Parliament.

A lot of people worry about chaos developing if there were more power to individual members of Parliament, but I don't worry about that at all. In fact, I would put much more power to initiate legislation in the hands of all party committees of the House. I think that on issues like the environment and Indian affairs, a group of elected parliamentarians working together would have more imagination than the present system, where these issues are treated as having a lower level of importance than budgets and other questions.

MPs' Individual Input and Influence

We would have a much better system if members of Parliament had more influence on the content of policy and were encouraged to use their ideas and had an opportunity to have them translated into policy. I think that can happen.

Now, we don't want to go to the American system because our own provides a means of control. That control comes down to accountability to Parliament, by being forced to answer questions in the House and going before a parliamentary committee to defend your estimates. I am the last prime minister — and I was the first — who ever took his own spending estimates to a committee and defended them before the Parliament of Canada, as other ministers should do. It is now unthinkable. I would do it again, though, because it is symbolically an indication of who's in charge: the members of Parliament and, through them, the people.

A Hope for Change

It would be a pipe dream to think that change is going to be initiated by the people who benefit now from the status quo. What is going to have to happen is a real demonstration in Parliament that the public will not put up with the status quo. I think there's increasing evidence that members of Parliament will not. I think there are enough members of

Parliament, in all parties, who favour a change that will put more power in the hands of Parliament and less in the hands of government.

There are two factors influencing why a prime minister might change a system that serves his interest now. The first is, believe it or not, at the end of the day most prime ministers are public-spirited people. They want the system to work well. While they are trying to maintain their own convenience, they would recognize if it is causing a fault in the system.

Secondly, they are not going to have a choice. I think that the system obviously doesn't work. That's widely believed by individual members of Parliament. It's also evident that our country is not functioning as innovatively or as competitively as other countries are. In terms of what is in the interest of the country and what the system will put up with, there is bound to be a change.

Consequences of a Failing Parliament

If things continue as they have, Canadians will simply drop out of politics. We've seen decreasing numbers in the voter turnout, particularly among young people. They see no point to the way Parliament now works and yet, as a country we are facing decisions that are not only complex but also very difficult. They can't be made unless the people making them have legitimacy and authority. If Parliament is not trusted and the people who have to make the decisions cannot do it with legitimacy, the whole decision-making capacity of the country is undermined.

A change in Parliament matters but there is no question that it's not a top-of-mind issue for most Canadians. Those of us who believe there has to be parliamentary reform have to argue hard to achieve that, but we have to demonstrate that a Parliament that puts more power in the hands of private members would also do a better job for the public.

The citizen is less part of the equation when the system doesn't work. The next question is, what do you do about that? Do you try to empower the citizen as an individual? Or do you try to build on the strengths of a parliamentary system? My strong vote is to build on the strengths of a parliamentary system because I think you need to have two things in a society that works. You need to have respect for different individual views, and you need to have some system by which different views can come together to support a decision. That's what Parliament, in the ideal, can achieve.

SCOTT BRISON

Scott Brison was first elected to the House of Commons in 1997, representing the riding of Kings–Hants (Nova Scotia). He was re-elected in the riding after a brief hiatus in the summer of 2000, when he offered his riding to Joe Clark. He is vice-chairman of the House finance committee and the Progressive Conservative critic for the departments of Finance and Industry. Mr. Brison is also an investment banker.

TOPICS:
His Place in Parliament
Defending His Constituency
Concerns in His Region and Riding
Representative Democracy: Party Loyalty and Public Service
The Role of an Opposition Critic
Committees Need Reform
Little Wins
An Effective Opposition Makes a Difference
How Concentrated Power Affects "Guardians of the Public Purse"

Ignoring Parliament on Budget Matters
Parliamentary Reform: Giving Power Back to MPs
Frustrations

His Place in Parliament

There's not a day that I don't look at the Peace Tower on my way in and think, "I've been entrusted with a lot by the people of Kings–Hants." They mean a great deal to me. I never take my place here in the House of Commons for granted, not between elections, certainly not during elections, and not after a hard campaign. I take democracy very seriously, and the opportunity for people, through democratic processes and institutions, to express their views and have their interests reflected in what we do in the House of Commons.

One of the most important jobs of a member of Parliament is not just speaking in the House of Commons, but listening in his or her constituency. When I'm in Kings–Hants I listen. When I'm here in the House of Commons, in either the main chamber or the committee rooms, I speak. And I represent my constituents to the best of my ability, as a member of the House of Commons and of the Progressive Conservative Party — sometimes pejoratively called "the fifth-place party."

In a well-represented democracy, sometimes you stand in the House and say or do things that perhaps your constituents don't agree with. I've done that a couple of times on issues of principle that I felt strongly about. I'm glad, not only that I was able to do so, but that my constituents felt comfortable enough with the quality of representation I provided to re-elect me. They didn't send someone to Ottawa to be a lap dog for the prime minister. They sent a representative to stand up for them.

Defending His Constituency

I feel very strongly about my riding. I grew up there, lived in New York and Toronto for some time, did business elsewhere and then came back to Kings–Hants with the skills that have enabled me to become a good member of Parliament.

In my first term people in Kings–Hants saw that I was vigilant in defending their interests — something they perhaps did not see in their previous representation by my Liberal predecessor, who was elected in 1993 and whom I defeated in 1997.

Concerns in His Region and Riding

Health care is my constituents' first priority. It's one of the most important issues to all Canadians regardless of income, but it's more important to people of lower income: they have a vested interest in ensuring that the Canadian health-care system stays single-tier. There's more to this crisis than can be solved by money. There needs to be a significant focus on long-term planning for health care, including palliative care, and certain issues require innovative approaches.

The twinning of Highway 101 is a very important issue to the people of Kings–Hants. I'm working with the provincial minister of transportation in Nova Scotia to advance the cause here in Ottawa. We've achieved a commitment to a greater level of funding for national highways. There's only about $500 million allotted for highways in all of Canada — a pittance compared to the $12 billion that the government takes in from gas taxes.

I live in an area of the riding where I see quite extreme poverty. Not far from Windsor, Wolfville or Kemptville, there are areas where there's severe poverty. I've been pushing for an increase in the basic personal exemption to $12,000. That would take 2.3 million low-income Canadians off the tax rolls and provide a tax break to everybody above that. It addresses the issue of poverty quite specifically and clearly.

Look at the government's response to some of these tax issues. When I first arrived in Ottawa as an MP, I would question the minister of finance on tax reduction. He'd respond that Canadians didn't need tax reduction. He said that our taxes weren't that much higher than in other countries, I wasn't accurate, and the Progressive Conservatives were out of line with the views of Canadians.

Well, tax issues are extremely important. We live every day in the shadow of a great economic engine to the south, which is about to embark on an even more aggressive tax strategy than in the past. President Bush is gaining support from key Democrats to move forward with his tax reduction plan.

Representative Democracy: Party Loyalty and Public Service

One of my other goals in Parliament is to have more free votes in the House. That doesn't necessarily contradict my strong party loyalty. Increasingly Canadians want a greater level of freedom and flexibility for their members of Parliament to represent their views and interests, and that's entirely consistent with my party's platform.

There are issues where individual caucus members, whether they're the opposition or the government, need to work together and sing from the same song sheet — particularly when it comes to fiscal issues. That's especially important for a government because a budget vote is, technically speaking, a confidence vote. There's a fine line between representing one's constituents in a fundamentalist, populist way and being an effective member of Parliament.

We're not only elected to represent the short-term views of our constituents. As parliamentarians in a representative democracy, we also have to represent the interests of all Canadians. That perspective is commonly referred to as Burkean, after the political theorist Edmund Burke. He said that during elections a member of Parliament belongs to his constituents, and between elections a member of Parliament belongs to his country. You have to find ways to bring your constituents' best interests in line with those of all Canadians.

The Role of an Opposition Critic

The House of Commons finance committee is probably the most powerful committee in Ottawa. As a member I can make a difference. I can contribute to the development of public policy debates that affect the lives of my constituents.

In my role as finance critic and industry critic I can defend my constituents' interests more effectively than if I were shepherded into the Liberal back bench and told what to do and say.

The prime minister has shown more than once that he doesn't even know the names of some of his backbenchers; he's called them by other names. It's hard to make a difference when the prime minister doesn't even know your name. He may not like me, but he does know my name.

I can't imagine how terrible it must be to sit in that Liberal caucus room and be given your marching orders once a week, unable to contribute to what's happening.

Committees Need Reform

Currently committees are being operated as branch plants of ministers' offices. Committees were not intended to work that way. If they are to work better, significant reform is required.

Committees are heavily weighed in favour of the government. It's hard to make a difference there, in the same way that it's difficult for the Progressive Conservatives in the House of Commons, with 12 members in a 301-member House. We're limited to four questions per day, when the other parties get a great deal more.

The degree to which committees are closely related to their ministers' offices is unfortunate — particularly for their chairpersons. They're not functioning as effectively as they should.

I'm on the industry committee, and the chairperson is running it as a branch plant of the minister of industry's office. She is his resident lap dog. A committee cannot be effective in that atmosphere. I'm also on the finance committee, where as vice-chairman I'm more active.

There's a great deal of co-operation between opposition parties, particularly on the finance committee, which works exponentially better than the industry committee. At the finance committee we've shown that though we're fewer in number, we can make a difference by being more effective parliamentarians as individuals.

Some exceptions exist: the foreign affairs committee, under the leadership of Bill Graham, is extraordinarily effective. If one knows the rules and is willing to work within those rules in a creative and professional manner, then one can make a difference on committees and in the House.

Little Wins

I didn't promise anything at election time that I couldn't deliver. If anything, I undersold what we'd be able to do on our constituents' behalf. If you're effective as an opposition member, you can make a greater contribution to debate in the House of Commons or at the committee level than a back-bench Liberal MP.

On a Friday in the House of Commons I asked the government, "When the government says that it's doing everything it can to fight the brain drain (the exodus of highly talented and educated Canadians to the U.S.), why is the government posting jobs in the U.S. on its HRDC Web site, a Canadian taxpayer–funded job search site?"

It was a painfully intuitive, commonsense question. The response was something like, "The honourable member is wrong. We're clearly not doing that. Why would we do something that silly?" On Monday I asked the same question again. The minister of labour said that the government's practice had changed and any such jobs listed — and there were 19 on Friday — had been removed from the Web site.

It shows a small but interesting way that one could make a difference in opposition. If I were a backbencher in the Liberal caucus, I wouldn't have had the chance to raise such a potentially inflammatory issue in the House. If I had raised the issue in a Liberal caucus meeting, the prime minister would muzzle me and they wouldn't do much about it.

An Effective Opposition Makes a Difference

This prime minister needs a strong, vocal opposition. We've seen the prime minister's arrogance a number of times, whether it's HRDC waste or calling the president of the Business Development Bank to get a loan for a friend in the prime minister's riding.

We've had a huge impact for a party that, in terms of members in the House, is disproportionately small. Over the last four years I've seen that many of the policies that were most vociferously opposed by the minister of finance when raised by Progressive Conservative members of Parliament have eventually been embraced by him. For example, reductions in capital gains taxes.

We don't always get credit on opposition benches, but we can put pressure on the government to respond to Canadians' glaring economic needs. We can make a huge difference by persisting with a well-thought-out and consistently well-delivered message. Even stuck in the far corner of the House, I do get my say. There's no such thing as a bad seat in the House of Commons.

How Concentrated Power Affects "Guardians of the Public Purse"

Since the late 1960s there has been a decline in the role of the member of Parliament and an increasing concentration of power in the Prime Minister's Office and in the executive Cabinet.

It's important to remember that before the late 1960s, departmental spending estimates were debated here on the floor of the House of Commons by the Committee of the Whole (where all Parliamentarians were part of the debate). That has changed. And that change has had a deleterious impact on individual members of Parliament's contributions to public policy, program development and spending priorities.

Traditionally the House of Commons has been the guardian of the public purse. But today when a budget comes out, many MPs feel that they have no say. I don't think that there's any coincidence there. If you track spending levels, you see that profligate government spending was commensurate with less parliamentary scrutiny.

Based on a whim, governments could indulge in extraordinary spending on priorities that did not necessarily reflect individual MP's constituents.

At the very least parliamentary spending estimates should be defended by ministers on the floor of the House of Commons. Ministers need to know where their departments are spending money. It was clear from the HRDC debacle that they don't. It was only the insistence and persistence of the opposition that forced the minister of HRDC to defend her departmental spending in some meaningful way.

Ignoring Parliament on Budget Matters

I'm particularly critical of the way the current government handles budgets. Paul Martin and the Liberal government made the arbitrary and irresponsible decision not to have a budget in 2001.

Without a budget individual MPs are denied the opportunity to debate, discuss and ultimately vote on the spending of taxpayers' money. This government has demonstrated an unprecedented level of arrogance. Their refusal to submit a budget effectively says that Parliament does not deserve the respect to debate, discuss and vote on the budget.

When the rights and privileges of MPs are denied, so too are the rights of their constituents. Instead government spending follows Liberal Party desires and whims, used to appease Liberal backbenchers or the pet projects of Liberal Cabinet ministers.

In the past we have seen governments spending indiscriminately and taking Canadian taxpayers for granted. But we've never seen the government doing so while denying an effective debate in the House of Commons. It's absolutely unbelievable.

Parliamentary Reform: Giving Power Back to MPs

Significant parliamentary reform should increase a member of Parliament's ability to make a difference on behalf of Canadians. But the government isn't really interested in that. Ruling governments are less than interested in the devolution of power, the return of power to its traditional place.

Liberal government backbenchers aren't given an opportunity to express their views, or those of their constituents, on policy issues. They're effectively herded in and out of the House to vote. That's terribly unfortunate because there are some very good people in this House, people with the greatest of intentions to make a difference.

The issue of parliamentary reform is starting to come into focus in Canada, and that's very positive. Many MP's who have spent a few years in Parliament realize the institution needs significant reform to raise the role of the member of Parliament to its previous standing.

Frustrations

There are two kinds of ambition. One is ambition to be and the other is ambition to do. For those who are ambitious to do, this House can be a very frustrating place.

My biggest frustration is that public service in general — Parliament and electoral offices — is failing to attract the best and brightest Canadians. To make a real difference this needs to be a critical mass of some of Canada's best and brightest. It shouldn't be some sort of holding pattern for the "schlumpy dumpies."

At one time there was a sense of noblesse oblige, when people would make sacrifices and look at it as a great honour and privilege to serve the public. That has changed. When you're sitting in a committee debating very important issues, at some point you realize that a lot of people are more interested in being re-elected than in making a difference while they're here. The House of Commons is not a make-work program. Anyone who is counting on Parliament for job security is in my opinion in the wrong business. You're here to serve. You're here to do your best. You're here to be principled and intelligent. If you do not match any of these criteria, then you should be somewhere else.

PETER MacKAY

P eter MacKay was called to the bar in June 1991 and subsequently
began a general law practice in New Glasgow, Nova Scotia. Mr.
MacKay assumed the position of Crown attorney with the Nova
Scotia government in 1993 and has prosecuted criminal matters at
the youth, provincial and Supreme court levels. Mr. MacKay was
elected member of Parliament for Pictou–Antigonish–Guysborough
(Nova Scotia) in 1997. He was subsequently named House leader for
the Progressive Conservative Party and critic for the departments of
Justice and the Solicitor General. He presently serves as a member of
the Board of Internal Economy and the Standing Committee on
Justice and Human Rights.

TOPICS:
The Need for More Free Votes and Less Party Discipline
Prospects for Parliamentary Reform
Power of the Prime Minister
Consequences of Not Changing Parliament

The Need for More Free Votes and Less Party Discipline

There has to be a change in attitude for members of Parliament, backbenchers in particular, to feel that they are a more important part of the process and have more power. That change would include more free votes in the House of Commons. There's a lot of talk about these things, but rarely do we see the leadership of a ruling party completely relinquish the reins of the party whip when it comes to voting on matters of conscience. Free votes are far too rare. In my memory there's been very few occasions where there's been a completely free vote.

Other changes that need to happen are, for example, have all private members' bills votable, give members of Parliament a greater ability to participate in debate and level out the time that members are given to debate certain issues.

In the grand scheme of things it's discouraging for the members who are here. I believe that we will not get the quality in individuals coming forward to serve in the House of Commons if they feel that their voice is not going to be heard or they're not going to be able to make a substantial change on behalf of their constituents. To that end it's very unfortunate.

Prospects for Parliamentary Reform

In terms of parliamentary reform, as with a lot of legislative initiatives, it's usually the House leader on behalf of the government who has the ability to make substantive change. We are in the process of having what they call the modernization committee. I don't want to prejudge what the outcome of that will be, but I'm sensing a bit of frustration around the table as to whether the final result will produce meaningful change. While it's incumbent upon the leaders of all parties to allow their members to have greater participation and greater decision-making power, at the end of the day it's the government that has the ability to force through or to vote down changes that would make this chamber and this Parliament more relevant. We're at a bit of a stalemate. The current government seems to want to entertain the idea of reform, but they don't want to implement any substantive change. I don't see a lot of prospects for that happening under the current prime minister's leadership.

Power of the Prime Minister

It appears, on the government side, that there is really very little genuine interest in relinquishing some of the power possessed in the PMO and in the Privy Council Office. If members are to be more relevant and play a more meaningful role in decision making, some of that power has to trickle down. That can only be demonstrated when the prime minister stops brow-beating members of his own caucus, preventing them from speaking their minds and standing up on behalf of their constituents on very important issues. We've seen it happen with the hepatitis C debate, where many members of the Liberal party did not support the government on the issue but were forced to vote for a policy they did not believe in. The ethics counsellor was another classic case where Liberals had to vote against their own party's 1993 *Red Book* election promise to have the counsellor report directly to Parliament, not the prime minister. I mean, Liberal members stood up in the House, ashen-faced, and were forced to vote against their own platform promise. It has to be completely humiliating for a member of Parliament to have to do that. Liberal members of caucus have repeatedly found themselves in that position under this prime minister's watch.

Consequences of Not Changing Parliament

Until Parliament becomes a place where Canadians can look for leadership, until the public honestly senses that the people they elect are not only acting on their behalf but are playing a significant role in the way that things are done in Parliament, then the whole institution is sullied. Unfortunately I feel that that is what has been happening. It's very frustrating. The reputation of Parliament has been steadily declining and people's faith in this institution is waning. We're reaching a critical juncture where we're going to have to do something to demonstrate that Parliament has relevance.

Chapter 6
The Bloc Québécois

RICHARD MARCEAU

Richard Marceau has been the member of Parliament for Charlesbourg–Jacques-Cartier in Quebec since 1997. He has held numerous posts for the Bloc Québécois, such as critic for international trade, Indian affairs and northern development, and intergovernmental affairs. Mr. Marceau is a high-profile sovereigntist and the Bloc's spokesperson overseeing relations with the rest of Canada. He has been a member of the standing committees on Justice and Human Rights, Finance and Foreign Affairs and International Trade. He is a graduate of the University of Western Ontario Law School.

TOPICS:
A Separatist in Parliament
The Job of a Critic and Spokesperson
Constituency Work: Keeping in Touch with Home
Taking Quebec's Concerns to Ottawa
Federal Money Comes with Catches
Subsidizing National Unity?

Canadian Parliament Is Dysfunctional
Three Levels of Politics
Jurisdictional Disputes and Centralized Power
Service Duplication

A Separatist in Parliament

I am a sovereigntist, and I am in politics to push for the independence of Quebec. That does not stop me from doing my job as a member at the local level.

In English Canada they have trouble understanding why a sovereigntist — or a party dedicated to Quebec's sovereignty — would go to Ottawa. You regularly hear, "What are you are going to do in Ottawa, destroy the country?"

Our answer is that elected representatives must represent the population as much as they can. It's important that the 45 percent of Quebecers who are in favour of sovereignty are represented in Ottawa. Sovereigntists had no voice in Ottawa before the Bloc Québécois. Could a sovereigntist vote for a Liberal government? No. The same goes for the Conservatives, the New Democrats and the Alliance. Now sovereigntists have a vehicle which represents them and their values on the federal scene: the Bloc.

The Bloc is not just about separation.

Of necessity, the Bloc deals with issues other than separation. For example, the debate on compensation for victims of hepatitis C. Liberal members wanted to vote for complete compensation, but were prevented by Prime Minister Chrétien. They stood up for the motion, voting with the government but against their consciences — in tears. That is something I will never accept and it is something which does not happen in the Bloc.

Take the debate on globalization. People ask questions like, "What sort of globalization? Is it being done in secret? Should it be done more openly?"

Increasingly the decisions about what we eat, look at, listen to, read and who will take care of us are made internationally. Countries sit at international tables. That's another reason I'm a sovereigntist: so Quebec can have a voice in determining the international rules that in the future will affect our daily lives.

I don't think that young people are uninterested in political matters. It doesn't matter where they get involved — a student union, a community — as long as they do.

The Job of a Critic and Spokesperson

I'm a busy person here in Ottawa. I have three main mandates. I'm the critic for intergovernmental affairs, critic for Native affairs and the main spokesperson for the Bloc for relations with the rest of Canada, something we call the Bloc ROC Committee.

My job as spokesperson for the Bloc is to show the rest of Canada that sovereignty is a legitimate project, an idea shared by almost half of Quebecers, and that there are logical reasons for it. In parts of Canada there's the sense that if you're a sovereigntist, you are stupid or mentally deranged.

Lucien Bouchard, for example, was portrayed in caricatures as somebody mad, emotional and irrational. But the project has a very solid legal, political and economical basis. After actually talking to people in New Brunswick and other parts of the country, the reaction was, "Well, I can't say I agree with you, but it makes sense." It is important for Quebec sovereigntists to have a dialogue with the rest of Canada.

To use an expression used by Theodore Roosevelt, I use my office as a "bully pulpit" to express my views on why Quebec should be an independent country.

Constituency Work: Keeping in Touch with Home

Ottawa is an entire world in itself, with its own rules. I try to get out, to see real people as often as I can, to stay connected with my electorate, the people I serve.

I have a column in my riding's local weekly paper. I send mail to a tenth of the doors in my riding basically every day. We have parliamentary bulletins four times a year. These are some of the ways I'm trying to reach my constituency. On the weekend I attend events in my riding.

Some people are intimidated and hesitate going into an MP's office. I don't know why, but they are. When they come to me and say, "I need your help, and oh, by the way, I voted for you," I say, "It doesn't matter." Once elected I must be at the service of the whole population.

Their political opinions are irrelevant: I'm at the service of the people, but they elected me knowing that I'm a sovereigntist.

Taking Quebec's Concerns to Ottawa

Running for office in 1997, at the age of 26, I ran into a lot of cynicism. So I said, "I'm not promising to change the world, but I will make these two promises: I will do everything I can and I will be very visible." And for three and a half years I have been very visible.

The federal election in Quebec is different from rest of Canada. It isn't a race between the Alliance and the Liberals — the Alliance doesn't exist here. It is a race between the Bloc and the Liberals. For various reasons people have to punish the government of Jean Chrétien. There are several federal issues at stake: access to employment insurance, the fight against organized crime, Bill C-20 (the Clarity Bill).

More than half the people paying for EI don't have access to it. That's totally unacceptable. The federal government doesn't put 1¢ into the EI fund. It all comes from employees and employers. We weren't going to allow the federal government to take money that doesn't belong to them. EI should be more accessible. If there's a surplus, it should go back to employers and employees through lower premiums because they're the ones who are paying for the system.

For the last few years the federal government has been putting money from EI in its own pocket. And for years the auditor general has said, "No, that's not legal, that's not correct. You can't do that."

With the bill that was tabled, soon to be adopted by the House, the federal government were trying to legalize, after the fact, what they did during all those years. They were trying to legitimize theft. The CSN, a big union in Quebec, even took the government to court on the matter.

Federal Money Comes with Catches

People ask me, "What do you want to do in concrete terms for us here in the federal riding of Charlesbourg–Jacques-Cartier?" I tell them, "When I get to Ottawa I am going to represent you well. I am going be your voice in the federal Parliament to raise the issues that affect you."

The national issues are less discussed than more local issues. Locally we are talking about developing the Quebec zoo, the Stoneham lodge (a ski resort) and the Trans-Quebec Trail. My election promise was to work for the Quebec zoo's renovation. My first option was to have federal money, but they decided to make a national unity issue out of it. They imposed conditions here that don't apply to similar projects in the rest of Canada. They asked for a Canadian flag and bilingualism, and the Quebec government said, "No. If you want to make a national unity issue out of it, we'll pay the entire amount."

So the provincial government has decided to put all the money into it. It's going to reopen in a couple of years, and that's what I was struggling and fighting for. It's done. We're not against English being spoken there or offering English services. But it smells fishy to us when the federal government says to do this when they can't bilingualize their own federal capital. You walk around Ottawa and it's basically English only. If they want to make an issue of bilingualism, they should start in their own backyard instead of imposing the Official Languages Act at the zoo.

The way the flag flap played in Quebec City was, "Why impose conditions on Quebec that you don't impose on other provinces?"

As a member of Parliament you're going to work for your constituency. Those are my underlying principles, and you have to stick to them.

Subsidizing National Unity?

The federal government's position on the Quebec zoo was part of a bigger propaganda machine. Since 1995 half a billion dollars were spent by the federal government in propaganda campaigns. They're trying to buy Quebecers' allegiance to Canada with Quebecers' money. We believe that money could be better spent.

Alfonso Gagliano, the Liberal minister responsible for Quebec, has said that members of the opposition succeed in attracting more money from the federal government than members of the government do. I know that Liberal federal MPs have no voice. They never open their mouths.

I'm disappointed that the federal government turns every development issue in Canada into a matter of national unity when it isn't. They look patriotic in the rest of Canada but come out badly in Quebec.

I think they assume the Quebec question is solved. Well, I read a couple of weeks ago in *La Presse* — which is very federalist — that sovereignty was at 44 percent. The younger generation tends to be pro-sovereignty, at least more sovereigntist than federalist. If I were the federal Liberals, I wouldn't put my head in the sand thinking we're done.

My constituents — and Quebecers in general — pay taxes to Ottawa. They should have the right to get something in return. It's despicable to attach strings to federal money, saying, "You have to promote Canadian unity and Canadian identity." It should be an economic development project and that's it. I'm disappointed with the federal government's attitude in this whole file.

Canadian Parliament is Dysfunctional

I'm going to a conference of the Law Society of New Brunswick called "Is Canada a Dysfunctional Country?" I'm giving a sovereigntist point of view, that Canada is indeed dysfunctional. The relationship between Quebec and Canada precedes Canada even being born. And I don't want to spend the rest of my life dealing with it.

In our system it's the first past the post. The Liberals won 40 percent of the vote and became the government. You can argue whether it's the best system or not, but it's the system we're in.

You have to be consistent before, during and after the election. That's what I'm trying very hard to do, and I think people appreciate that, even people who disagree with me politically. You can't be half pregnant — you're pregnant or you're not. So you're a sovereigntist or you're not. You can't have it both ways.

Three Levels of Politics

During the last federal election in Quebec the Liberals made a provincial issue into a federal issue: municipal mergers. The Parti Québécois government in Quebec had passed a bill forcing municipal amalgamation. The Bloc and Parti Québécois (PQ) are brothers in arms for Quebec's independence. So people said, "If we want to send a message to the PQ, instead of waiting until the next provincial election, we'll tell them now through the Bloc."

As a result, we had to fight not only the Liberals, but also the coalition of suburban mayors in and around Quebec City. Lots of money was involved — not just the usual Liberal war chest, but money from the municipalities. The Saturday before the election there was a fluorescent sign next to each sign in my riding that read, "Block the Bloc on November 27th, we don't want municipal mergers." It must have cost tens of thousands of dollars.

For a federal candidate to say, "Vote for me, I am against the municipal mergers," is being dishonest. The day after an election, what does this new Liberal MP do to prevent mergers? Tell the House, "I want an emergency debate on the mergers?" He'll only hear, "Buddy, you're in the wrong legislature." Campaigning on that is intellectually dishonest.

Now there's a backlash taking place. People are saying, "It's an issue we'll settle in the next provincial campaign." In the meantime the issues we have to talk about are employment insurance, organized crime, the health system — in short, issues that involve the federal government, and not the municipal mergers.

Jurisdictional Disputes and Centralized Power

It goes back to the Social Union Agreement, signed by nine provinces out of 10 — Quebec opted out. It gives the federal government the power to intrude into any provincial jurisdiction. The pattern is of a federal nation-building process, with the true government in Ottawa annexing provincial governments.

The more the federal government sticks its fingers into provincial jurisdictions, the more federalist Quebecers — who still harbour some hope of remaking Canada with a committed Quebec — will give up. They'll say, "If it's the only way we can give Quebec more power, I'll vote 'yes' in a referendum for sovereignty."

There have been federal intrusions in education, training, environment, family and parental leave. The Quebec government has proposed a very strong parental leave program, much broader than the federal government's supposed plan. Under the federal program the self-employed are denied EI and therefore can't get parental leave benefits. But the self-employed tend to be young — the same people who are having kids. So a big chunk of the young generation in Canada has no access to a good parental leave program.

If the Quebec program was in place, the self-employed would be covered. If the rest of Canadians are satisfied with that program, fine. In Quebec we set ourselves broader objectives than Ottawa. Just send us the money, we'll add some of our own, and let us administer it. We'll be better for young Quebecers who want to have children.

The irony of it all is that when the federal government intrudes into provincial jurisdictions, federalists who usually defend the division of powers say, "We don't care. We're invading you." And sovereigntists counter by saying, "Well, you know, as long as we're in Canada you might as well respect the document on which our relationship is based." So you have the sovereigntists defending the letter and the spirit of the Canadian Constitution, which is so weird, so surreal.

Service Duplication

Duplication of federal and provincial services is a problem. We transferred responsibility for employment to the Quebec government, except what is known as "Youth Strategy." A young person who wants a job is stuck in this schizophrenic system. Who looks after it, Quebec or Ottawa? Some programs overlap, some contradict each other, and it makes you want straighten it out.

This is a concrete example of the need to achieve the independence of Quebec. That is, we have to get rid of this constant constitutional bickering. We are going to have an open door for young people, where they will need to apply for government assistance or programs and which will have the answers to everything, and not have the young person feel like they are being sent down various government garden paths.

SUZANNE TREMBLAY

Suzanne Tremblay was a university professor and has been a Bloc Québécois member of Parliament for Rimouski–Neigette-et-la Mitis in Quebec since 1993. As an outspoken supporter of a sovereign Quebec she has been the BQ's official critic on Canadian heritage. She has also been an active member of the heritage and official languages committees.

TOPICS:
Daily Routine
The Research Team
Caucus and Teamwork: How They Work
Last-Minute Information Overload
Objectionable Bills
Conflicting Responsibilities
The Opposition and the Party Line
Absenteeism as Protest
Following the Party Line
Can the Party Line Change?

Daily Routine

The day starts very early in the morning. I have to be at a meeting at 8:30 a.m. on Mondays, Tuesdays and Thursdays, and 8:00 a.m. on Wednesdays and Fridays. I'm a member of the Question Period committee and we prepare for Question Period. So we need to listen to the news, read the newspapers and go over the press releases, just to find out what's going on that day, what's in the news, what's important. Sometimes we have to go through documents that have been prepared for us by researchers, for example, because of the administrative agreement that the provinces have signed with the government.

I am on two committees, the Canadian heritage committee and the official languages committee. To be prepared for these meetings we have to go through the papers that witnesses send to us. Sometimes they send them just the day before, sometimes a week in advance. We also have to study bills, read them article by article to see if we are going to make amendments or if we agree. We also have to study documents for the party. We have to be in the House on duty once in a while — we share the duty time because we need to have at least 15 percent of the party in the House at all times. So we have duty days, each of us. It's the same thing for all parties.

We also have to read documents, to be able to make speeches on the bills that are presented and discussed in the House. There are all sorts of meetings in the House every day, five days a week, and each member is in Ottawa four days a week. There are many things to do, a lot of reading, a lot of work. Not all the MPs do all that by themselves; some have people to help them.

The Research Team

We have a team of Bloc Québécois researchers because we MPs cannot go through everything ourselves. We must have great confidence in the spokespeople of all of these departments to make sure that studies are well done. We have a budget to hire qualified research people, but we don't have enough money to hire researchers for each department. The researchers have a lot of work, and it's a good thing that these young people with a university background are very keen to help us find points that are more important than others.

The researchers aren't green, they're experienced. Some are under 30, but they have accurate training at the university level. The director of the research is a person over 50, and many who are working with him are over 35 and they have experience in the field as researchers. Some have experience in politics because they have been working with MPs, in their office here in Ottawa or in their ridings. These are the people who do the research, the background information that brings the law. We also have people in our office and in the leader's office, many people working to be sure that we have the information we need to make decisions.

Caucus and Teamwork: How They Work

We hand the paper to the caucus to explain to our colleagues what the main issues in a bill are. With all the experience of these people together, we finally make a decision. A spokesperson may have a line to propose to us, and when we discuss it we may point out things to be careful of. Also, we may sometimes change our mind with the caucus. For example, we may have originally been in favour if we followed the recommendation of the support person, but after discussing together with the support person, we come to the conclusion that we need to have another position on the bill. So we change it without a problem.

Last year we had to discuss the creation of a park up in Nunavut, and it was a question regarding the border. Of course the border didn't make any difference for us, but it was important to hear what the people want — the people of Nunavut, the First Nations that live there above the 54th parallel. It's so far up north, and they know what it is to live there, so we thought it was better to defend their ideas than those of the minister, who never set foot there and doesn't have a clue what it's like.

With that kind of thing we don't need to have everybody very well informed on the matter. They have confidence in the work we are doing with the research department, and we just inform them that this is going on. I don't think one person can get all of the information required in his or her head. That's why it sometimes happens that years later we have to change a law because there was a mistake which we did-n't catch because we didn't have time to go deeply into it. Remember that lawyers write the laws, and they like to go into court to find out the correct way to interpret the interpretation. It's not always easy to under-stand a law the way it's written.

Last-Minute Information Overload

As I said, committees sometimes get the paperwork at the last minute. All the paper we have to read and go through is a real problem. Sometimes we lack basic information. For example, we had the CNA (Centre national des arts) in front of us at the Canadian heritage committee. We were hearing what the president read for the first time. We knew a little bit about the problem, but we did not have information on how many members were on the board of trustees. I realized that we should have asked the clerk to give us some minimal information about the CNA. If we want to have it, we can do the research ourselves, but sometimes we don't have the time. If we have the general report today, for example, and we have a committee tomorrow; it's impossible to go through everything and prepare questions to ask the government. It's difficult to be keen because we don't have the time.

From what I've heard, it has always been like this — it's kind of a tradition. So the Conservatives are in a bad position to say to the Liberals, "You shouldn't do that," because they were doing it before. The Alliance Party, the NDP and the Bloc would never be in government. We can point out problems within the system, but nothing changes. It's very rare that we have documents well in advance to make decisions on these issues. In addition, we must also deal with the journalists. If they know we have an important paper, they want to get the content before, and some committee members may feel pressure to leak documents.

It's difficult to know exactly the best way to handle this information. Some MPs who have been here for a long time know all about it. So we sometimes feel that if we go on with the questioning, it would be boring or stupid. You don't want to look stupid, so you don't ask the basic questions that could be important. It's not easy, but of course we are ordinary people and we do the best we can.

Objectionable Bills

Sometimes we have surprises. We have to get involved in bills other than those which are our main subject. For example, the minister of finance had a bill called C-44. This was a large bill and one we had to go through to find out everything that was going to be changed in the Finance Department. About halfway through the bill we found an article that introduced what we call an "ejector seat" for the chairman of the CBC, the chairman of Telefilm Canada and the chairman of the National Film

Board that may not have looked very important to the person responsible for finance. That's why it's quite difficult for an MP to go through all this stuff — sometimes we have to speak about things that we know little about. However, if we discover something, we are going to speak about it.

I remember C-28, which was this kind of omnibus bill. You could find everything in it. And we could find a direct link between certain articles and the minister of finance's shipping company. I felt they put a few articles in that look stupid or unimportant but had very big consequences. Initially, when we went through that kind of bill, we didn't really have the time to look at article after article very deeply to find out the whole process. We discovered that the Canadian government had made an agreement with the American government for retired persons who had worked in the United States and had a pension from the U.S. government. Many Canadians who were living across the border had trouble with that, and we had to work very hard so the government would come back on that decision.

Conflicting Responsibilities

In Bill C-55 that Ms. Copps put in front of the House, we discussed magazines and Canadian ownership of them. In my own riding people who earn their living from lumber wrote to me and said, "Be careful with C-55, we would not like to have trouble with the United States with the exportation of lumber." So I am in a position now where I must decide what is good for them, and what is good for Canadians. It is often difficult to decide which way to go. Of course we bring forth the intrinsic problems of our constituency, but we also have to think of the whole situation. I must choose — do I need to protect the culture or do I need to protect the few businesses affected by this?

We discussed C-55 a lot because it was a problem for many of my colleagues in the caucus with paper companies in their constituencies. In our caucus we discuss the orientation of the session, what we are going to look after, what's going to be important for us and what's going to be important for the interests of Quebecers. Most of the time the interests of Quebecers are also interests of Canadians. So if we get close to the interests of our people, most of the time it has an implementation in all other parts of Canada.

It was difficult to decide which way was better, but we thought we must face the challenge of the United States. In this instance we thought it was more important to defend the culture of Canada and to be against the United States on the matter of magazines. Therefore we voted with the government on that one.

The Opposition and the Party Line

The opposition to the government is something very easy because it depends on the party line. Most of the time we are not against the Liberals just to be against them. When we were the official Opposition we were with the government on 44 percent of the votes, and we were the first official Opposition to work so closely with the government. Any time the government presented something that was good for Canadians or Quebecers, we were with them because we are not an opposition trying to become the government. We are here to defend the interests of people and of course we want sovereignty for Quebec. We are working to have a good government, the best we can have for Canadians. So sometimes, if what the Canadian government proposes is all right with us, we vote with them without a problem.

I have the opportunity to speak every morning at Question Period. I don't have any problem expressing myself. As for the party line, I'm part of it because I am working to decide it. I do not have frustration with that. Like anyone else, sometimes I make concessions — I may not completely agree with the party line, but I understand that it's OK for me to vote for it.

Absenteeism as Protest

If there is a party line that I cannot support at all, I won't be in the House to vote against it. I will stay in my office instead. There are ways to vote while you're absent, if you accept to be paired with a person of the opposition or with the government. It's like being in the House. Personally I refuse to be paired — I would rather be completely absent from the House if I'm not voting. If a journalist asks if I was absent from the House because I was against the vote, I would say yes. I wouldn't have any problem with that. It's very rare — it happened only once under Mr. Bouchard's leadership. The vote wasn't in accordance with my principles, and I couldn't support it because it wasn't a good law.

Following the Party Line

Frankly, sometimes I go in to vote on something and they give me a paper which indicates that "we are going to be for that bill, for such-and-such reason," but I never saw the bill before. We all are like this, and sometimes I'm discussing with members of the Liberal Party, and they ask me, "Why did you vote for or against this?" Sometimes they discover that there were problems in the law. They just approved it because they had to — they're backbenchers and they don't have a clue about what they're doing there, except voting like the prime minister told them to vote.

In politics, if you don't go along the party line, you may be excluded or punished. I don't think it's worthwhile because I think it can be useful being a spokesperson for Canadians. I think it's better to stay in my office rather than to say, "I'll stand up and vote against my party." Look what happened with Mr. Nunziata and other members of the Liberal Party who decided to vote against the government. The political parties don't support this kind of rebellion. We try to stay low profile when we decide against something. It's more important for me to be able to wake up the next morning and be happy to live with what I am, rather than what I should have done.

Can the Party Line Change?

The party line will only change on the day many people in one caucus start to say, "Well, listen, we're not children. We have consciences." My first line is my conscience, and that's the thing I will have to live with all my life. We have agreed now to have more freedom and we are more accepting of the possibility for members to be outside the party line. A change is coming, but if you want to change the situation, you must change it yourself.

As long as all members of all parties want to follow the party line because they're afraid of being punished, it's not going to change. If you can stick to your principles and say, "No, I'm not going to vote for that," you will be able to change things. Mr. Duceppe once asked me, "What would you like us to do if we want you to vote with us?" I said we must take the engagement and make a promise that we are going to have a private bill to change the government bill. So he said, "Oh, that's nothing, we'll do it." So we are working on a private bill to try to change the law. That is important for me. My conscience is safe, the party line is safe and my constituents are happy.

We must find ways of compromise and agreement to have that happen as much as possible. It takes time because you must discuss and you must be able to have your own clear ideas to discuss with other people. If you have the courage, it will change. It depends on the way you are. I prefer to stand up for my principles and discuss as much as I can.

PART TWO

Insiders and Outsiders

Chapter 7
Historians and Academics

ANNE COOLS

A nne Cools is a member of the Senate representing the division of Toronto–Centre–York. She was appointed by Prime Minister Pierre Trudeau in 1984. She is currently a member of the Legal and Constitutional Affairs Committee and the National Finance Committee. Prior to her career in politics she worked as a social worker and community organizer.

TOPICS:
Canada's History of Parliament and Responsible Government
The Weakening of Parliament and the Growing Strength
of Government
Concentration of Power in a Few Hands
Parliament's Forgotten Role: Control of the Public Purse
A Stacked Deck: Why Parliamentary Scrutiny of Government Is
Escaping Canadians
Does a Citizen's Vote Count When Parliament Is Weak?

Canada's History of Parliament and Responsible Government

Canada is a monarchy. Many Canadians do not understand this. The prime minister, who does not really exist in law, is really Her Majesty's first minister. Her Majesty's government in Canada is a system of responsible government. Responsible government is an aristocratic concept, really. What it means is that the king, the sovereign, must choose his ministers and must choose his government from members of Parliament. That, in its day, was truly revolutionary. It was intended to be the most wonderful system of government that had ever been devised by human beings.

This really is our Constitution. Nowadays we think the Constitution means the Charter of Rights. In point of fact, when we used to say "our Constitution," we used to mean this system of governance, which meant the king, the prime minister, the Senate and the House of Commons. It is a mighty system.

Parliament is really supposed to be the mightiest representative institution of the nation, the high court of the land. It's where the opinions and the views of the nation are brought forward, discussed and debated and voted upon. The conclusions of Parliament are supposed to be the representative opinions of the citizens.

I have to admit that the system is failing in many cases. Parliament in many instances is no longer holding ministers responsible or accountable. I wish Parliament would assert itself a lot more in this respect. I'm not telling any tales out of school to say that Parliament is probably in its weakest stage of its entire history. And remember, Parliament is a very ancient institution. I do not believe, in any of my readings of history, that I have ever known Parliament to be so weak.

The Weakening of Parliament and the Growing Strength of Government

Parliament has many roles. One of them is obviously the legislative role. Everybody knows that. We pass bills. But what is not so well known is the administrative role, which is the overseeing of every single department of government. So whether it is Justice or Defence or Energy or Health, Parliament has a duty to oversee the administration and the internal, day-to-day running of those departments.

It is fair to say that in our modern, contemporary society, the size of government has grown at an enormous rate. Executives of government have grown and expanded their influence. Yet Parliament has not grown and developed at the same rate.

The business of Parliament is supposedly to be able to contain and to control the administration and the government of the nation. That is what it's supposed to do. However, Parliament has become little more than a legislative machine which pumps out so much legislation. Votes are held every several weeks on an appointed day, where members come running in to vote as they're supposed to.

The concentration of power is slipping away from Parliament to the government. Some of the symptoms may be the same as some of the consequences, but symptoms are perfectly evident. For example, we have bills that are passing, daily, in spite of marked opposition from great numbers of the public, or in some cases a majority of the public.

For example, I was part of the famous Senate filibuster on the GST. The Senate at the time adopted a position that the GST was a bad tax. Under the leadership of Senator Allan MacEachern, a former minister of finance, we endeavoured to fight the Mulroney government on that issue. It was pretty evident that the entire country did not want the bill. The public did not want the tax. The Senate said very clearly that it did not want it. At the time Mr. Mulroney opted not to face the public and go to an election. That's what he should have done if he had come into conflict with the upper chamber, the Senate. But he used an unusual section of the BNA (British North America) Act to appoint an additional set of eight senators and ensure his legislation got passed.

The consequence of this new concentration of power away from Parliament is that a lot of bad legislation has been passed. People are not getting the kind of quality of governance that they deserve. Parliament needs to take back its powers and to exercise them more vigorously. They need to defend the public's interest a little bit more strongly.

Concentration of Power in a Few Hands
We have to be mindful of governance, as opposed to government. The governance of a nation is an extremely important function. We also have to remember that most human beings are pretty good people. However, we cannot exist in a system where you depend on the extremely virtuous because the extremely virtuous are few and far between.

Remember what Lord Acton said: "Absolute power corrupts absolutely." Parliament and the system of governance are supposed to understand that human beings with absolute power, or governors with unbridled power, invariably will abuse it. The business of Parliament is to make sure that power is always exercised very properly and in a very orderly way on behalf of the citizens of the land.

However, if you were to look at the history of Parliament and the history of the development of responsible government, it was all about wrestling power away from non-responsible, non-elected bodies — kings, usually. Now we see the situation ticking slowly, but certainly and surely, back to something akin to the old system.

I've made it my business to study this institution of Parliament because I love it and I believe in it. It took about 1,000 years to get certain powers away from the king. Supposedly they were to come to Parliament. It took about 50 years to give those powers back to a prime minister. I sincerely believe that that is the case here in Canada.

This is a social and political question that is commanding study and demanding examination — the total buildup and accumulation of powers. It's not only in the prime minister's hands, but also in the hands of the Prime Minister's Office. You now have a situation in this country where the executive, meaning the Cabinet, exercises the king's powers, the governor general's powers, the Senate's powers, the House of Commons's powers. I think that we should always be diligent about the accumulation of so many powers in so few hands. It worries me.

Parliament's Forgotten Role: Control of the Public Purse

The government today spends close to $170 billion per year. Amounts of money like this are really beyond the comprehension of most human beings, beyond even their grasp. I sit on the national finance committee because it was my job to bring in the government supply bills. The numbers are staggering — $10 million for this, $10 billion for that, $50 million, $800 million for that. And all of these huge amounts are one-line items.

Parliament really is about two things, just as government is really supposed to be about two things. It is about the authority to raise and spend taxes. In other words, who is given the power — by being voted in, in an election — to dig into the citizens' pockets, to take out money, and who is given the authority to spend it? We used to call that, in Parliament, the "control of the purse." *That used to be the most important role of Parliament.* And it is our job as Parliament to hold governments accountable for every penny that they spend. That's what we're supposed to do.

It is part of the whole phenomenon of supply. That definition of supply, like so many parliamentary terms, is now somewhat arcane. Governments have grown increasingly remote and distanced from people. The fact is, supply means the lifeblood of government. In other words — money. The business of supply is the parliamentary business of voting on money to allow a government to function.

Not voting on supply will bring a government to its knees. If a parliament ever wanted to cripple a government, or to force a government into a state of resignation or defeat, all that the parliament has to do is to cut off supply. It was through this process that the genius of the British constitution excelled and made itself felt. It was through this process of supply, and what we called in Parliament "confidence votes," that despots and absolutists and improper tyrants could be removed without shedding a drop of blood, or without even too much conflict.

It is a fascinating historical process and it was the genius of the parliamentary system. It had a way to excise tyrants and it had a way to excise absolutists, bad rulers, with just a vote of the parliament of the land. All that the vote had to say was that this chamber has no more confidence in those ministers or in that government.

It's a mighty process but I fear that this critical role of the parliamentary system is slipping away from us. Its very knowledge seems to be becoming more distant to so many, particularly members of Parliament. The business of mastering this process of controlling money, of even understanding it and being able to guide it — swerve it, correct it and challenge it — is so enormous that it inhibits most MPs and many shrink back from it.

We have a duty to be stewards of these institutions, and we have a greater duty to be the protectors and the stewards of our population. For example, when government says they are instituting a gun registry, a member of Parliament should be persuaded to vote yes or not based on the information that is put before them. So if a government tells Parliament that this gun registry will cost $85 million, and then X years later we hear the number is up to $500 million and climbing, then I think it is in order, within the best country in the world, to ask the very best questions. The best questions are, "Why did the government tell us that it would cost $85 million and why is the evidence pointing in an opposite direction?"

A Stacked Deck: Why Parliamentary Scrutiny of Government Is Escaping Canadians

The mastery of parliamentary rules and procedures over government in itself is a difficult task. It is very demanding and needs a fair amount of exertion and a lot of study. Sometimes it's a bit difficult for members of Parliament because they have a lot on their plates. Members of Parliament have very limited resources.

I have two staff and myself in my office, that is the totality of my resources. And then I am up against a minister who, in the instance of the Department of Justice, has 1,200 lawyers on staff and a host of other resources. So you begin with a stacked deck. Many members have difficulty maintaining a position or even any sort of a posture in that sort of uneven situation. I have had some success at doing it. There have been times when the ministers, with their 1,200 staff and all their resources, were no match for the two loyal people in my office. My two wonderful staff and myself on some occasions have succeeded in holding them accountable and bringing forth the public interests. I'm talking in particular about families in divorce and the entitlements of children to be able to have relationships with both their mothers and fathers.

I sincerely believe that it is the duty of each and every member of Parliament to hold government accountable. It's a difficult, challenging and daunting task. But it is one that must be done. Not to do it is to undermine democracy.

Does a Citizen's Vote Count When Parliament Is Weak?

The citizen is at a very serious disadvantage because the citizen has no mechanism to express opinions. The citizen goes to the polls and votes once every four years. The citizen is supposed to be represented on the floor of the chamber through his members. We are now dealing with a situation where the magnitude and size of government, with all its resources, is making even asking questions difficult. Members of Parliament don't have the resources and members come and go. It could easily take a new member two or three or four years to begin to know the ropes, much less seek change. In the long run the only correction for this sort of thing is an informed public.

What worries me, and it is a point that I keep harping on, is that so many sections of our population are now marginalized. There is a state of remoteness between the regions and Ottawa, between the citizens and Ottawa. I am always trying to do my little bit to bring this information to the public. One of the biggest reasons for these developments in our political condition is because our citizens have become impoverished. Successive governments of this country have impoverished our citizens of the knowledge of how these systems work, and even of the language of Parliament.

What is really needed is a reacquaintance between the citizens and government, between the citizens and Parliament. We must simply bring this language and this process close to people. If we say we believe in the citizens, and if we say we believe in democracy, we simply should give people the tools that they need to follow what is going on. An informed public is a sharply politically charged public and a prudent public. I'm not a great admirer of pollsters and polling. My view has always been, "I am the best pollster that I know," because it is up to me to measure what people tell me and to be able to read what they say, what they think and what they believe.

I'd view myself as a classical 19th-century liberal. So to my mind the problems of Parliament are not insurmountable. We have a vast body of principles in our background. All that we have to do is to bring them out, shine them up and put them into operation. We would have a far happier system of governance, a far happier Parliament and a far happier electorate. I do believe this, but maybe I am an idealist.

JOHN STEWART

John B. Stewart was summoned to the Senate by Prime Minister Trudeau in 1984 and served until his retirement in 1999. Prior to his time in the Red Chamber, Stewart was a Liberal MP, elected in 1962, 1963 and 1965 (three minority Parliaments — one Conservative minority under Diefenbaker, and two Liberal minorities under Pearson). Serving as an MP during minority governments significantly impacted his thoughts on power in the House of Commons and changes to the committee system. He has held various committee positions as an MP and senator, as well as various parliamentary secretary positions within the Pearson government. In addition to his political career, Stewart has also authored four books, including *The Canadian House of Commons*, published in 1977. From 1968–84 he was a professor at St. Francis Xavier University.

TOPICS:
The Importance of How Our Government Spends:
The Business of Supply
Government Oversight of How Money Is Spent: Reforms of 1968

The New Committee to Oversee Money: A Disappointing Outcome
Other Committee Problems
Consequences for Voters of a Lack of Budget Scrutiny

The Importance of How Our Government Spends: The Business of Supply
The spending estimates of government are extremely important because it's through the Estimates — through the control that the House of Commons has over money — that the government is kept responsible to the House of Commons. Unless the Estimates are dealt with properly, that responsibility gets thinner and thinner.

The business of supply is fundamental to responsible government. A government could go perhaps years without changing the ordinary laws of the land or even the tax laws because they continue from year to year. But the rule of the Constitution is that supply lasts for only one year at a time. That's why the business of supply is so important — it is the lifeblood of government.

Parliament could absolutely not carry on without supply. Supply — money — has to be voted to the government at least once a year. It is voted only one year at a time and it is the main means by which the responsibility of the executive government to the House of Commons, and thus to the people of Canada, is enforced.

Government Oversight of How Money Is Spent: Reforms of 1968
During the late 1960s I was an active member of an all-party committee that dealt with the reform of the rules of the House of Commons. I was not re-elected to the House in 1968. My constituency had disappeared but Mr. Trudeau asked me to stay on a year to finish the reform of the rules. So I did. There were various intentions, but I think the most important thing was to assure that government spending estimates were dealt with more adequately by Parliament. Prior to 1968 spending estimates were treated in a committee of the whole House (which included all MPs), called the "committee of supply."

There were two things wrong with the old system. First, the opposition — Liberals or Conservatives as the case might be — was using the budget votes and debates just to delay all the operations of the House of Commons. Second, the spending estimates were not being examined with the kind of detail they deserved.

We wanted a better process. We decided to send the spending estimates for each individual government department to an appropriate standing committee, then give the opposition parties a number of days in the House to deal with supply business. That was the scheme of the reform.

It wasn't a unilateral change — it was a unanimous decision of all the political parties in the House of Commons in the fall of 1968. Where previously supply business (the oversight of money) was dealt with by a committee of the whole House of Commons, now the spending estimates for each department — Agriculture, Fisheries and so on — were to be sent to a committee which dealt with only with agriculture, fisheries and so on.

The idea was that there would be much more intensive examination of the Estimates because the committees would be composed of people who knew something about agriculture or fisheries. It would enable MPs to get away from the general discussions that characterized the old committee of supply.

The reforms did remove the annual supply roadblock that was holding up all the other House of Commons business. But overall the outcome did not match the intent.

The New Committee to Oversee Money: A Disappointing Outcome

The outcome of the 1968 changes is rather disappointing. The work of the committees is not what we hoped it would be. We were hoping that putting fairly expert members of Parliament to analyze the estimates of areas such as agriculture, fisheries or foreign affairs would result in close examination of government policy. We had hoped it would enable the ordinary members of Parliament to influence future policy. My impression is that the members of Parliament have not given much attention to government spending estimates since that time.

I think it's a well-accepted impression that the committees have not gone into the non-partisan examination of public policy in the way we had hoped. Intensive discussion of particular policies by expert members of Parliament is lacking. That is a disappointment. In many instances they are not transmitting to the ministers the proposals for improvement in government policies and performance. One thing we have to remember is that an awful lot of the members of the House of Commons are there for a relatively short time, so they do not catch on to what opportunities the rules and procedures give them. So perhaps we expected too much from them.

Most members don't really know what it was like before 1968. Week after week there were trivial discussions of estimates in the chamber, with a relatively small number of members in the opposition asking questions. But the reforms didn't engage the vast number of back-benchers as intensively as we would have liked. The disappointing outcome has virtually nothing to do with the rules; it has a lot to do with the fact that the committees tend to be rancorous and the time is divided between too many parties.

Other Committee Problems

We have five or six political parties, which shatters the time available to a committee. There is too much political rivalry in the work of the committees. This means that a committee is not performing as efficiently as it might if there were only two or three parties. As well, committee work does not get the kind of media coverage that a well-placed question in Question Period gets.

Consequences for Voters of a Lack of Budget Scrutiny

Prime ministerial power does not like intensive examination by back-benchers on either side of the House. I don't think the government has any zeal for careful scrutiny of its operations. Yet the supply business, which deals with voting money for the government, is essential to the system.

If members of the House of Commons and backbenchers on both sides are not exercising their control, the executive government, through no fault of its own, goes unchecked. Then mistakes made by ministers and bureaucrats in past performance are not detected and made public, and the programs for the future can't be improved without the input of members of Parliament. It means that our system isn't working nearly as well as it should. It could be a lot better.

Voters ought to be very concerned if members of Parliament are not following precisely what is being done with their money, which is supposed to be spent to provide good programs to the people of Canada. First, it's the taxpayers' money that is spent. Second, it is being spent on programs. Almost every taxpayer in the country has a real interest in ensuring that those programs are as sound as they can be and as well administered as is possible.

Without money there are no programs. It's very important that those programs be properly scrutinized by members of Parliament. Otherwise we could be spending a lot of money and not getting adequate return in the form of good health care, support for our fisheries or agriculture — you name it. Parliament's job is to scrutinize the supply business and make sure that those programs are sound and are properly administered. There could be major improvements but I think there are fundamental problems that make it very difficult for MPs to perform this essential duty.

DONALD SAVOIE

D onald Savoie is the author of *The Politics of Public Spending in Canada*, the definitive book on the concept of spending in the Canadian political system. From 1974 to 1982 he held various positions with the Department of Regional Economic Expansion and he was an advisor to prime ministers Mulroney and Chrétien. His latest book, *Governing from the Centre: The Concentration of Power in Canadian Politics*, is a critical assessment of how Canadian government operates today. Savoie is currently a professor of public administration at the University of Moncton in New Brunswick, where he is the senior fellow at the Institute for Research on Public Policy and holds the Clement-Cormier Chair in Economic Development.

TOPICS:
Accountability in Government:
A Stacked Deck Against Parliamentarians
Accountability over Money:
Why Parliament Must Guard the Public Purse

Central Agencies
Power of the Prime Minister
Centralized Power
Centralized Power: A Weakening of Cabinet
Centralized Power: Quick Decisions but Little Democracy
Centralized Power: Consequences
On the Role of the MP
The Role of the Media
The Role of the External Media on Canadian Policy
Mechanisms of Accountability: The Public Accounts Committee and
the Auditor General
Cost Sharing and Blurred Constitutional Lines of Accountability
Cost Sharing and First Ministers' Meetings
Accountability of Government: Crown Corporations
Crown Corporations: Accountable to Whom?
The Subsidy Game
Government Subsidies: Regional Development
Globalization and External Pressures on Parliament
Marginalization of Canada
Morale in the Public Service
Trends in Government over the Last Decade

Accountability in Government: A Stacked Deck Against Parliamentarians
Holding government to account is probably the most fundamentally
important role that Parliament has to play. The role of Parliament is to
ensure the government is accountable. That process will determine if
the government has done what it said that it would do and if it has delivered. Sadly, I think we are seeing a change for the worse. Accountability
has become far more complex. It's far more difficult for a member of
Parliament to understand government programs and policies and to
seek out where the public funds have been spent. So the process has
taken a turn for the worse.

It is also disingenuous to make the case that the best accountability
we have in Parliament is having the ability of the back-bench member of
the ruling government to stand up and vote the government down if that
MP disagrees with what the government is doing. Which government
caucus since 1867 has stood up to vote the government down? It doesn't
happen. That's not the way it works. If the only way to hold government

212

accountable is to defeat it, then we haven't held any government account-able for a long, long time. People who make that case are vested with power, so of course the status quo suits them fine. The system serves them well. Yet I think if you ask a member of Parliament, "Are you happy with the state of Parliament?" he or she will likely say, "No."

Accountability over Money: Why Parliament Must Guard the Public Purse

Accountability is important in the raising and spending of public funds because it is to citizens what market share is to the private sector. It's the only way we really know if things work out the way they ought to work out, or if something that was done was not appropriate. To hold people to account is to determine if they have done what they said and to ensure they haven't played fast and loose with the public funds.

There are all kinds of examples of a lack of accountability in spend-ing money that I can share with you, depending on the prime minister. Jean Chrétien, for example. We now know that the $2 billion he put into the Millennium Scholarship Fund was something that he designed with a few key advisors. They decided to run it by Paul Martin to make sure that money will be put aside. Cabinet learned of the $2-billion expendi-ture no sooner than you or I did. It was the prime minister's initiative. He decided on the program's scope and ran with it. Now, is he account-able? Members of Parliament can ask questions in the House of Commons, and he'll answer as best as he can or as best as he wants. Is that accountability? I don't think so. I think we've concentrated those decisions too much into the hands of too few.

Central Agencies

Central agencies are there for a single purpose: to assist the prime min-ister in running the government. The Privy Council Office is his depart-ment. It has no programs. It's not distorted in its views. It can focus exclusively on the needs of the prime minister; it shapes what goes into Cabinet; it determines what's decided in Cabinet; it dictates the deci-sions made in Cabinet; it writes them and sends them to all depart-ments. It becomes the focal point of decisions. The Prime Minister's Office is there to assist them. The Prime Minister's Office and the Privy Council Office will be there to advise the prime minister in terms of appointments. They sift through all kinds of names and decide who makes it into the Senate and who becomes a senator.

Central agencies are there to assist the PM in all of his functions. The Department of Finance has a minister, of course, but the Department of Finance also has a special relationship with the prime minister because he dominates the budget process. Key decisions fall in his hands, so the Department of Finance is there to advise him as well. Central agencies — and there are three or four of them that are well staffed by the most senior and competent public servants — are there to assist him. Again, this increases his levers of power.

Power of the Prime Minister

The Canadian prime minister is an extremely powerful political person. In fact, he holds in his hands all the key levers of political power. Indeed, if you compare his power to that of the president of the United States, the prime minister of Great Britain or the president of France, I would make the case that within the federal government, he holds more power than his counterparts for three or four reasons.

First, it seems he has the power in his hands to appoint everyone. He appoints Supreme Court judges, senators, Cabinet ministers, deputy ministers and so on. He holds in his hands the power to decide who makes it in the upper ranks and who does not. He sets the public policy agenda. No other person in this country can shape the public policy agenda to the same extent as the prime minister. He decides over the public purse. Key decisions of the budget are made in his office and by him. He is also the centre of media attention. If the media is going to focus on anybody in this country, it's on the prime minister. He dominates the media pages. So for those reasons he is far more powerful than any of his counterparts elsewhere.

In theory the Cabinet should make up the executive. Cabinet is the official decision- and policy-making body of the Government of Canada. In theory it should be, but in practice it doesn't quite work like that. The prime minister chairs all Cabinet meetings and the prime minister will dictate at the end. If the consensus goes his way, there's no problem. If it doesn't go his way, he can hold it up. He can say, "Well, we'll come back to it in a month." So Cabinet has become more or less policy advisors, much like his staff. But something has changed. A minister of this government observed that it's no longer a decision-making body, that Cabinet has become a focus group. I think that defines the problem.

It's safe to say that the Supreme Court and the Senate no longer belong to Canadians. They belong to the prime minister. The prime minister will decide if somebody becomes a Supreme Court judge. It's the prime minister that will make a decision on who becomes a senator. I think 30 or 40 years ago it might have been appropriate, but today, as citizens become better engaged and better informed, they will want a say. It is their institution. It doesn't belong to a single politician. So there's cause for a great deal of concern.

In many ways the prime minister is his own boss. It's true that every four years he has to face the Canadian people. If he or she decides not to run again, then there's very little check in terms of political power. But important forces that influence what he or she does are at play. For example, the 10 premiers have a voice in terms of public policy, especially if we're dealing with health care, education and so on. It's their sector, their jurisdiction. They can shape the views of the prime minister to a certain extent.

Centralized Power

When power is so centralized the implications are clear. Canadians do not understand how the process works. It's a hidden power. A lot of the decisions are made by a few key advisors and policy makers. Canadians are for the most part on the outside looking in. They don't have a sense of ownership. They don't understand about the process. It is no longer their budget process. It belongs to politicians and a few advisors. That's the problem. Parliament still sits, Question Period still exists and elections are still held. However, we're moving away from Canadians having a sense of ownership in their government and that, in my mind, is serious.

A lot of people in government are paid to "fall on hand grenades." That enables the prime minister to focus on four or five key issues and make them happen so that everything else is kept running. The PMO doesn't want any problems; it doesn't want any mistakes and it doesn't want the media to catch on.

If power is concentrated around the centre, and the prime minister can naturally only handle four or five pet projects or issues at a time, the other issues and policies are left at bay. They're left hanging. The prime minister will focus on only certain key files. For example, Pierre Trudeau and the Constitution, Brian Mulroney and free trade, Jean Chrétien and the deficit situation and the foundation for innovation.

These are the files that each prime minister will carefully embrace and work on.

What is expected of the rest of the system is for it not to make waves — to ride the issues out without making any big mistakes, to make sure nothing makes it in the media as a scandal. The prime minister will tell his ministers and deputy ministers, whom he appoints, "Look, we're focusing on those four or five key priorities. Your job is to make sure we don't rock the boat, that things go smoothly, and I don't want your name on the front page of *The Globe and Mail* saying something is screwed up." The rest of the issues are held at bay to enable the prime minister to have his way on four or five key files that really matter to him.

Centralized Power: A Weakening of Cabinet
Ministers used to have a greater say in spending. First off, there was more money to spend and secondly, the process was far more open. You had an envelope, ministers went to Cabinet, and in fighting it out they would say, "Well, I'll help you here if you help me with the harbour in Halifax." There's less of that now because there's less money, but also because the process has been really centralized. It's now in the hands of the prime minister and the minister of finance. They call the shots. It's far more difficult to do horse trading with the prime minister than it is with a Cabinet colleague.

Centralized Power: Quick Decisions but Little Democracy
Since power is so concentrated, it enables the prime minister and his key advisors to turn around and make a decision fairly quickly. They don't have to worry about Congress. They don't have to worry about other forces inside. The downside, of course, is that because power is concentrated and because they control so much, there are a number of issues and errors that somehow don't surface. Canadians don't know exactly what's taking shape inside. Hence it cuts both ways. On the one hand they're able to turn around very quickly, but on the other hand it enables the prime minister to camouflage a number of issues that he doesn't want to see surface.

We're still able to say to the prime minister every four years, "We'll pass judgment on you." The problem is, to do that properly we need opposition parties that can become viable alternatives to the sitting government. We don't have that at the moment. So there is a great deal of concern. Is there anything that we can do about it? I think the solution lies in all of us. It lies in Canadians. We have to engage. We have to become empowered. Nobody's going to do it for us. The more citizens learn about how government works, the more they'll be able to articulate what they want and how changes should be made.

Centralized Power: Consequences

I think part of the problem here is that we do not let regional concerns surface — instead we just manage crises. There is a big difference. If Atlantic Canada and Western Canada were free to surface their concerns, free to voice some of the criticism, free to explain what doesn't work in their regions, knowing how government and government programs work, I think we'd have a healthier Canada and a healthier government. That's not the way it works. We don't let those concerns surface. We don't see tradeoffs taking place in Parliament, where these concerns ought to be raised.

On the Role of the MP

The priority of a member of Parliament sitting in the House is to get re-elected. A member of Parliament would push and pull every lever that he or she can to make sure he or she appears well in the public eye. That having been said, the role of a member of Parliament is not to govern. The role of a member of Parliament is not to say, "We will spend money here or there." The proper role is to say to the government, "You said you would do this and you haven't." The proper role of a member of Parliament, in Parliament, is to hold the government to account for its policies.

Again, sadly, that accountability for the raising and spending of public funds falls virtually nowhere. You have to understand that a) they have no resources and b) we're dealing with a budget of $140 billion. For a member of Parliament to get a handle on that budget and to have an appreciation of what's being planned within a few weeks is an impossible task. Unless we equip members of Parliament with the proper resources to go through all these numbers and programs, I think we're whistling in the wind.

Another fundamental problem is that MPs do not have the resources to hold the government to account. The government has 100,000 public servants or more. They have Crown corporations. They have access to all kinds of consultants, whereas Parliament has only

80 non-partisan policy researchers. You can't really do battle with 80 non-partisan policy researchers serving both the Senate and the House of Commons, trying to hold 100,000 public servants and Cabinet to account. There's a complete mismatch. The challenge, I would argue, is to fix that.

The lowly MP has a great deal of struggling. He has a great deal of work. Really, if he or she wants to hold the government to account, they have to put forth an incredible amount of effort. They don't have the kind of resources that the prime minister or Cabinet has. They have access to very few experts so they fly by the seat of their pants. More often than not they will be concerned with the interest of their riding, as well they should because it's their riding. It's their people back home who will decide if they're going to be re-elected or not. Hence their attention is divided a great deal and they simply do not have the resources to say to the prime minister and to the government, "We'd like to hold you accountable on this program." They don't have the time, the resources or the expertise to really understand that program and how it works.

The Role of the Media

I think the major change we've seen in terms of MPs' emphasis in Parliament has been driven by the media. If you want to understand the role of a member of Parliament, look at the media because the member of Parliament will play to what the media wants, to the 15-second clip on TV. You can't understand a government policy or a government program in a 15-second clip.

The media has changed as well — it is now 24-hour news. It's a more aggressive and less deferential media. So a member of Parliament will try to sniff out what it is that the media wants or what the flavour of the month is. That tends to defocus a lot of members of Parliament and I think that's a fundamental change. But to really get at a government program and for an MP to hold a government to account, you have to do a lot of homework. The question is, will a member of Parliament be willing to invest that kind of effort to hold a government to account on a given program? In most cases the answer is no.

The Role of the External Media on Canadian Policy

The Wall Street Journal ran a piece during the budget process in 1995 saying that Canada was close to hitting the wall in terms of public spending. Mexico had hit the wall and *The Wall Street Journal* said Canada, the neighbour to the north, was next in line. That sent a bolt of lightning into Ottawa. The prime minister and the minister of finance were trying to curtail and cut spending. That article was a tremendous help. It gave them the levers to make sure what they wanted done was done. They were able to cut spending, programs, review 50,000 job cuts and so on. That was a critical moment. It was an external force that came from New York but it was a powerful force that influenced and shaped the kind of decision making that takes place in Ottawa.

Mechanisms of Accountability: The Public Accounts Committee and the Auditor General

There is one mechanism of accountability that stands out and that is the public accounts committee. It stands out for two reasons. First, the chairperson of that committee is an Opposition member of Parliament, not a government MP. Therefore it has a degree of independence that other standing committees do not have. Secondly, it has access to a lot of resources. The Office of the Auditor General plays a hand in that committee, so it can draw on a number of resources. It can also look at past spending patterns. At the moment the public accounts committee appears to have a free rein to move where it wants to move. It can wreak havoc with a lot of government programs. The political centre, the prime minister and his office as well as the Privy Council Office, has a great difficulty in exerting power over the public accounts committee.

Cost Sharing and Blurred Constitutional Lines of Accountability

Accountability in cost-sharing arrangements between governments is also not obvious. In an ideal world accountability is relatively simple. In an ideal world either the federal *or* provincial governments would be responsible for a program like health care.

The fundamental problem here is that the federal government, in constitutional terms, has no business in the health-care field. It doesn't belong there. It has no proper role. Constitutionally it shouldn't be there. It's been there because it raises taxes for the public purse. The federal government has money, so they walk into the provinces and say, "We'd like to cost-share medical services." Initially they advised the provinces that they would pay 50 percent of the costs. It's now down in the range of 15 percent. So the federal government's only role in health care is through taxpayers' money. That's where the confusion stems from. The federal government provides some money. For what? Nobody really knows. There are five basic guidelines under the health-care act. Every year they send a cheque, and the provinces complain. The federal government advised that we're spending more than we did a year ago. The provinces say, "Not true." It's confusing. The average Canadian really doesn't understand who's doing what. Nobody really knows who is responsible for what.

The federal government provides money and the provinces are the implementers of the programs. So you have many trying to figure out who's accountable for what. In health care it's like grabbing smoke; you can't do it. It's very difficult for a member of Parliament to tell the prime minister (in a health-care crisis) that it is ultimately the provinces that should deliver the program, while the only thing that the federal government should do is provide money and some basic guidelines.

The problem is, the provinces say to the public, "Well, we'd like to be helpful, but Ottawa's not providing enough money for health." Meanwhile the federal government says to the public, "We'd like to be helpful, but we're not the providers of health care. We only provide money." So trying to hold somebody to account in health care is, again, like grabbing smoke. It is very complicated.

Cost Sharing and First Ministers' Meetings

The 10 premiers meet every summer at premiers' conferences. They go over the issues, and they're saying amongst themselves, "What are the key issues here? The key issue is health care because there's not enough money. There is a crisis in health care. Who can help us?" There's only one level of government who can help, and that's the federal government. They agree to knock on the door of the federal government. The federal government is sitting there saying, "Well, we'd like to help. It's not really in our jurisdiction but because we think there's a national purpose here, we'll provide some money."

Accountability of Government: Crown Corporations

Crown corporations were set up a long time ago mainly because it was felt that the private sector could not accommodate some of the needs out there, such as the war effort, radio and television, air travel. If you recall, Trans-Canada Air Lines was set up because Canada felt it needed a national airline. Canadians looked south and saw big American firms that could provide air travel services to all parts of the States, but the Canadian private sector at that time was not big enough to take on the task. So Crown corporations were established to set up Air Canada, CN, CBC and the like — things that it was felt the private sector could not do.

Regular government departments were too cumbersome, too caught up in red tape and too close to political power, if you like, for them to do the job properly. Some of these jobs needed to be arm's length. They needed to be as close to the private sector as possible and away from political influence. Hence we established Crown corporations. Then Crown corporations expanded even more. They expanded so much that at one point we lost control. We didn't know how many Crown corporations existed in this country — we actually did not know the specific number. It was a crisis. So, as we typically do, a royal commission looked into this and advised that it was a mess that needed to be straightened out. We set up rules and regulations and guidelines that required Cabinet approval in order to set up another Crown corporation. Also, Parliament has to be informed. So we now have some stronger guidelines.

The scope of Crown corporations expanded so much to cover so many policy fields — whether it was research and development, art, culture, banking, foreign trade and so on — that we then established a series of different Crowns. We had Crown A, Crown B and Crown C. Crown A was a tighter control, if you like. Crown C was as independent as a private sector firm. We started asking questions about accountability. How do you hold these Crown corporations accountable? They're not government departments. In fact they were set up not to be government departments. They were set up not to have a minister dictate policies and processes and grants. We gave them a lot of leeway and a lot of independence. This begs the question: how do we ensure that we can hold them to account?

We established guidelines. We established a board of directors. So now a Crown corporation has it's own board of directors responsible for setting the broad policy framework.

Crown Corporations: Accountable to Whom?
At least in a government department we know that the government department has a budget. It's accountable its minister. That minister

goes in the House of Commons and has to answer questions in Question Period. The minister responsible for Crown corporations answers general questions, but specific questions are rarely dealt with at the political level. So there is a question of accountability.

If the board of directors of a Crown corporation is responsible for setting a broad policy framework, where does Cabinet sit? Good question. Where does the member of Parliament that has an interest in the Crown corporations sit? Where does he or she take his or her concern? Good question. Who controls these Crown corporations if they draw from the public purse? It's not as clear-cut.

In defence of Crown corporations, they *are* involved in private sector activities, whether to promote trade or what have you. They will argue that they can't be treated like a government department in terms of access to information because some of the information is of a commercial nature so it has to be in some private quarters. However, all too often Crown corporations use that as an alibi, as an excuse not to answer questions. They give you the runaround. I think there is a growing concern that some of the information Crown corporations should provide to Parliament and to Canadians is not there. They hide under the veil of necessary secrecy and that has become the problem.

Who in government can hold these Crown corporations to account in direct policy? The answer to that is the prime minister. The prime minister appoints a board of directors, a chairman of the board and CEOs. By the process of appointment the prime minister has a direct hand in Crown corporations. This begs the question: given the centralization of power, does it make Crown corporations even more accountable or less? I would argue less because the prime minister has only so many hours. He only has so much time. He can only deal with so many fouls. He'll appoint a CEO. He'll appoint a chairman of a board of a Crown corporation, then largely forget about it — unless there's a mess. If there is no mess, they go on their own and do whatever they do. Through the appointment process, the prime minister is the only one that can really influence what a Crown corporation does.

The Subsidy Game

The government recently announced that they were getting out of the subsidy business. Now, a lot of programs provide financial assistance and you supposedly have to pay back the government the money it gives you, but they're still in the business. The one thing I would add is that the subsidy business has become more of a fraud now. It's not as pure and as clear as it was 25, 30 years ago. It's all over the map. It makes no sense. There's no coherence to it. Sorry to be so harsh, but we now have agencies running amok. There's no central purpose.

The federal government is not out of it. The Department of Industry is anything but out of it; it has a multibillion-dollar budget each year. It throws its weight around, and it supports all kinds of things. Look at the export market and what they do. They subsidize loans — a subsidy is a subsidy. If it walks like a duck, quacks like a duck, it's pretty well a duck. We have a number of ducks here. So they can say that they don't give out grants enough. That's fair. Some of it is repayable, but if you apply for some form of assistance and you get $100,000 and you repay at zero or one percent, that is a form of subsidy. They can't really make the case that there's no assistance. If there's no assistance, then why have a multibillion-dollar budget?

Government Subsidies: Regional Development

Private firms and businesses benefit from what these subsidies accrue, and there's not a region in this country that's purer than the next region when it comes to getting regional development dollars from government. The biggest benefactor of regional development policy at the moment is the province of Ontario, followed by the province of Quebec. In 1968 when the first regional development initiatives were launched in the heyday of the Trudeau years, it was made clear that if you spent less than 80 percent of the regional development budget east of Trois Rivières, then you'd be making a tragic mistake. We have made a tragic mistake.

If you want to see the most ambitious regional development programs now, you'd have to look to southern Ontario — and that makes absolutely no sense. I mean, here's an economy that's buoyant, that's heated, that's been overblown for the past several years, and yet the federal government has been there, present with money. Look at money going to Bombardier, De Havilland, and in Kanata, Ontario, the high-tech sectors. Those are not market forces dictating where the money is going; that money is being used as a public policy instrument. So the federal government has lost its way. It just doesn't know really what it wants to do in terms of regional development. It's all over the map.

Not to be overly cynical here, but it appears that a lot of this is driven by political considerations. They can count numbers and see Ontario has 103 seats in Parliament. It becomes the focus of the efforts and it's creating problems in a number of the regions. They see that something has been distorted, something has gone amiss, something has turned into a fraud.

Globalization and External Pressures on Parliament
Globalization, which is a new phenomenon in terms of the marketplace, has had a tremendous influence on government. The prime minister cannot operate in complete isolation from what the president of the United States does or the British prime minister. Wall Street has also had a tremendous impact. The market, in terms of interest rates, comes into play and the prime minister has to deal with it and has to push and pull any levers of power that he can to accommodate it, yet still have his own way.

External influences like NAFTA and free trade have affected the government. We're able to gain markets, but we've lost a bit of our sovereignty. Let's be clear about that. Twenty-five years ago the prime minister wanted to launch a program to assist the Maritime provinces to do certain things and he was relatively free to do so. Now it's not that simple. There are trade rules that govern what kind of national programs can be put in place, so we're inhibited. There are all kinds of better examples. In terms of the environment we now have a global perspective. This country, much like the United States or Britain, is expected to do its part. So there are a number of key decisions being shaped from outside forces rather than from internal forces.

Canada will react to these external pressures certainly in one way: our economy is getting tied into the American economy. It's becoming clear to me that both economies are gelling. We see Americans buying firms that 40 years ago would not have been acceptable. So we are merging two economies, which gives tremendous levers and tremendous influence to the Americans and how they look upon Canada.

We're about to see a major public debate launched in this country about fresh water, oil and gas. A number of Canadians are saying we should keep that fresh water, we should keep oil and gas. But the Americans might say, "Look, our economies are mixed into one. We need to buy some of your water." It will force the hands of the prime minister and the Canadian government and the provinces to open up and sell water, which we may not want to do and which we may not have wanted to do 30 years ago. In 10 years from now we may have less of a choice. The point is, when you enter into these agreements, into globalization, you lose a bit of your sovereignty, and that's what we're seeing now.

Marginalization of Canada
Apart from political power, there is a real risk that you could see power concentrated in the hands of people in Chicago, in New York, in Boston, in Houston, and Canada becoming a branch plant. When you have a downturn, which plant are you going to close first? It's the branch plants. Where are you going to concentrate your power? It's where head office is. We've seen it move to Montreal and Toronto. In the future people in Toronto might see a move to Houston, Chicago and New York. It's an interesting question and I'm not so sure we have a full handle on it. It is, however, cause for a lot of concern.

There may be a parallel between the loss of autonomy in the Maritimes and Canada's loss of independence through globalization. If success breeds success, where will success take place? In 1867 the Maritime provinces experienced *the* economic boom of this country. Slowly but surely success moved west because of national policies, because of the war effort, because of fiscal policies and so on. If you duplicate this again and concentrate power, not so much political power but economic power, in Tokyo, in New York, in London or Paris, then do you run the risk of seeing Canada become like a Maritime province, in terms of the rest of the world?

There are indeed measures to prevent this from happening but it won't be painless. You can say we're going to have a national policy, we're going to protect our private sector and we're going to put in place measures to protect the national economy. It can be done, but there's a cost. Our standard of living may drift downwards. We may not have as much revenue in the government caucus as we want. Are Canadians prepared to put up with that cost? That's a very good question but I can't answer it.

As Canadians look at globalization and see the powerful forces out there, the implications are fairly serious. They might come to the conclusion that there's no sense in trying. Global forces are so powerful and they dictate their daily lives so much that they can't shape them. So you might see signs like less voting. In the last federal election we saw a steep decline in terms of voting participation. That might be a signal that Canadians are giving up. What's the point? If the public service gave up, saying, "We're not going to speak truth to power. Our purpose now is to help politicians," this is an important change. If Canadians come to the conclusion that they can't speak truth, that they can't change or impact on powerful forces, they may well give up. That would be a sad commentary.

The remedy is a strong political power with a sense of vision and purpose, a Canadian that would rise up and say, "Look, this country is beautiful. We love it from sea to sea and we want to keep it intact. There are some difficult choices here. Here is where I want to lead you in shaping this country." I think you would have a chance of saving it. You have a chance of engaging Canadians with the options. For that you need a lot of political will and strong leadership with a sense of purpose and a sense of vision. Assuming that the political will is also generated from the public, would things like referenda and recall and putting the fear of God into these MPs help initiate this public role?

We've reached a point where we're beyond that, where there's a sense of urgency. If you start with referenda, recalling a member of Parliament, you're playing at the margin. We are living in some very difficult times with global forces. We can accept them and in terms of economics draw a lot of benefits from them. Or we can say, "No, that's a bit much. This country is far too important. Globalization is important, but let's shape it for our own purposes." That's what I would like to see. If we want that then we need strong political leadership with a sense of purpose, a sense of vision. Recalling a member of Parliament is something we can do later. I think the time has come for a sense of purpose, a sense of coherence, a sense of leadership and a sense of vision.

Morale in the Public Service

I think there are all kinds of implications about a morale problem inside the public service. I suspect it's not because of pay and perks. Public servants are decently paid. They have good pension plans and so on, but there is a morale problem because managing crises and camouflaging things saps away at energy and creativity levels. Instead of bringing creative talents to solve problems, they spend a lot of their time massaging, taking care of the minister, hiding things, not in a morbid sense, but in a way that doesn't let the media get access to a potential crisis. So it speaks to the fact that Canadians are not fully aware of what exactly goes on inside government. They don't know the tradeoffs. It's done internally. They don't have access to it. It is less their government then it could be if it were more open.

The most puzzling aspect about the public service is that we clearly have a morale problem. If you read the reports, if you look at surveys that are done, there is a serious morale problem. And you have to wonder why. I don't think it's a question of salaries and perks. I think there's another factor here. Surely the fact that the ranks were toned down or cut back didn't help matters, but there's a more serious problem at play here. It is to define the proper role of a public servant in Canadian society. I don't think we have quite figured that out yet. It's changed. We don't know what the new role is. Until we do we will still be plagued by a serious morale problem.

The problem is that the role of the public servant is not clear-cut. If we can ever come to terms with it and define what is the proper role of a public servant in terms of advice and managing programs, then we will make some serious headway. Until such a time it's difficult. Everything is in a state of flux inside the public service. One day they're responsible for spending $1 billion. The next day, if it's raised in Question Period, they can't even change a single window because it becomes a political crisis. So public servants are walking on quicksand all the time. It's that degree of uncertainty that makes it extremely difficult. They just don't have a proper framework from which to spring into action.

In the early 1980s there was a lot being said, that bureaucrats were running the whole country. If you recall, even ministers in the Trudeau government were saying that bureaucrats were too powerful. They wanted to recapture some of that power. In the Mulroney and Chrétien years there was a lot of effort on the part of ministers to recapture that power. I think they bullied a lot of public servants, whereas in the 1970s it was less obvious. A lot of public servants stood up and said, "Minister, we'll speak truth to power. Here's what we think. You want to make a mistake? Go ahead, but what I'll do is this."

There's less of that now. Public servants are less certain about their proper role in terms of policy advice. They want to please the ministers and they haven't quite figured out the best way to go about it. I think public servants were hurt in the 1980s when they said bureaucrats were too powerful. They became uncertain. They lacked security. They lacked confidence about the ability of their institution to respond. When you lack confidence and you wonder what's out there, you circle a lot of the wagons, and that's what they did. Co-opted is a strong word, but they became far less certain in providing policy advice.

There is definitely a connection between the morale and uncertainty problem and the centralization of power in the hands of very few in Ottawa. You hire a public servant fresh out of university. Bright, master's degree, whatever, and they want to make a difference. What they're being asked to do is to manage crises, to keep it on an even keel and not to upset things. And a lot of the key policy- and decision-making power is centred in the hands of a few. Public servants for the most part are on the outside looking in. And that can't boost morale.

Trends in Government over the Last Decade

We've seen several significant political changes in the last six years. First, in 1995 we were primarily concerned with the deficit. Clearly the debt is still a problem, but the deficit has been cornered and corralled and dealt with. In terms of the change in the attitude concerning the deficit, I think we're more than riding a good wave. I think Canadians in the early to mid-1990s said to the government, "Enough is enough. Deal with this problem." They were quite prepared to take on a number of sacrifices and government got its cue. So they were able to make some tough decisions.

It wasn't just circumstances that allowed government to gather more revenue. They made some very difficult choices. That explains in large part why they were able to get into a situation now where it's no longer a problem. And neither is it one returning in the foreseeable future. The one area of concern is that we still have a substantial debt. We're still paying down that debt. If the interest rate should fly up and grow to 15 percent again, then clearly we'll have to crank up a lot of the spending to pay for the interest. But in the foreseeable future, I don't think the deficit is a problem. The debt is still a serious kind of overhang that has to be dealt with.

The second big change I've seen in the last six years is the forces of globalization. They are far more serious and powerful today than they were six years ago. By globalization I mean that most things involve several countries now, whether the discussion is about the environment, monetary policy and so on. There's a global texture to a lot of the things that we do. Discussions have included creating one dollar — marrying the U.S. dollar and the Canadian dollar. Twenty-five years ago nobody

228

would have dreamt that, but now we're talking about it. Imagine what it's going to be like in 10 years. Thirdly, the forces of regionalism are far stronger today than they were six years ago. Regions are starting to ask fundamental questions about the kind of arrangements under which they deal with one another. So those three forces are new, different and far more powerful.

Edward (Ted) McWhinney

Ted McWhinney was elected to two terms in the House of Commons between 1993 and 2000, representing Vancouver Quadra as a Liberal MP. He has a worldwide reputation as a scholar of international and constitutional law. During his tenure in the House of Commons he served as parliamentary secretary to the minister of foreign affairs and international trade and to the minister of fisheries and oceans. McWhinney was one of the last MPs to have served in any branch of the military; prior to being elected to office he was a member of the Canadian air force. In his professional life he has been a Crown prosecutor, royal commissioner of inquiry, consultant to the secretary general of the United Nations, and constitutional and international law advisor to several Quebec premiers, the premier of Ontario and the federal government. He has been a member of the Permanent Court of Arbitration, The Hague, and special advisor to the Canadian delegation to the United Nations General Assembly. He recently completed a two-year term as president of the Institut de droit international in Geneva.

TOPICS:
Background and Entry into Politics
Early Challenges and Goal Setting as an MP
Understanding the Executive and Legislature: The Inherent Flaws
Executive Power: Curse or Benefit?
Committees: A Canadian Parliamentary Weakness
Committees: A Comparison of the American Versus the Canadian System
Parliamentary Committees
Committees: Wasted Talent
Prepared Speeches
Parliament as Political Theatre
Going into Politics Today

Background and Entry into Politics
I'm a graduate of Yale University and was very strong into constitutional law, and I did my doctorate on legislating supreme courts. Not surprisingly my first books were on constitutional law, but I have also written about half my books on international relations. I've written four books on terrorism. I also wrote the first book in English on the German constitutional court. So comparative federalism has been with me all my life, and it's on that basis that the Quebec and Ontario premiers sought my advice. I served the Ontario premier for 10 years as constitutional advisor.

I remember giving a Quebec premier a report on an issue of language policy, and he said, "This is a brilliant report. It's got everything there, but you didn't tell me what to do." And I said, "No, I'm a specialist advisor. It's not my function to tell you what to do, that's for your political advisors. What I do is analyze the problem and quantify the alternative costs of the various solutions put forward. I lead you right up to the solution, but not the final choice." He said, "The problem with my political advisors is, they're so emotionally engaged that I can't trust their views because they get coloured by their emotional preferences." So I said, "On that basis, if I were in your position, I think I would do this." And he said, "Fine." He accepted 50 percent of the advice and went ahead, and it was quite successful. So if you advise somebody, you sit next to them and if you are competent, meaning you don't try and exceed your function, you find people saying, "Would you like to be a political candidate?"

For the last 30, 40 years, people of different political parties and different provinces have asked me if I'd be a candidate, but I've always been too busy. I am writing the next book on nuclear disarmament, or a new study on international terrorism. I'm dealing with experts in other areas. Finally it happened in 1990–92, when the country was in a mess federally because the Meech Lake Accord had failed, the Charlottetown Accord had failed and the divisions were very clear, very bitter. Two national leaders came to me and said, "Would you be a candidate for our party?" They actually said in each case, "You've given a lot of free advice, now you should put up or shut up, come into the arena." There was a window of opportunity and I took it. I made the condition that I would serve one term, two at the most. I would postpone a few things, but I would go back. That's how it worked out. I left politics before the 2000 election.

When I was asked to be a candidate nobody offered to appoint me. In fact, John Turner, my predecessor, said, "It's the kiss of death in British Columbia to be appointed, you've got to win it." So I had to go out and learn how to win a nomination for a party — a contested nomination with four or five other candidates who had been working for a year or two. I had to learn how to win an election, and then of course how to be re-elected. It's a science, and if you apply intelligence, you can do it. And we did it. It took me about six or eight months to win the nomination and then the election. Intensive work. I haven't worked as hard since I was a flying cadet as a 19-year-old.

Early Challenges and Goal Setting as an MP

When I became a candidate in 1993 it was assumed that the Progressive Conservatives would possibly be re-elected. So I was looking forward to being in opposition. I think I would have enjoyed myself more in opposition than in government. A majority government in its first few years tends to ride with its electoral mandate — it's very confident, it usually doesn't do very much. Trudeau, for example — his first term wasn't his best term. Some say his best term was his second term, the minority government. So there really wasn't much to do, and one of the conclusions from the 1993 campaign was that people, even though they'd experienced Meech and Charlottetown, were just bored with the Constitution. They wanted to bury it, and so that large area was out. There was no discussion. There's been very little happening on it in Parliament since 1993.

Similarly in foreign policy, when the Berlin Wall had fallen in 1989, a lot of the ideas I had put forward, scientifically and nationally, were already in operation. Nothing much happened in foreign policy, so we were left with a budget on which I had strong views. We needed fiscal responsibility — the $42.8-billion deficit budget we'd inherited was absurd. It couldn't be tolerated.

We also needed to focus on how to make economies that keep things going. Medicare, education, advanced research — the provinces were strapped for funds, so I made my main objective to get pure research supported federally. A massive inflow of federal funds was needed in spite of the need to balance the budget. My first test case was the Triumph project at UBC. I got the university $167.5 million to continue particle physics research at a time when we were paring the $42.8-billion deficit budget down to about $30 billion.

I set myself goals — tangible, realizable goals. I discussed them with my constituents very fully, and we agreed and we won. We got federal money for pure research; we got money for higher education. We basically got the universities back on a track of competition with leading institutions elsewhere. I don't regard my time as wasted, but it was essentially bilateral, dealing within the government. I would go to a minister I had good relations with and was confident in. Paul Martin, the finance minister, knew he had to make his austerity budgets, but he believed in higher education. The industry minister, John Manley, impressed me enormously with his capacity to read briefs and understand problems in which he had no background.

I discussed with the first transport minister, Doug Young, ways of keeping Canadian airlines alive, which was very important to my constituency. We basically succeeded. There were very few targets that I set that we didn't achieve. By the end of each year I felt I'd done enough.

Frankly, nobody's a nobody unless they give up. Within the caucus, if you know how to raise an issue properly, you can win. The thing you don't do in caucus is make 20-minute speeches. Three minutes is about the maximum tolerance level. You've got to explain complex issues in very clear language, and you've got to keep coming back again and again, and go directly to the minister. When you see a minister in your field, you've got to be better informed than the minister, so you've got to study, read the files. It's a science; it can be done.

Understanding the Executive and Legislature: The Inherent Flaws
Canadians mix up the executive and the legislature, and I'm not sure it's very healthy to mix them these days. The qualities required to be elect-

ed as a member of Parliament are not necessarily the qualities to be a good executive (prime minister and Cabinet ministers), and certainly the reverse is true. I've seen many excellent people in industry and labour who would be very good members of a Cabinet in the United States, but couldn't possibly be elected in Canada. They don't have the personality, the patience or the discipline to go about being elected. So I think the executive talent available in Parliament is very much weaker than in the United States.

Correspondingly, since our executive members of Parliament are already into this double function (having to get elected, as well as being an executive in the Canadian government), their potential of being elected and re-elected is limited. I don't think they're able to do the time in the legislative process.

Executive Power: Curse or Benefit?

It was always said, of course, that under a strong prime minister, the parliamentary system produced an executive stronger than in the United States. Great Britain under Lloyd George, for example, or Winston Churchill, or in recent times Margaret Thatcher, had a stronger executive power without the constitutional restraints you get in the United States. It's the periods in between where you have the problems, where you get a weak prime minister and don't get the support from Parliament.

Consensus building in the United States is through the elected Congress. The executive is selected for totally different reasons. You select them for their specialist confidence or their overall capacities. I couldn't have seen Colin Powell being elected, for example, as a senator or a congressman. He would not have the patience to put up with that, but I think he will be a great secretary of state. The only way we can bring these people into our system is to create a by-election, get somebody to retire, put them in our appointed Senate — which is a joke by comparison with the American Senate — and run somebody.

The case of General McNaughton is the best example. Poor General McNaughton was commander of the Canadian Forces in World War II, and Mackenzie King wanted him in the Cabinet. He tried twice to find him safe seats, but he was beaten each time. He was totally hopeless as a communicator, but in terms of the direct conversational exchanges with the prime minister or others as commander-in-chief, he was excellent.

The American Congress is a permanent consensus-building institution. The Cabinet comes and goes according to the changing political attitudes of the country, but the president has an enormous freedom of choice. Even where the president's party is in a minority in the Senate, so that you might say that the opposition party controls his veto over Cabinet selections, the rules of the game are at par except in an extreme case of confirmation.[1]

Every president leaves his mark. In Ronald Reagan's first term he inherited people and it wasn't much of a term. In the second term his staff was there. The people he selected were excellent, and they carried him into history.

Committees: A Canadian Parliamentary Weakness

Because our Parliament and how it operates is tied into this British parliamentary executive, the committee system is weak and ineffectual. The membership of committees is controlled by the party whips. I don't know how often they organize their talent banks and see what resources are available, but there are some committees that are favoured because they have large travelling budgets and travel to exotic places. You find people ending up on committees because they go to the whip and ask to be put on it, not because they're necessarily expert in the field. Foreign affairs is prized because it has a lot of money for travel, and you will end up in interesting and not unpleasant places in the spring before the snow has melted in Ottawa, so there's intense lobbying to get there.

I think under the American committee system, if you get somebody who's been on a committee for 10 years, there's a lot of expertise there. I think on the American committees in general there's been a gravitation to areas of some familiarity for the people concerned.

Committees: A Comparison of the American Versus the Canadian System

A strength in the United States is the ability to summon witnesses. I've been a witness, and American committees have sought my testimony. Their range is very wide, and they at least read what's being written and say, "Well, we need something to balance our viewpoint, let's have it." Here in Canada I found very little sophistication in the opposition in bringing forward witnesses who might have a different viewpoint. This is why in some respects one would like to have maverick MPs around, those who don't follow their party lines. Svend Robinson was not always popular in his own party, but he did ask the unexpected questions. With the Bloc, I found that they were well-educated, thoughtful people, and they were very helpful in committees, but foreign affairs doesn't have too much impact on traditional Quebec sovereignty issues. It does occasionally, if we get into the issue of recognition, but on the issue of the Balkans, is there a Bloc Québécois position or not?

The Canadian committees pale in comparison to American committees. The work that gets done in the United States on legislation just isn't done in any comparable way here. I have friends in the United States who are U.S. senators, and they'd much rather be a senator than be in the Cabinet. The only two posts in the United States that rank ahead of being the senator of a big state would be secretary of state and possibly secretary of the treasury. But there's no job more pleasant than being a United States senator: frankly, if you organize yourself in your six-year term, you are very fully informed.

As an MP I dealt directly with a lot of United States senators and congressmen. They were very well informed, very well disciplined, and if they themselves didn't have background in an area, they had the staff. And so did the committees. Opposition members, or Republicans if they were the minority party, would have their own council, their own staff. The quality of the questions is very much better. The handling of the issues is better; the policy maker is much more effective.

Parliamentary Committees
I was a member of the foreign affairs committee, then parliamentary secretary. As a parliamentary secretary I was a representative of the government. I was a member of the committee and I would communicate to the chair who was always, of course, a government member (except on the public accounts committee). It was my obligation to communicate government positions. I'm not sure that's constitutionally a good plan. In the American system a member of the government wouldn't be a member of a congressional committee, but they were evenly balanced in terms of numbers. In our case both government and opposition choose the members.

The minister doesn't have much choice in who the members of the committee are. This is good in one sense — that the minister shouldn't put yes-men or women onto the committee. But it does mean that you get a committee that doesn't necessarily have any expertise in foreign affairs.

Committees: Wasted Talent

It always puzzled me why the whips didn't use their talent better. If you get justice committee or fisheries committee, there are MPs with expertise in these areas. It may be specialized expertise, but you say, "This man knows fisheries. I'll put him there." I never saw this happening in Ottawa. I hate to say it, but I think it's a way of keeping backbenchers in one's own party and the opposition leaders keeping their backbenchers happy.

Our committees don't have a great deal of expertise. The majority members of the committee, who represent the government's side, control the calling of witnesses. The opposition — because they don't themselves use their expertise to the fullest — are also not very helpful in putting forward useful, interesting witnesses who will differ from the government line.

It was not my role as the parliamentary secretary for foreign affairs to produce balance among the witnesses. All I could and did suggest — and I met no resistance when I did this — was say, "Look, we need more information, here are some interesting people." For example, during the Balkan war I knew we had some Canadian experts in this country who could speak on the issue. Yet we were always relying on the representatives of government-funded non-governmental organizations (NGOs) to speak to our committee. I always had the awful feeling that some of these NGOs might be "singing for their supper," telling us what they thought we wanted to hear, when they appeared as witnesses.

As an ex-lawyer, the other thing that always puzzled me was, why didn't the opposition raise the issue of a lack of expertise by various witnesses who appeared before our committees? If you are a lawyer, when you get somebody introduced as an expert, you ask, "Well, what's their expertise?" If you go into a court you say, "This is an expert on heart diseases," and you examine them and find their medical practice has all been in maternity cases, they're dismissed as an expert. I never found any great sophistication in government.

Prepared Speeches

When I was in the Fisheries Ministry I was parliamentary secretary, before I went to Foreign Affairs. The ministry used to write these speeches and they'd start out with platitudes: "Canada stands on so many oceans, and the frontier extends from one ocean to another," and I said, "This is junk, why do you do this? Who does it?" The answer was, "Well, retired civil servants are paid to do them." I said, "Why do they write this junk?"

"Well, they seem to think members expect this."

Personally I had a rule when I spoke in the House of Commons — I only spoke on the issues where I had something to say. Yet the research bureaus attached to the political parties and operating through the government whip's office prepared many of the speeches, on both sides of the House of Commons. I made a point of reading the speeches, just to make sure I knew what government policy was, so I didn't get off the party line unconsciously. I liked to know what they said, but I wouldn't use them.

I gave my own speeches, and the whip accepted that.

Parliament as Political Theatre

I once sat as the commissioner examining the legality of televising parliamentary debates. It was commissioned by the B.C. legislature while Dave Barrett was the premier. There weren't really any legal problems — Parliament has enough discipline and decency to control abusive use of time — but the problems that have arisen due to televising parliamentary debates should have been anticipated, but they were not. Once televised, Parliament turned into theatre, a soap opera in a certain sense, and Question Period now has come to dominate everything.

For 45 minutes each day everybody's there. You get two-thirds of the members of the House present, you get the galleries packed, usually by school children and others, who sometimes come out in horror. But you get this bear pit, this theatre, which has very little relationship to reality. Questions are asked, but the answers are non-responsive and everybody knows that. The questions and the answers are framed rhetorically. Some ministers are not very good on their feet, others are excellent. I mean, one of the best is Herb Gray because Herb had developed this capacity for giving a boring non-response, deliberately low-key. He's one of the brightest members of the House, but you know, it's theatre. It isn't reality.

When I was a parliamentary secretary, one of the roles was substituting for the minister in Question Period, so the briefings for me would begin with the ministry. Even in areas that I was well acquainted with, they'd come at 11:00 and I would already have read the government books. We'd begin discussing potential questions and answers, and we would go right on until 1:30 p.m. Then you would go in the Cabinet room and rehearse the sort of answers to give to questions and make sure your answers co-ordinated with government policy. I would see the

Bloc Québécois people begin work at 8:00 in the morning on Question Period. So between 8:00 a.m. and 3:00 p.m. their time is taken up with this. Is it an efficient use of time, when other problems in Parliament should be addressed?

Television has accentuated this trend, and Parliament has been transformed even more.

Going into Politics Today

Part of the problem is that we are certainly not getting the interesting, bright people that we used to get, say, 30, 40 years ago. It's a very obvious comment.

Can we turn it back? I don't think so. I think the fundamental reforms of Parliament probably really have to go to issue a complete change in the Constitution, separation of powers, American-style and European-style. The country's certainly not yet ready for that. It may occur in the future, but you can see the weakness of the system and the frustrations it brings.

People ask my advice and I say, "If you go into politics, go in while you're in your 20s." I say, "You're young enough to serve a couple of terms here. You'll qualify eventually for a pension that you'll get at 65 or 55, but you've got time to save enough; then you could study medicine or get a career." It's really a career only suited for very young people — of whom the BQ and the Conservatives have a very considerable contingent. Bright kids who are into one or two terms, or people who are basically retired, sufficiently independent to be able to say, "I'm not going to bother running again, I've done my bit." In between you're not getting the people you want in Parliament, for example, the 40-year-old CEO of an air-space company.

You're not getting interesting, dynamic people anymore because there's more competition in going into a multinational company.

If they leave by the time they're 30, they'll never go back to politics — they've had enough experience. When I left politics, if someone asked if I would be interested in such-and-such a position, I said, basically, "I've got enough entries in 'Who's Who.' What does it add for me that I was minister for revenue? I didn't go in to get an office. What would have been the point of it?" If you go into politics expecting promotion, you may be wasting your time.

The whole point in going into politics is to put your ideas into operation. It is mastering the techniques of communicating. I never had any difficulty in getting directly to the prime minister on a matter of importance, but I didn't abuse this. I didn't go to his office every week, or even necessarily every month. On big issues I would give him a written memorandum, ideally one page. So everything's compressed — "This is an issue we should take up." I've had no problem in that and I think this is the way to look at it.

Power is participation in decision making. It's not an office you hold. Look at our Cabinet response to the September 11 terrorism — who's in charge of it? The foreign minister. Does the minister of revenue have anything to communicate on that, or the fisheries minister? If you have a different view to the government line and you're in Parliament, you can say it. You can go to the prime minister and go to John Manley and say, "Here's what I think."

That's a crucial issue of the constituency, the sort of person you're seeking. I look at the bright people — Stephen Harper, who made the decision after one term to leave the Alliance and go on. I know a senator here, John Nichol, who's a very good friend, but he committed the never-heard-of act. He was appointed by Pearson to the Senate, and after six years he left. He was under 50 then, but he felt he could be more useful outside. People these days are more interested in doing things, in making decisions, rather than going after particular offices. If you're worried about getting a pension, you're in the wrong profession. You should be out in business.

NOTES

1. Even if the president of the United States has a minority government, the odds of him getting his selected appointments approved to the U.S. Cabinet are still good. The U.S. Congress, which consists of the Senate and the House of Representatives, must approve presidential appointments to the Cabinet, but there is an understanding that the executive branch of the government needs to operate. Therefore the president has freedom of choice and the "rules of the game" are still equal even if he has a minority government.

PATRICK BOYER

Patrick Boyer has been a journalist in Ontario, Saskatchewan and Quebec and a lawyer specializing in communications and electoral law. In the 1980s he became a parliamentarian representing a Toronto constituency. He was a parliamentary secretary in the 1990s, first at External Affairs and subsequently at the Department of National Defence. He is a past president of the Couchiching Institute on Public Affairs and current chairman of the Pugwash Thinkers' Lodge in Nova Scotia. He is the author of more than a dozen books — from biography and legal texts to historical and political works on the governing processes in Canada. He holds several university degrees (in history, law, economics and politics) and currently is adjunct professor in the department of political science at the University of Guelph.

TOPICS:
Parliament: Theory and Practice
Personal History

Responsible Government
Parliament and Government
Traditional Role of MPs
MPs as Government Mouthpieces
MPs' Speeches
The Government Line
Historic Changes to the Role of MPs: Efficiency and Ambition
Parliamentary Committees
Foreign Policy
Parliament and the Military
Role of the Military
The Oka Crisis
Morality and Character

Parliament: Theory and Practice

Are Canadians satisfied with the representation they're getting in Parliament, and should they be? I simply have to report to you, as a veteran of our House of Commons, that what goes on in Parliament is not what we're teaching the children in civics courses. The gap between the theory of our system of parliamentary government and its actual practice is so wide as to constitute a credibility gulf in the way that Canadians see their government and the way it's actually functioning.

Personal History

I was in the Canadian House of Commons for a decade, but in fact I'd spent most of my life preparing to be there. I was, I think, about 10 when my dad was elected to the Ontario legislature. I came to a view that our Parliament would be the centre of the country, where great issues would be debated, and men and women from many different regions and walks of life would gather there to have a major say in the policy that would direct our country. So I grew up believing that, and also training myself to be a member of Parliament. I was 39 when I was elected from this district, and I was there for 10 years.

I don't think I went into Parliament naive. Not only had I grown up with a father in politics, not only had I read Machiavelli — who taught us that we have to deal with people as we find them, not as we dream they could be — but I had been a student of realpolitik and worked in elections, including in Quebec. Still, I think I went into the House of

Commons pretty dry behind the ears. Yet even so, it was still a sobering revelation to discover what I did there.

Responsible Government

The Constitution of Canada has two main features. One is the concept of responsible government and the second is the division of powers between different levels of government. Of course our Constitution has a lot more in it, but those are the two fundamentals. Responsible government, really, is about the prime minister and Cabinet ministers being answerable in the Commons to the elected representatives on questions of the day, and being held accountable for everything from government spending to decisions on how the military is being conducted.

What I've realized, and I think most Canadians who are sitting back observing come to a similar conclusion, is that when you study the functioning of responsible government in Canada today, it is really a sham. It is a hollow exercise of what the principle says because we don't have responsible government in this country. We have partyism in Parliament. We've seen the ascendance of organized party discipline, the intense role of the party whips controlling who says what and when and how, on issues from foreign policy down to something like satellite dishes or acreage payments for wheat farmers.

It doesn't matter what's going through Parliament, there's a strict line that's adhered to. There was a time when people, including in this country, would invoke the name of Edmund Burke and his great speech to the electors of Bristol, in which Burke said that an elected representative owes the people who elect him or her the best of his or her conscience and independent thinking. Well, point to examples in recent memory of conscience and independent thinking in the Canadian House of Commons. If you can find them, you're also going to find examples of people who were placed under the thumb of the whip, the party structure and the party leadership. So in fact we have less responsible government in practice today than probably going back to the days of the Family Compact, the Château Clique, Lord Durham's report, and the invention of this concept that we should in fact have an accountable executive. Today we do not have that.

Parliament and Government

I think a lot of Canadians misunderstand the role of a member of Parliament, including many MPs themselves who sense that they are part of government. Parliament is not government — Parliament is a separate body. It's our national legislature, and its role is to be involved in law making, dealing with legislation and holding the government to account on the issues of the day, if it chooses to. And that's not new. Gladstone said that in England in 1851 when addressing Parliament and some people who thought that they should be having more of a say in running the country. He pointed out that Parliament's role is not to run the country; that's the role of the government.

We have this concept that the government, at least the Cabinet ministers and the prime minister, the political executive of our country, have to be in Parliament. That's where we fuse them, that's the buckle that joins the two together and brings through accountability. So the potential is there, but where do we see it displayed? Only in Question Period today could you say, "Do people think that they're getting accountability?" Sometimes, whether it's on the tainted-blood scandal or certain other issues, you can see that a government's feet are being held to the fire by a sustained effort on the part of the opposition, and there is accountability. You get commissions, you get corrective practices going on. But in the main, the problem is that people are elected as representatives to Parliament and think that somehow they're part of the government. They're not.

Traditional Role of MPs

The examples that I think many of us grew up with, and I'm in my 50s now, were major parliamentarians in this country. You didn't just know the name of the party leader. The television news at night, when that developed, didn't just show the party leader and his or her turmoil and every last utterance. There were many members of the parties who were strong spokespeople for different points of view and different regions. It truly was a Parliament — a gathering of mature, informed, seasoned Canadians with different outlooks, discussing, debating and crystallizing points of view on the issues that would affect the future of this country.

In contrast to this recent difficult period that we're finding our national politics in, if you go back and read *Hansard* up to the 1950s or early 1960s, as I have done, what you'll find there is very informed and intelligent discussion by parliamentarians about issues. Cabinet ministers would bring new legislation before Parliament. They would explain what the problem is, why they're trying to address it with these measures, why they think it's going to be successful and what their reservations are about increasing this tax a little more or adding a further bit of regulation over there; presenting it as the best possible shot at this thing at the moment and asking what do others think. Then you would see opposition members, and indeed other members on the government side, weighing in with their points of view and consideration from their own experience. It was a place where thoughtful adults were speaking together with the objective of being law makers and generating legislation that's going to be the most effective at this point in time for Canada.

Today, do we have that? Not at all. What I found in my time in Parliament, routinely, were speeches crafted on opinion polls, based on policy that had already been decided by the government and that was being laid out as the perfect solution to the problem at hand. No doubt. No hesitation. It's forced through: "You accept it, and by the way backbenchers, fall in line and support it. And incidentally, if you're on the other side of the House of Commons, fall in line and oppose it." This is a fairly dumb exercise for mature adults in a self-governing democracy.

MPs as Government Mouthpieces

For many years when I was in Parliament, people would be handed speeches written by the senior policy speechwriters from the government departments, whoever's legislation. If it was a transport bill, a defence bill, if it was something to do with agriculture, these potted speeches were handed out, and the term used was "modules." There would be various paragraphs or modules that you could move around, but there were key messages. And of course, who crafted these? Well, there were speechwriters, working in concert with opinion polls, who had pretty much determined where the tolerances were for the Canadian public to be receptive to this message.

Now, if I'm an MP and either in the House of Commons or somewhere at a public event across the country I'm taking and reading one of these speeches, what's wrong with this picture? Well, what's wrong is that it's not me. The person that's written these words that I'm mouthing has not been at the caucus meetings and heard the cut and thrust of different philosophical and practical debate on these issues. He or she has not been around the electoral district and felt the heat and the views of the people who are actually living, working and making this country operate. That speechwriter is not someone who is imbued with the traditions and the philosophy of the political party that, in my case, I would have been representing.

No, this is someone who is a wordsmith, good at crafting the nice phrase. Someone who knows what the opinion polls state on the issue of the day. Someone who knows the position the government has already arrived at and is trying to sell it to the public. And for sure this is somebody, working at a senior level for a Cabinet minister, who wants to ensure that above all the Cabinet minister is not embarrassed. They want to ensure that the government's policy is going to be adopted and that the prime minister will watch the whole unfolding little drama with a sense of approval. Does that speechwriter have the interest of the MP or the Canadians whom that MP is representing at heart? No. Does that speechwriter even have those concerns in mind? No.

So the result is, we have seen the public representatives in our national Parliament rendered into vacuous ciphers. There may be different marionettes whose strings are being pulled, but the same play is being performed. And that is not a Parliament. That is not representation of the people. That is a complete functional abdication of the role of being a representative of the people of this country in our national public life.

MPs' Speeches

In terms of how these speeches are written and then also how they're delivered in Parliament, it's kind of fun. I suppose it's why the Shakespearean festival at Stratford is such a booming success. All seats are sold out; it's in the black. People like theatre in this country — well, we've seen our national Parliament become a version of political theatre. And the actors and actresses are doing tolerably well in front of the cameras with the scripts that have been handed to them. As I remember, different times one would finish reading the speech only to be succeeded by another parliamentarian reading kind of a continuation of the same text — inasmuch as it had been crafted out of the same minister's office by the same speechwriter—complimenting one another on their fine thoughts and their great contributions. Well, actors like to compliment each other on their roles, but it's also a different issue here.

I used to work in newspapers. We'd actually have filler copy: "We're coming to the deadline, here's another half page that's got to be filled in." You'd have some filler copy to put in there to use up the white space.

Well, often the parliamentarians are filling up the space for the debate, talking out measures that maybe have been introduced by opposition, that would challenge the government's position. It's a kind of a Canadian version of a parliamentary filibuster to have these innocuous speeches just filling up the space.

The speeches that are given by rank-and-file members of Parliament are not getting on the national news. It's only what the prime minister, the Cabinet minister or a leader of the opposition has said because the media themselves have just focused on the very apex of power. Which is a self-defeating circle over time, in terms of a representative democracy.

The Government Line

There's another point about the government line. What a pretence it is to think that at one moment a government of the day has got the perfect insight as to the solution to the problems of this country. Canada has major, enduring problems, and we have to constantly be busy with them. Whether it's the Canada-U.S. relationship, the continuing relationship between the French- and English-speaking communities in our country or the issues of our geography — this vast landmass with relatively few people — and so our transportation and communications issues. These are things that have been, before Confederation and ever since, and well into our future will always be, our three defining national issues. So you don't have final answers to any of these, nor indeed to most other issues. This is a parliamentary system where there's ongoing discussion and refinement — new ideas come up and we do the course corrections. That's what a self-governing country and a self-governing system of government is all about.

Now there's the government line. In my time in Parliament I saw it all too often, that a prime minister or ministers would stand up and present a policy as if it was the best thing that the human mind could invent and the greatest solution for all Canadian problems. You had to support it, and you couldn't criticize it because this was perfect. And of course the corollary of that attitude on the opposition benches was, "For heaven's sakes, you've got to oppose this. It's the worst thing that could happen."

It's kind of like a sports team. We've carried what we do on the hockey rink into our Parliament. You're either wearing that red sweater or that blue sweater. And if you're wearing that other-coloured sweater, we're going to skate you into the boards and maybe even elbow you in the corner because you're on the wrong team. We've carried that mentality into our parliamentary life, to its great detriment.

Historic Changes to the Role of MPs: Efficiency and Ambition

It didn't happen overnight that somebody got out of bed and said, "I think I'll convert from being a robust, thinking-for-myself Canadian and just become a lackey on a leash for the system." It doesn't happen that way. But a couple of the long-term trends were a quest for efficiency in government — that we saw through the 1960s and 1970s — and the great force of personal political ambition.

Now, dealing with that first one, if you're running the Government of Canada through the 1960s and 1970s, spending is just going up by billions of dollars from year to year. You're hiring, not thousands more, but tens of thousands more people into the public service. And you've got programs for everything that moves in the country. There's a point where you start to say, "We've got to get efficient about this huge organization." And rightly so. But a part of our national government is Parliament. So what happened was, especially during the period that someone like Michael Pitfield was secretary of the Cabinet under Prime Minister Trudeau, there were a lot of new proposals brought in to streamline and make government more effective on its own terms, including, for example, the way that Parliament always seemed to talk about things endlessly. So rules were brought in to limit the amount of speech time that MPs would have.

How about approving the departmental spending? Well, sometimes that took a long period of time, way into the summer. Wouldn't it be more efficient if we knew by sometime in May what the approved spending for a department was? So rules are changed, and by late spring the departmental spending estimates, billions of dollars in thousands of categories annually, are deemed approved, whether Parliament looks at them or not. So in that context government is starting to look very efficient, but Parliament has been eviscerated in terms of one of its most traditional roles, which is the control of the public purse, control of spending, authorizing taxation and so on — all the money-related functions fundamental to why we even have a Parliament. Gone. So that was one of the factors.

Combined with that is the reality that a lot of people go into political life because they are ambitious to advance their careers. The great thing, probably, about the Parliament in England is that there are about 700 parliamentarians. So most of those folks know they're never going to get to be in the Cabinet and never even going to get to be chairs of parliamentary committees. They're cool about that, and they just spend time being parliamentarians — questioning things, running around holding officials to account and what have you. In our Parliament, with 300 members, and given the fact that a number are in opposition, you might have 160 to 200 of them on the government's side. By the time you've got 30 or 40 in Cabinet, and then another 30 or 40 as parliamentary secretaries, and then another dozen or two chairing committees, and then some others being deputy chairs of committees, plus the whips and so on, there's only a relatively small number of parliamentarians left on the government's side who aren't in positions of power.

You must remember that every chair of a committee sees herself or himself as becoming a junior Cabinet minister. Every junior Cabinet minister sees himself becoming a more senior Cabinet minister. And most senior Cabinet ministers aspire to become prime minister. So what we have going on in our Parliament is this wonderful game of political ambition that's motivating people every step of the way. They're learning how to hold their tongue, how to be polite and deferential to the one who can appoint them higher up. So they're not becoming critics. I've seen this so many times: even though they've got fundamentally different views on what's going down, they don't express them because they don't want to imperil their advancement to a higher position. So those two factors taken together have resulted in our Parliament being really just a little drama centre where nothing of true significance is actually going on.

Parliamentary Committees

The Americans talk about "oversight," meaning that they're going to look over everything that's going on and supervise and monitor it. In Canada, and in our English usage on this side of the border, if you say "oversight," that means you overlook it, you miss it. "You didn't see it happening right in front of your face, you fool." The role of our parliamentary committees, whether on justice or on defence or on foreign affairs, is to deal with issues that come up. They deal with contemporary issues that need to be focused on and have hearings to look at the spending practices and the policies of that department. Committees are the watchdog that actually sees what's going on, on the ground, holds the government accountable for it and contributes new ideas and new thoughts to policy. It's a functioning part of a self-governing country. Unfortunately we often find that the role of parliamentary committees is simply off the radar screen as far as the prime minister and those around him in the PMO are concerned.

Foreign Policy

When Canada decided to join the Organization of American States, what could have happened, at a minimum, was that the parliamentary committee on external affairs, chaired by John Bosley, a seasoned parliamentarian, could have held some debate in Parliament, perhaps some hearings across the country. It's fine that if the senior levels of government decided this is an important thing for us to do, we should proceed that way. But still, there are 30 million Canadians — you have to bring public opinion with you. Part of the reason that Canadians today feel so distanced from their government is that we've had a run for 30 or 40 years of leaders who thought that the way of the government was to make the big announcement. Don't do it in Parliament, do it at a press conference. Here's the big announcement, folks, and "Oh, guess what? The prime minister just announced something."

Well, in a democracy it's very important that the governed consent to what is going along. We believe in informed consent: in medicine, in sexual relations and also in government. Informing people of why something is going to happen has been the traditional strength of Canada's Aboriginal communities, of Asian communities whose style of management and leadership we've written great books about in North America. Why, in contemporary North America, do we have this kind of "Got you!" surprise approach? As if everybody, MPs included, should click their heels, fall in line and say, "Wow, isn't that great."

Bosley and the foreign affairs committee could have held hearings. We could have heard the pros and cons. We could have understood why in the past Canada had decided to not participate in the Organization of American States and what had changed so that now we were going to. It would have been a better exercise for remaining informed about our national purposes and how collectively, as a people, we chose to pursue them as one.

Parliament and the Military

When you raise the question of the Canadian Armed Forces and their relationship with Parliament, we get to see all these issues that are played out on the domestic scene in much sharper relief and more dramatically. Because all of a sudden something much bigger is at stake. It's a bit like the surrealistic experience when we look at Canadian domestic politics, but sometimes it's actually a little grimmer than surrealism. Sometimes it's as if we're in a theatre watching a drama being performed, and then later, to our shock, we discover that up there on the stage it wasn't just great acting — they were actually killing people. Those sobering moments are the kinds of things that transform you into realizing, "No, this isn't just theatre, this isn't just drama. This is real life. Actions have consequences. Policies carry with them the fortunes of nations and the lives of people." Particularly when it's outside of Canada involving the Canadian Armed Forces, the role of Parliament is fundamental to seeing that there is true accountability.

What we're seeing with the evolution of Canada's Parliament is perhaps very well demonstrated by the 180-degree reversal in what's required when Canadian men and women wearing that Canada patch on their uniform are sent beyond our shores bearing arms. Let me give you the long view of Canadian history. There was always a policy from the very beginning, from colonial times, that while people would be mobilized for military service within the country, no one would be sent outside the borders without there first being authorization by the legislative assembly. So much so that the first time that this happened after Confederation, which was the time of the Boer War in South Africa, Wilfrid Laurier, who at that time was leading the official Opposition, urged that there be a referendum in Canada to authorize the sending of our soldiers to South Africa. Not just a vote by Parliament, which Laurier and all the other leaders of the day knew was a necessary precursor for any of our military personnel to leave the country, but taking it even beyond, to all the people. Because the view then, as it ought to be today, was that in a democracy no question can be too big for the people.

We saw that same approach continue in August of 1914, when Prime Minister Borden was at long last with his wife on a vacation in Muskoka, after years of unrelenting work in Ottawa and across the country. What he thought might have been a week of great Muskoka vacation was cut short because the storm clouds had broken over

Europe. He went back to Ottawa by train. Parliament was summoned and a vote was taken on a resolution to declare war and to commit the military of Canada to service overseas. The same approach continued into World War II. The Mackenzie King Liberal government, having won re-election in 1940 on a pledge that there would not be conscription for overseas military service, discovered by 1942 that the direction of the war seemed to require conscription. So honour-bound was Prime Minister Mackenzie King to that mandate from the people that, again, in the middle of the war, they went back to the country with a national referendum — a ballot question directly asking the people whether they would release the government from its prior commitment. Yes or no? That's how serious it was. It wasn't just holding a referendum. It was doing it in the middle of the war.

By the time we got to the Korea campaign, as it was called in the early stages, we began to see a shift toward more executive management of these decisions. Parliament was not so centrally involved. By the time we get to the Gulf War, here is Patrick Boyer, parliamentary secretary at National Defence, up at Lake Couchiching attending the summer conference. I am standing beside someone who is a ranking officer in the Canadian Armed Forces and we both are watching Prime Minister Mulroney on television — not meeting Parliament in session to vote on whether our Armed Forces are going to be dispatched overseas, but at a press conference announcing to all of us that a commitment had been made to dispatch ships and planes into the Gulf War. A 180-degree reversal, documenting, in the process, how Parliament had totally been eclipsed and was irrelevant to any of these decisions, and leaving wide open the question, "If Parliament isn't part of this process, where in the name of democracy in Canada is accountability for the government being enforced?"

Role of the Military

The connection between the military and the people is something that has frayed over the last number of years. We've mostly lost the generation of people who fought in the First and Second World Wars. We are now dealing with a generation of managerial people who have very little experience and exposure to the Canadian Forces. The military and the people have got to be reconnected. Obviously the connection has to come from Parliament, as the representatives of the people.

It's very interesting to ask to what extent Canada is a country that really has a place for the military, in our heads or in our hearts. We are not a warlike people. We have not sent our armies abroad to make war on others. You'd be very hard-pressed to define exactly what the role of the military in Canadian political life is, in contrast to just about any other country. We absolutely believe in and live by the concept that the military forces, like the police forces, are subject to civilian control — that's a fundamental of our system. A second reality is that our Armed Forces have always had their role defined in relation to the greater military might of other nations — initially the French and the British, and in the 20th century the Americans — to the extent that Canadians, unlike many other countries with comparable size of geography and population, have largely had a free ride because we came within the umbrella or the ambit of the defensive policies of other countries.

A third and important element has been our approach in adopting collective security. We didn't try to go it alone as an independent nation, but sought partnership through military alliances and collective security, whether it was United Nations, NATO or other organizations that we've been party to. Part of it was the idea of forward defence. We wouldn't just defend our borders, but we would be out in the world trying to keep the peace and defend ourselves from insurrection or invasion by anticipating and dampening down hostilities and conflicts where they arose. And we could, as we had seen from our own history, whether the old British approach of trying to put down these Dutch farmers in South Africa or the Balkans skirmish in 1914 that triggered all these alliances of the imperial European powers.

We have seen and learned that young Canadians could be taken out of the farms and forests, out of the offices, away from the factories and schools, put in uniform and sent overseas to eat the machine-gun bullets being fired at them from other nations' armies. And die senselessly, in many cases, in the mud of foreign trenches in Belgium, France, Germany, South Africa, wherever. So coming out of that visceral experience was a strong Canadian feeling that we did not want a part of war. Like Franklin Delano Roosevelt, we had seen war and we hated war. And yet there is a need for defence. The eclipse of Parliament, cost-cutting measures by the government and our ability to get a free ride under the American defence system meant that, more and more, the role of the Armed Forces in this country was right off the radar screen as far as the

Canadian public, and necessarily the Canadian Parliament, was concerned. No accountability if you're not in sight. No accountability if there are no questions.

The Oka Crisis

I can remember being parliamentary secretary of defence at the time of the Oka crisis, the movement into Quebec of the Canadian army to stand and maintain the peace. The Canadian people were galvanized by this television image of a young, strong, clean-cut Canadian soldier in uniform, facing down a warrior with his face covered and the nickname "Lasagna," and were very proud of the strength of character of the Canadian Armed Forces to keep the peace. Two things happened. One was that in the wake of that, applications for enlistment in the Canadian Armed Forces increased all across the country. People were proud of this. Secondly, at the time that those soldiers were marshalled to go to Oka in Quebec, it didn't leave a single available person anywhere else in the country. Our resources were so strained and limited that if there'd been a boatload of armed insurgents arriving on either of our coasts, we couldn't have dealt with it. In other words we'd been pared to the bone at that point. We were still getting great service, and the good character of what Canadians in arms are all about was being displayed for us. But it was from the rank and file, who were doing their best in very difficult circumstances.

Morality and Character

Is there a deficit of morality in the country? I don't know how you measure morality, to know if there's too much or too little. I think that whether we're talking about an institution, a country or an individual, these questions of character, morality and conscience are only tested and proven out when there's some kind of crisis. I teach at university, and students do not study for exams that they don't have to write. I'm also a lawyer, and lawyers don't spend a lot of time preparing to argue a case that's never going to court. I don't think that, in the abstract, countries are all sitting neat in their synagogues, temples or churches, getting their morality right for the moment that they might someday, theoretically, be called on to give an accounting. I think the only way that we know about the moral fibre of a nation, of an institution or of an individual is by the specific acts that we see day to day.

It's what our great historian Donald Creighton referred to, all history being the result of the interaction of character and circumstance. Those are the two grand elements. You know, we all know that we don't really choose the conditions in which we live. There are some givens: the broad economic systems, the systems of religion and culture that are around us. And yet within the parameters that we can control we do make decisions that affect our own life and the lives of others around us.

I think the question of character, if it were tested, wouldn't just be confined to our national Parliament. It would be to the people who are running our professional sports teams, the captains of our chartered banks, the people who are in charge of our health-care systems and running the hospitals and those who are directing the police forces in the streets of our cities. It would also go to the leaders of the agricultural organizations in the farming communities all across Canada, to those in the oil patch, and on the Prairies, and elsewhere now in the new areas of Canada that are opening up with renewable and non-renewable resources, and the kinds of decisions that they're making. Including whether there's concern for the environment. Where does the floor revenue go? Who's benefiting? Is this just another chance for greed to prevail? Or is there going to be a sharing with the whole community? All of these issues come up every time any one of us makes a decision in any walk of life.

I don't think that we can look at our Parliament and those who are in it — the 300 men and women today who are members of the Canadian House of Commons — as being distinct or separate from the other 30 million of us across the country. We are a very special people, the Canadians. We are made up of fragments of so many other cultures, and in our long walk, the natural rhythm of evolving into a new national community in a new society, we are tested daily — morally tested with attributes of character as to how we get along with different religions, cultures, economic values and philosophies. That is really the measure of a nation, but it's ultimately the measure of each of us as an individual.

PETER DOBELL

Peter Dobell is founding director of the Parliamentary Centre, which he launched in 1968 after serving for 16 years in the Canadian foreign service. The centre aims to strengthen legislatures in Canada and around the world. Mr. Dobell also currently sits on the board of the Institute for Research and Public Policy.

TOPICS:
Is Parliament Relevant Anymore?
Member of Parliament: A Once-Noble Profession
How Polling Has Changed Politics
Parliamentary Committees:
Where an MP's Influence Is Supposed to Rest
A Potential for Change in the Parliamentary Committees
Power of the Executive (A.K.A. the Power of the Political Party)
Parliament's Major Flaw: Accounting for the Money It Spends
Question Period: The Good, the Bad and the Ugly
MPs: A Building Frustration

Alberta:
How a One-Party Province Ensures Its Elected Members Are Heard

Is Parliament Relevant Anymore?

I believe that the public takes less interest in Parliament than they used to. Yet when there's an issue that they want to promote, they certainly go to their members of Parliament. They go to the opposition political parties. They will bring petitions to Parliament. The number of people voting has diminished, but I think Parliament is still an institution to which they turn.

The notion that Parliament is failing would be a pretty dramatic statement. I'd be prepared to say that the role of members of Parliament has been in some degree diminished, but Parliament itself is still a place where the issues are raised. If it didn't exist, we'd be worse off.

A different question is, how do we get people more interested in the political process? That's pretty tough. It used to be that people felt that government was the most important agency or instrument in society. For instance, when I was young joining the public service was my highest aspiration. My son, however, would not be dragged into working for a government. He wanted to get out where he felt the real decisions were being made, which was in the business world. I think that's a pretty general view.

Will people continue to seek to be elected members of Parliament? I think finding people to run for political office is not a problem. A lot of people would like to be a member of Parliament. However, I have never seen a profession where someone who has been encouraged to run for office by colleagues, or by a political party leader, spends less time asking what the job involves.

Member of Parliament: A Once-Noble Profession

To appreciate all the changes to the role of a member of Parliament, you have to look back to the 1950s. Back then members of Parliament were the primary source of information on how the people in the region in which they lived thought about public issues. This was the avenue by which Cabinet ministers found out how people thought about issues. For that reason, back then Cabinet ministers would normally attend most debates in the House of Commons. This meant that when a member of Parliament was speaking, he or she felt that what they were saying would be listened to and possibly have an influence.

Cabinet ministers no longer listen to what members say in the House of Commons. They may pay some attention to what they say in their party's caucus, or they may accept that a member comes in and has a private meeting or talks to them on the floor of the House.

For the members of Parliament, when they participate in discussion of a policy issue, they should be allowed to approach it as intelligent individuals drawing on their experience. When they come to a common decision on a national issue, they should be listened to. That doesn't happen now. From the point of view of the member, that is what is so frustrating. It's particularly frustrating for opposition members because the ruling government members do have the opportunity, through their party caucuses, of having occasionally some influence on what the government is going to do.

On the other hand, the government members have the disadvantage that they are discouraged from speaking their own mind. When they are asked to speak in the House, they are often given the text by an aide to the minister on the issue on which they're speaking, and they're told, "That's what you've got to say." If they have a matter that really troubles them, it's hard for them to get to the floor. The opposition members have the satisfaction of getting up and attacking, but they have no influence. For both of them, for different reasons, they have frustrations.

How Polling Has Changed Politics

Polling has, in my view, significantly reduced the influence that members of Parliament used to have.

Prior to the advent of polling (when it became possible for a government or an opposition party to get precise information on how the public would react to various policies) governments were dependent on only two principal sources of information. They were dependent on their connections with local media — editors, people who wrote the editorial columns — and they were dependent on the members of Parliament who lived in their constituencies and followed things closely. Once polling came in, that changed the significance of MPs in the House.

There's some sense that MPs have lost the balance of power. I think members of Parliament had influence. They never had power. The ministry has power, but MPs have less influence in how the decisions are taken.

Parliamentary Committees: Where an MP's Influence Is Supposed to Rest
Now that government is bigger and Parliament has become busier and
there is more going on, it has moved much of its work into committees.
Yet part of the problem in committees is that the media pays very little
attention unless a minister is in trouble and is going to be there. In the
1960s and even in the 1970s, when a committee was meeting the media
would be all over it. It would get well publicized, so the members who
were participating would feel that they were making a contribution.

It was also the case in those days that a committee received what is
called an "order of reference" from the government, indicating that they
would like the committee's views on that subject. So when the members
were working on it they felt that what they were doing was going to be
listened to. And indeed it was. Now, when 20 or more committees are
meeting all the time and when they can meet by their own decision,
there isn't the same focus on issues. There is less of a sense that the government is interested in having their views.

Nowadays the government already has its agenda set. In the past the
government would assign issues to committees and listen to their recommendations. Today the committee decides on its own agenda. That's
the first problem. The second problem is that the issues come to committee when the government has already made up its mind on issues,
and so the members on the committee from the government side feel
compelled to follow the party line.

If you can change the dynamic, if you create a condition where the
government members don't feel they have to defend what has already
been endorsed by the government, that would also free up the opposition members on the committee. They wouldn't always feel they have to
oppose the government because there would be no set government policy to attack. So if you can move in that direction, I think you would see
an improvement.

A Potential for Change in the Parliamentary Committees
I was involved in a fascinating experience back in the middle 1970s,
when the government was very concerned about immigration policy.
They decided to ask a group of experts to produce an options paper,
which is called a green paper. It would identify various ways of addressing the problem. They decided to refer this to a joint committee. What
was interesting is, it took about two months for the opposition members

to recognize that the government was genuinely looking for advice and had not made up its mind. It wasn't looking to have the Liberal members endorse a policy they had already decided on. The dynamics of that committee were totally different. When they came to vote they divided not on party lines. There were some 300 votes. I drafted the initial report, so I followed it very closely. They divided between big cities and smaller communities. They divided between cities where there were a lot of recent immigrants and constituencies where there were just either anglophones or francophones who had been there for a long time. And then finally there were some ideological differences. But you had a man who was then a Conservative, David McDonald, voting with Andy Bruin of the NDP.

One of the things I've been advocating is for the government to return to bringing green papers to committees. There haven't been any since 1975. Or they could do what the British Parliament is now experimenting with, which is drafting legislation that has not been approved by Cabinet. Bringing it to a committee, the minister is saying, "This is the advice I received. I'd like your reactions."

Power of the Executive (A.K.A. the Power of the Political Party)

With the current system in Ottawa, the political party in power tells backbenchers how to vote. In Britain's Parliament they have a number of levels of voting discipline. If it's something on which they campaigned and where they had taken a strong position, then the government members are expected to support that and are in trouble if they don't. That's called a three-line whip. Then you have what they call two-line or one-line and that means some encouragement to vote with the government party, but not an order. You wouldn't be in real trouble if you didn't do it, particularly if you could demonstrate why your vote was different. I think our problem in Canada is that we haven't given our MPs enough latitude in voting. The power is coming from on top. Once the decision is taken, MPs are expected to vote the party line.

The executive is good at keeping MPs in line in the House. First of all, have you ever seen how they vote? They stand up, one after another. Their names are called and they go down the line. It takes enormous courage for someone to fail to stand up or to stand up and say, "No," if all of his colleagues are saying, "Yes." That's one form of discipline.

What other things can they do? Well, they can remove someone from his committee. There was a rather dramatic example some years ago, when Warren Allmand, an MP with about 25 years' seniority, was chairman of a major committee. He was simply withdrawn from the committee. So that's another discipline. A third form of discipline? They could not expect to be included in a delegation travelling abroad. They might be looking for some assistance in their constituency. It would become harder if they were on the government's side. The opposition parties have fewer powers because they don't have as much to give, but they can still remove a member from a committee.

Parliament's Major Flaw: Accounting for the Money It Spends

Accountability of public spending hasn't been very effective for the past 50 years. But it is certainly ineffective now.

One of the biggest failings of Parliament today is that it never really has been very successful at reviewing how government spends money. Part of the problem is that government finance is now extraordinarily complex, so that you'd have to spend a great deal of time and have very large staffs to do it effectively. There is a feeling that it was better in the past because the Estimates had to be approved in the House and were debated in the House. But that ended in 1968. It had reached the point where Parliament was approving government expenditure one month at a time. It had become a system for holding up the government until the last moment, but always paying it at the last moment. Quite often the only thing they'd get is that one department would have some cuts made to it. It wasn't a very thoughtful analysis of how the money was spent.

Do we need a better system of scrutinizing spending before the money is spent in our Parliament? Well, the timetable for producing information about proposed expenditure is pretty tight. It's recognized that if you look at the spending estimates and have three months to review them, you're not going to be very effective.

One solution is the potential area of activity by parliamentary committees to look at reports from departments and review their proposed plans so that their proposals would influence next year's expenditure. Then the government would find itself with enough time to react and Parliament would be able to judge whether the government paid attention to their recommendations.

The problem is, members of Parliament can never be like an auditor. They have to decide on where the policy emphasis should be, where the money should be spent. If committees would concentrate on offering advice on future expenditure, they would then have something to judge when the Estimates come down six or nine months later. Then they could really go after government. They could make that politically quite difficult.

Question Period: The Good, the Bad and the Ugly

I don't admire the current Question Period. But it does one thing — it forces the minister to inform himself or be informed by his advisors about problems in his department or her department, and if it's a serious problem, to try and rectify it or correct it. Question Period does give the opposition a focus of attack. Unfortunately the media now really only follow the Question Period. It gives the television media, particularly, something that they can use.

I would judge that 95 percent of the impressions formed by the public about Parliament are based on what they've seen of short clips from Question Period. The problem today is how to change it.

What's interesting is, 50 years ago Question Period lasted about 10 minutes a week. Ministers were questioned on some subject about which there had been late-breaking news and about which the opposition reasonably considered that they should find out a bit more. The questions were what you might call open, honest. And the answers were open and honest. The system began to change in 1956, when Diefenbaker used it as an instrument for attacking the government on the Mackenzie Pipeline debate. He used that day after day, and quite effectively. It changed more when the Liberals were decimated in 1958. There were what were known as the "Four Horsemen" — Lester Pearson, Paul Martin, Sr., Lionel Chevrier and Jack Pickersgill. They used the Question Period so aggressively on Diefenbaker's government that sometimes it lasted all day. It was at that stage that they negotiated and agreed to limit it to one hour a day.

MPs: A Building Frustration

There are MPs who talk quite a lot about unhappiness with the system. They don't do anything because you can't easily organize change. How would they do it? So the problem is, they have real distress. The power to change requires a majority of members and all parties agreeing. If you can't get all of those people together, you aren't going to get change.

Unless the system improves, our members of Parliament really won't feel as though they are making a contribution. They'll continue to be frustrated. This current Parliament is particularly frustrated because they had a relatively small turnover. Almost 85 percent of the members have been here for one or two or three previous Parliaments. So they know what the problems are.

That members of Parliament now have less influence in how decisions are taken should be of concern to voters. However, I think a number of people say, "That's beyond me." The people who have concerns more are the members of Parliament themselves. I mean, it's embarrassing for many of them. They fight a campaign. They say, particularly the new ones, that they're going to Ottawa to change the system. That's what happened when the Reform Party came in. But they discovered that not only could they not change it, they began to conform with it because that's the way the place worked.

That's why I'm persuaded that ultimately there has to be a change that is agreed upon by most of the members. The prime minister doesn't have to lead the change, but he certainly has to agree. Parliamentary reform can come directly down from the prime minister or it can come from a slightly lower level, say, the House leader of the ruling government party. It must have not only the prime minister's approval; it must have the approval of the other parties.

I don't think change is going to happen in the next year or so. It is quite possible it might happen when a new prime minister comes in.

Alberta: How a One-Party Province Ensures Its Elected Members Are Heard
Alberta has a different system. Alberta has had this consistent phenomenon of the government party being almost the whole House. The current system was developed by Peter Lougheed when he was elected premier back in the 1970s. There were no opposition members whatsoever. He had the whole House. So he devised a system which called for every piece of legislation that the government proposed to be submitted to the government caucus. There was an exhaustive internal discussion.

Even now the Progressive Conservative caucus in Alberta meets every day when the House is in session or for long as they feel it necessary. Unlike our federal caucuses (although I think the NDP may vote this way federally) the Alberta caucus accepts a motion from any member of the caucus. So if you are pressing a certain case, you submit a motion saying that the caucus favours this. That is voted on and the majority determines how the party is going to proceed. The premier may even be in the minority, although he probably tries hard not to be. Compare that with the federal system where there are no motions and the party leader concludes discussion with his perception of the consensus. Woe betide a member who says, "That's not the way I heard it."

To go one stage further, in Alberta every piece of legislation that's going to come to the House goes to caucus. Approximately one-quarter of all the bills are sent back to the department with directions as to how they're to be modified. So providing you're in the government party in Alberta, you have a significant opportunity to contribute to the development of policy.

Unfortunately if you're in the opposition, by the time it gets to the House the whole thing has been cooked. Opposition parties have even less influence than in Ottawa, and that's reflected in their committees. The opposition are not members of their committees. It is ministers who are responsible for that area and some back-bench members. It's a totally different system.

Chapter 8
Advisors and Civil Servants

STANLEY HARTT

Stanley Hartt is the chairman of Salomon Smith Barney Canada Inc., based in Toronto. Prior to joining Salomon, Mr. Hartt was chairman, president and chief executive officer of Camdev Corporation (now O&Y Properties Corporation) from 1990 to 1996. Hartt served as deputy minister in the Department of Finance from 1985 to 1988, and from 1989 to 1990 he was chief of staff in the Prime Minister's Office. Before joining the civil service he was a partner with the law firm of Stikeman Elliott, from 1965 until 1985.

TOPICS:
Role of the Prime Minister's Office
Realities of Working in the Prime Minister's Office
The Prime Minister's Office:
Keeping the Prime Minister's World in Order
The Power of the Prime Minister's Office: Balance and Responsibility
The PMO:
Pubic Opinion, the Media and the Microscope of Question Period

The Game of Politics:
Polling, Television and the PMO's Measurement of Success
The PMO: Managing the Media
Party Discipline and the Four-Year Dictatorship
The Citizen's Vote
Party Loyalty: A Matter of "Confidence"
MP Loyalty, the PMO and Internal Debate in Caucus
The PMO and Party Discipline
Power of the Cabinet Minister
The Prime Minister's Power of Appointment:
How It Leads to Complete Party Loyalty
The Canadian System of Government
The Canadian System of Government Versus
the British and the American Systems
Government Checks and Balances: A Case Study on the GST
External Influences on Government:
Lobbyists and Special-Interest Groups
The Public Service
Changes in Public Perception over Time

Role of the Prime Minister's Office

The Prime Minister's Office has an almost impossible job. It's supposed to help the prime minister develop policy that is consistent with his platform. It's supposed to attend to his travel, speaking and schedule needs. It's supposed to worry about image, press and communications. And it's got a tiny staff to do all that. It does have the benefit of working with the Privy Council Office on policy matters. But what I found was there's an awful lot to do with a very few people.

I think it's very easy to blame the Prime Minister's Office because the PMO is almost partly there to be blamed. You don't want to stand up and say the prime minister is mean. So you say the Prime Minister's Office is mean, they're tough, they're not respectful of democratic rights. It's very easy to pick the PMO as the whipping boy. The PMO staff doesn't wield any power. The distance is given to them expressly and by delegation from the prime minister himself. The second he wants them to stop doing anything that they're doing, he says so, and they stop.

266

Realities of Working in the Prime Minister's Office

I wouldn't say it was fun working in the Prime Minister's Office. I would say it was the hardest job I'd ever had. It was harder than being a lawyer with a very complex corporate and securities practice. It was harder than running a huge bankrupt real estate and retail company with 110,000 employees and getting them out of bankruptcy. It was harder than dreaming up brilliant investment and banking ideas, which I do now, for a vast variety of companies. It was the hardest thing I ever did by far, way harder than being deputy minister of finance. There are so many pressures on you from so many different directions. Your reaction to them had to be so instantaneous, and you had so few allies that you could count on; that was very difficult.

There are certain talents that you have to have. First of all, you have to understand the political process. Second, it helps in the Prime Minister's Office if you have a strong tie to or tradition with the ruling political party. I realize that neither I nor one of my successors and my predecessor had particularly strong ties with the party, but that does help. It helps to know the MPs personally from other activities that you've been engaged in, so that when you go to talk to them you're not necessarily there as the threatening guy from the PMO. You're just a friend who wants to help the party succeed, stay in office and prosper.

The Prime Minister's Office: Keeping the Prime Minister's World in Order

I think the prime minister's personal role is totally leadership driven. His staff has to pay attention to stamping out fires. That's a lot of what we did. I found that personally, when I got there, I was distracted by the fact that we had emergency after emergency. I don't know if people will remember, but we had a rumour that turned out to be true, that a Chilean terrorist had put cyanide in our grapes. We had to recall all the grapes on every grocery shelf in Canada and examine them, and we found two that indeed had cyanide in them — not at levels that would have hurt anybody, but we couldn't take that chance.

Then we had a Lebanese terrorist hijack a bus in Montreal, drive it to Parliament Hill with 11 people on it and threaten to blow it up. We had to surround Parliament Hill with sharpshooters and talk him out of the bus. Then we had the budget disposed of by a printer in a casual way, which led to it being exposed publicly before the date the budget was supposed to get read — and on and on. I did have the impression that we were distracted from helping the prime minister build a platform of legislative ideas that was consistent with his platform, would appeal to the public and keep his popularity high.

The Power of the Prime Minister's Office: Balance and Responsibility

The Prime Minister's Office seems to wield power, not because they arrogate to themselves the chance to do this or the need to do that, but because the power comes from our structure. It comes from the power the prime minister himself or herself wields. The prime minister is powerful in our system because the prime minister is by definition a leader of the party that has the most seats in Parliament. The party with the most seats in Parliament gets called on by the governor general to form the government.

The prime minister is then given prerogatives to use discipline, which will keep the loyalty of his party members so that they stay in Parliament. For example, he can decide when the election is, unlike the American system, where you can predict the next 5,000 American elections just by using the calendar going forward. In Canada that prerogative lies with the prime minister. Why does that lie with the prime minister? Because if he gets dissident members in his caucus objecting to what he wants to do, he can say, "How would you like to run an election? How would you like to defend your seat again? Do you think you'd win your seat tomorrow? I'm confident that I'd win mine. If you don't want an election tomorrow, stand up and vote the way I tell you to vote." His prerogatives are on purpose. They're part of our system to help him keep the discipline so that he can keep his majority. So if he's that powerful, of course his office in his name and under his aegis has to help him wield that power.

The PMO:
Pubic Opinion, the Media and the Microscope of Question Period

Public opinion affects the Prime Minister's Office instantaneously. Our routine used to be that we would meet at 7:00 in the morning, the entire staff, having read a précis of every newspaper in Canada basically. We had a cutting service that worked for us all night, and these very thick books were delivered to our homes before 6:00 a.m. We showed up at the office by 7:00, having read them. So we knew what was on the mind of the press all across Canada. That was helpful to prepare for Question

Period. Invariably Question Period is based on matters that are already running in the press, in order for the opposition member asking the question to have some legs to his question. Or so that they'll be at least some reporters interested that he's asking and interested in the answer, and they'll write another article the next day. Knowing what was on the mind of the press also helped us to manage where public opinion was. We were very interested in public opinion and in keeping ourselves abreast of it.

Unfortunately the relationship with the press makes the PMO job hectic. You have to have smooth, no-error baseball. You can't say, "Well, look, we'll play an ordinary nine-inning game, or we'll take six or seven errors, as long as we get 12 hits, a couple of which are home runs, that's a good game." We have to play error-free baseball. What makes it hectic is the pressure from the press not to create a rabbit that's a distraction from what the prime minister wants to achieve, namely getting his agenda in the public's mind and then through Parliament and into legislation.

The Game of Politics:
Polling, Television and the PMO's Measurement of Success
I believe that television has made the leader a more important part of our governmental system, and it has made his electability and his acceptability — measured constantly through instantaneous polling — more important. The more important he becomes, the more important to keep his image, his prestige and his acceptability high. That's the job of the PMO.

If the prime minister and his party are high in the polls, the PMO has been successful. If the prime minister and his party are low in the polls, the PMO has been unsuccessful. The PMO deals with its failures very swiftly, in the sense that politics is a profession in which you don't have a lot of scope and time for error. If you make a mistake, everybody makes a mistake. If you make a mistake, you fix it right away. If it can't be fixed, then it causes damage that can be either serious or permanent.

So it's a very fast-moving game. It's almost like a cameraman trying to follow the puck in a hockey game. If he takes his eye off that puck for one second, he has no more idea where it is than the viewers at home. You've got to move quickly. There are thousands of issues coming up, and you have to deal with them as best you can. Being prepared helps. Seeking the advice of the Privy Council Office is essential on policy issues. Knowing what you're doing from past experiences is helpful, but it's a very fast-moving, fast-paced game.

The PMO: Managing the Media

We were not telling 150 newspapers what to print. We were reacting to what they put in the papers. There was a communications department in the Prime Minister's Office that tried to plan how we could present our initiatives in the best possible way. That's only normal, and every prime minister has always done that, whether he had a formal apparatus to do it or not. Every press release, every ministerial announcement, every photo opportunity was designed to get people to understand why the government thinks that it's doing the right thing.

I don't think that's media management. It's getting your message out in a way that the public might be receptive to — that people might actually get to understand why you're doing all these strange things, like the GST. Even today you've got to explain to people why we have that excellent policy. Most people accept it, but the people who really understand — economists and businesspeople — love it as policy. Most ordinary people are resigned to it, but they would still like to see it removed. I think they'd be wrong. So obviously we haven't managed the media.

Party Discipline and the Four-Year Dictatorship

When the voters choose their members and they give an overwhelming majority to one party, the voters have said, "We want you to have all that power." Nobody makes up the rules after he gets into office. The voters know how powerful the executive council or the Cabinet is in our system when they vote. When they give an absolutely overwhelming majority to one party, they know they're electing, in effect, a dictatorship for four years. That's because of party discipline and the fact that we have the rule that you have to maintain the confidence of the House, that is, if a bill doesn't pass, you have to resign. They know that the prime minister and his Cabinet will use that power over the members in order to get them to vote for what the Cabinet decides policy ought to be and they'll brook no contradictions. Voters know that when they vote for these members.

The Citizen's Vote

A citizen votes every time there's an election through the mechanism of voting for the nominee of the party that he wants in office. In effect he votes directly for the prime minister. It's very rare that an individual's charisma, character, personality, record and appeal get that candidate elected irrespective of the party that he or she's in. The candidate is elected because the voters want the Liberal, the Conservative, the Alliance, the NDP or the Bloc member elected so the leader of that party has that much more chance of being chosen prime minister.

Our vote by definition matters only when the prime minister calls an election — that is his business. He does that for his own reasons. By definition citizens' votes only count in elections. Citizens do not go to Parliament and stand outside and vote personally on every issue before Parliament, and they shouldn't. Anybody who thinks that would be a better system hasn't seen a mob before.

The citizen knows all of this. For example, if the citizen thinks that's all bad, all the citizen has to do is vote strategically, talk to his fellow citizens and say, "Hey, why don't we give the opposition more clout? Why don't we elect more opposition members? Why don't we have a minority government? Why don't we elect so many opposition members that the government has to stay on its toes and really listen." But when the citizens say, "We don't like any of the opposition choices. We really, really love the government, to the extent of a vast majority," the citizens are conveying that power to the government. The citizen knows those rules before the citizen votes.

The citizens are making a perfectly valid democratic choice to give those dictatorial powers to the prime minister for four more years, watch him closely, count mistakes up, write them down, try not to forget them and if they don't like what he does, kick him out. I happen to believe it would be healthier if the prime minister got kicked out more frequently. But the citizens don't agree with that. The citizens have re-elected the present prime minister three times. The citizens vote knowing the consequence of their vote. They're extensively happy with the result. If you take a poll today, you don't find the citizens bitterly unhappy with what the present government has done.

Party Loyalty: A Matter of "Confidence"

The Prime Minister's Office doesn't, generally speaking, control the whip or the House leaders. Those people are elected officials who report to the prime minister without going through his office. If on a policy issue it's known that member X is out of step, doesn't agree or has grave personal, maybe even moral, reservations about the issue at hand, it is not unknown for a member of the Prime Minister's Office staff to go and sit with him and try and explain to him that, first of all, there are mechanisms for him to convey his disagreement. That's called the caucus. It's behind closed doors. You don't disagree with your party in public because the system is based on maintaining the loyalty of a majority of members. So when your loyalty becomes questioned and you reveal that publicly, you're already raising doubts in the mind of the governor general about whether or not the prime minister really does have a majority in the House of Commons.

So it's not unknown for the Prime Minister's Office staff to go and sit with a member and say, "On this bill we'd like to talk to you about the fact that you've been known to have said, first privately and now a little bit publicly, that you disagree, and we'd like to talk you out of that. Not necessarily because you don't have the right to disagree — there's a time and place to disagree — but once caucus has decided to back a bill, you're supposed to stand up and vote with your party on matters of confidence."

We still have not in this country redefined what a confidence matter is. Almost all government initiated bills and certainly all money bills are deemed to be matters of confidence. If we want the MPs to have more independence, there are lots of ways to reform parliamentary rules to give them more independence.

MP Loyalty, the PMO and Internal Debate in Caucus

Parliamentarians have been elected. Ipso facto, that gives them a right to have their views taken into account over and above unelected appointees. And I must tell you, when I was in the Prime Minister's Office my staff were very conscious of the fact that parliamentarians had to be listened to. The disdain of parliamentarians for the PMO comes from the fact that the PMO's job is to make the prime minister look good even when he's doing tough things. Even when he's doing things that aren't necessarily popular but that he thinks need to be done. They need to convey the impression that the party is still united, that what the party is doing is good. So if a member disagrees with something, sometimes he gets the feeling that this message is conveyed to him on behalf of the prime minister in a way that is inconsistent with his rights as a democratically elected representative.

What the member of Parliament's supposed to do about that is not fight with the PMO. What they're supposed to do is go to caucus and say, "Cabinet has presented us with a legislative initiative that we, many of us, more than one or two isolated ones, disagree with. And we don't want that bill to go forward as a government bill." It's in caucus that that discussion takes place. That's not a fight that members have with the PMO. The fight with the PMO's only after caucus has decided that a bill should go through, perhaps with some dissent, which is never quantified or revealed publicly.

The PMO and Party Discipline

If an MP is out of line with the party, he or she will feel the heavy hand of the PMO, which will say, "Wait a second buddy, we sign your nomination papers next time. Funding from the centre comes through the central party organism with which we liaise. If you're not going to help the party, why should the party help you?" Sometimes that heavy hand makes MPs feel unhappy.

MPs are rewarded for toeing the party line. That's how party committee chairmanships are given out. That's how parliamentary secretary jobs are given out. Ultimately that's how Cabinet jobs are given out. You will find invariably, no matter what party is in office, that if an MP is consistently out of line, doesn't agree with his party's policy, says so publicly, is a difficult MP for the whips, the House leader and the PMO, that person is not going to get promoted to one of those plum jobs.

Power of the Cabinet Minister

There were Cabinet ministers and there were Cabinet ministers. The leading Cabinet ministers, those that ran the central agencies — like Deputy Prime Minister Don Mazankowski or the minister of finance, Michael Wilson — were extremely powerful in my day. All Cabinets have to work on the basis that the minister of finance has a veto at the Cabinet table because otherwise the spenders will have him every time. His fiscal framework, his budget, will just be blown to smithereens within days of its announcement in the House. So there are some very powerful Cabinet ministers. There are other ministers, not just with lesser portfolios, but who by their personality don't command the respect and loyalty of their colleagues to the same degree. They don't have the same control of the reins of power as the central agencies have. Those ministers may often have to fight for visibility.

The Prime Minister's Power of Appointment: How It Leads to Complete Party Loyalty

The prime minister intentionally — when I say "intentionally" I mean by the framers and makers of our Constitution — has these powers to appoint. Technically the power to appoint is Cabinet's power. Cabinet does ratify all the so-called prime ministerial appointments. None of these are individual calls. But it is intentional that the prime minister has the power to make large numbers of so-called patronage appointments, that is, appointments to people whom the prime minister wants to reward for either service in Parliament, service in the Cabinet, service in the public service or service to the party. This is so that he can maintain the discipline on which our system depends. Remember, when he loses the support of the majority of the members of the House of Commons, visibly and externally as opposed to in their hearts, that's when he loses office, and all the government loses office.

The PMO doesn't have power of patronage. It may make recommendations to the prime minister, who will check with key ministers whether certain appointments ought to be made. I think it's a myth that the PMO makes these appointments without asking anybody. They may ask, What are their qualifications? What risks are there to making the appointment? That is to say, what might come out about the past and other aspects of the person's life? But they don't make these appointments.

Parliament is the object of those appointments, not the mechanism of those appointments, in order to keep individual members voting the way they are meant to vote, according to the mandate they receive from the voters and the internal democratic processes of the party that establish what's in the platform. What's a Cabinet proposal to caucus? It's what caucus has approved to keep those members in line. They don't get to make the appointments. They are the objects of those appointments. They will either get them or not get them, depending on whether they vote the right way. But that's our system. Our system depends on that. Because if our members were independent and could vote any way they wanted, the government could fall daily. We would have elections weekly, and we can't have that. We don't have the American system in this country.

The Canadian System of Government

I'm not arguing that this is the best system ever devised, or that it couldn't be improved. One suggestion would be to not make bills matters of confidence just because they come from the government benches. Have three confidence bills or three confidence votes a year. The Throne Speech, the budget and one matter raised by the leader of the Opposition, his choice. Every other bill would not be a matter of confidence. All of a sudden, with that simple rule change, you would change everything in terms of the relationship between the centre. In the centre I include not just the PMO, but also the House leader, the deputy prime minister, the whip, the Cabinet and the caucus, which wants members to vote loyally so as to preserve them in office. Since it would no longer be necessary to have their votes to stay in office, members could feel freer. There'd be nothing wrong with that, but that isn't our system today.

The system is built, first of all, by a first-past-the-post system of elections (where the MP gets elected in a "winner takes all" system of voting, no matter what percentage of the vote their party gets). We have no proportional representation (where the number of seats in Parliament would be decided by the percentage of votes cast to each party) to militate toward a majority government.

The majority government is meant to stay in office for a full term. In order to stay in office for a full term, it is meant to have the powers in the hands of the leadership — duly elected leadership — that keeps people in line. As I understand, the democratically elected MPs may sometimes say, "Since my people elected me, I don't have to stay in line." But that isn't our system. For example, the recent defections from the Alliance Party do not bring credit to Parliament. I think that the dissidents in their hearts truly believe that they are the democratically elected representatives of their constituents and if their constituents are momentarily unhappy with the leader, the right thing for them to do in our system is to leave the party and to demand publicly the leader resign. In our system that is absolutely the wrong thing for them to do.

The Canadian System of Government Versus the British and the American Systems

All the citizens are making a choice. They like that. I'm not sure I hear from the citizens the complaint that I'm hearing from journalists: that there's something theoretically wrong with our system. Power isn't centralized in the Prime Minister's Office. Power is centralized in a few central agencies and that includes the deputy prime minister, the whip, the House leader and some small group of Cabinet, usually the members of our priorities and planning committee. Power is centralized because our system requires that power be managed in a way that militates decisions getting made and, once the decision is made, decisions being carried out. You can't have a hand-wringing, endless debate at every step of a process, trying to get something done. You would never have any legislation passed. That is our system.

This was not done without thought. Originally the British parliamentary system was developed as a counterbalance to the power of the king and the power of the nobles. That's why the House is called the House of Commons. It was designed as a counterbalance. But the essence of our system of responsible government is, you put a bill in the House, you lose the vote, the government falls and we have to have an election. And that militates having a strong leader who tries to avoid that circumstance.

You could look at the American system and say, "How does it work?" Well, the American system was designed to get nothing done. The checks and balances are so important in the American system that it is a miracle any legislation ever gets passed. The only reason it gets passed is if the president, using the bully pulpit, can convince Congress, including his own party members. He has no such discipline and no such whip authority over the individual members of Congress or the Senate — that they better vote for it because the people want it. If you think that's a better system, then we have to change our Constitution. But the point is, that isn't our Constitution today.

Government Checks and Balances: A Case Study on the GST

Canada has its own checks-and-balances system that's very different from the Americans. When issues are being discussed there are various interests that have to be conciliated. I think I can best explain this to you by giving you an example. When we were designing the GST we thought that one option might be to include food among the things that were taxed, that is, not exempt food. There was great tension among the Department of Finance, where this tax was being designed, the Department of Revenue, where it was going to have to be applied, the political authorities in the Prime Minister's Office, the minister of finance's office, and the provincial ministers of finance.

Here's how it worked. The Department of Finance thought that a much lower rate, say, three percent, could be obtained if you taxed everything and you didn't have any exemptions. The Department of Revenue thought that it would be easier to import if you didn't have silly rules like six doughnuts are food because you're taking them home and five doughnuts are a restaurant meal, so you have to pay tax on them. To avoid these silly demarcations would be an important thing in getting public acceptability for a tax. The PMO said, "You are not going to tax my grandmother's grocery run. You're just not going to do it."

There was no way to sell that publicly. Members of Parliament shared that view. Just before Christmas in the year before we actually announced the design of the tax, Mike Wilson yielded to the members of Parliament who said, "We can't go back to our riding and say, 'Look, don't ask us why, it's just better policy to have no demarcations. The tax isn't on books or on medical or on food. It's on consumption. Just trust me, it's better and the rate will be lower.'" Mike couldn't do that. So he said to his colleagues in caucus, "I'm going to take food out of the base." When he told his provincial ministerial colleagues, they said two things. One, "It's your problem because we didn't have the guts, frankly, to join you. We should have joined you. This would be better if it was a national tax. But we think that it's a big mistake to raise the rate and create this vast, difficult exemption of the demarcation lines."

So here you had perhaps the wrong policy decision, interestingly enough, brought in as a result of discussion between political forces — members, and the PMO, and the ministers' political staff, and the Finance and Revenue departments that were designing the tax, and their provincial counterparts. Every one of those forces played a role. It came out as a seven percent tax, exempting food. It was probably the wrong decision but politically the right decision.

External Influences on Government: Lobbyists and Special-Interest Groups

The interests that affect government are not just in the government. They're also outside the government. They're lobby groups, they're interest groups and they're non-governmental organizations. The government has a vast array of people who care about its decisions. I would say, "Thank God," because if the government were irrelevant we'd have a real problem. The government cannot just say, "I'm going to do this and I really don't care who disagrees." They have to consult, depending on what the policy issue is. They have to, if they can't bring people on side, at least explain to them why they're doing it and take their views into account, perhaps as to how it should be done.

I find there's some truth to that sentiment that government is very large and therefore unwieldy. I find that happens in large bureaucracies, even in the private sector. You can have a company that is so large that sensible ideas get lost because they bump up against general policies that don't pass the commonsense test but are policies. They're passed down by somebody up above, and nobody quite knows why.

The Public Service
What struck me when I first served as deputy minister was how hard the public service works and how good it is. I had shared the view common on the street that civil servants are in a bit of a boondoggle. They don't work very hard; they go home at four o'clock; they push paper; there's too many of them; they don't really take responsibility; and they play bureaucratic games. What struck me immediately was how untrue all that was. Parliamentarians work extremely hard. Their days are endless. They're away from their families, living sometimes in shared, cramped quarters, which I don't know how they put up with. Bureaucrats are extremely talented, extremely dedicated, loyal, and are basically taking a permanent pay cut from what they could achieve in the private sector. You can have bureaucracy in the private sector as well as in government. I think the answer to why that exists would be that it's intentional. In other words, process is very important in government to make sure that nobody runs off half-cocked with an idea that hasn't followed the appropriate path to getting adopted, approved and accepted by all those who need to be consulted; process exists so that there are no freelancers (i.e., workers independent of a "boss" and therefore not subject to checks and balances). Although there still are freelancers in government, despite all that caution and those safety mechanisms.

Changes in Public Perception over Time
Because so many interests in and out of government have to be concili-ated, by definition a government is a big apparatus that can't turn on a dime. It has to turn slowly like the *Queen Mary*. But it does turn. If you

look at the past 20 years, we've gone from a culture of "Spend it, who cares, it doesn't matter. We only owe it to ourselves. What's a deficit?" to "The deficit is extremely important, and we don't ever want to go back to that world again. We're going to manage our money with reserves so that any risk of an economic downturn won't put us back into a deficit." That's a cultural change.

The citizen thought, under Prime Minister Trudeau, that the deficit didn't matter. Why did the citizen think that? Because a great leader, much admired, pushed it up to $38.6 billion and never said a word about the fact that it was a problem. Mr. Mulroney got elected with a very difficult job of changing public perception. I must tell you, I still believe he paid a terrible price for having to change that public perception. On day one he didn't have a big audience, but he had the guts and the leadership abilities to try to persuade people that governments are not very different than individuals. They are bigger. They don't die. And they can tax and print money. Aside from that, they still do have bankers who sooner or later phone them up and say, "Sorry, fellow, no more money."

That was happening to the Canadian government in 1984 when Mulroney took over. Mulroney changed all that. Now the Liberals, who never mentioned deficit ever — Paul Martin voted against every single deficit-reduction motion that Mike Wilson put forward — they're the champions, successfully, thank goodness, of deficit reduction, and the culture is completely changed. Its leaders have led the public to a different mindset. There's nothing wrong with that.

Harry Swain

A s former deputy minister of industry, Harry Swain led the preparation of Canada's microeconomic agenda for the incoming Liberal government in 1993–94 and set up Canada's first renewable energy program. He was also deputy minister of the Department of Indian Affairs and Northern Development in 1990–1991, and while in the Privy Council he was secretary to the trade executive committee, chaired by former prime minister Brian Mulroney, which guided Canada's negotiations on the original free trade agreement with the U.S. in 1986–87. Recently he chaired the Walkerton inquiry commission panel in Ontario.

Swain has taught at the University of Toronto and at the University of British Columbia and was a project leader at the International Institute for Applied Systems Analysis in Laxenburg, Austria. He holds a doctorate from the University of Minnesota and was awarded an honorary degree by the University of Victoria. From 1996 to 1998 he was a director of Hambros Bank Limited, a U.K. merchant bank, and CEO of its Canadian subsidiary.

TOPICS:
Power of Deputy Ministers
The Duelling Roles of a Deputy Minister
Politics and the Civil Service
Political Pressure from Above
Influence of the Media
Accountability: Dealing with Parliament and the Committee System
Power of the PMO

Power of Deputy Ministers

Do deputy ministers have too much power? Well, they sure have a lot of responsibility. Of the senior people in the game, they're the only ones that are full time. Politicians have a lot of other responsibilities — to their party, to their constituents, to public communications, the hours they spend in Parliament, in Question Period. Deputies don't have to do any of that. Deputies have to worry about making sure that the policy advice that ministers get is first class and making sure that the delivery of programs is first class. They do that full time.

Is politics a game? At some level it is. It's an immensely enjoyable human experience. It's also played to win by a lot of folks. Ideas matter. People care a great deal about outcomes. So gamesmanship sometimes becomes part of the game. It's part of the operation. But in another sense it's not a game. It's very serious. One is playing with the public trust, with public resources, and one is playing for very high stakes — usually things that matter a lot to the country as a whole. If that's not done well and done seriously, everybody suffers.

The Duelling Roles of a Deputy Minister

There have been times when I felt that things ministers decided to do were not terribly smart. But on the other hand, they were the folks who were elected to make those decisions. At the end of the day, after I'd given all my best advice, if they decided they were going to do something else, my obligation was either to deliver it to the best of my ability or to resign. I never did find an issue that I disagreed with enough about to resign. I'd argue about it, but I never had a minister who did anything that was really destructive to the country.

From time to time I thought those things that ministers did, or Cabinet did, were less than the best available decision. But then again, my judgment on that was not the one that folks paid for. To be fair about it, ministers have to make decisions with political popularity and electoral success in mind — doing what it is that the people want. Sometimes what the folks want may be in your opinion shortsighted or wrong-headed. That's life.

Deputies are responsible for making sure that ministers have the most complete arguments about alternative courses of action. If they are bound on a course that's unwise, you can warn them, you can advise them. You can, in a pinch, go to the person that appointed you, the prime minister, and say, "Sir, we're heading for trouble here." It's another thing that I'm glad I never had to do, but it's a theoretical possibility. But at the end of the day, if all those things are unavailing and you think that the minister is bound on something that's really bad or dangerous or illegal, you have no choice but to resign.

There are some formal mechanisms for going around the minister if you do. This is very high-stakes poker, and one hopes that it never occurs. But if, for example, you have a minister who is bound and determined to do something which is against the stated and recorded policy of his own government — and this happens occasionally — or in the extreme, something which may be improper or even illegal, you have an obligation first to have the most straightforward conversation with that minister. If that conversation is unavailing, the deputy usually has a word with the clerk of the Privy Council, the deputy minister of the prime minister. The clerk may intervene directly. He may call the minister concerned and say, "Look, sir, don't you think that we should think about this again?" In the limit you or the clerk may go to the prime minister, who appointed you both. The prime minister's decision is of course final. If at that point a deputy still has deep problems of conscience, there is only one choice.

There are a lot of people who work in government who feel frustrated because they don't think their talents are being used optimally or their ideas aren't getting enough running room. To a degree that's true. But a deputy minister must be willing to serve whomever it is that the people put in office, with a full heart. If you can't do that, you shouldn't be in the business.

Politics and the Civil Service

A deputy minister is political in the sense that he or she has to understand the currents of the day. But a deputy minister must not be partisan.

I won't give you names of people that I've seen who have acted in a partisan fashion. There have been a few examples in Ottawa. They usually wind up being fired by the next government that comes in. That by itself is destructive of the ideals of the public service, I believe. It is all too common in the provinces. There have been a number of provincial governments which in my view have been just about ruined by partisan appointments at the deputy level.

The relationship between a minister and his deputy has got to be a relationship of complete trust. It doesn't necessarily have to be friendship. The minister may not ever want to deal with the deputy on a social basis. That's quite understandable. But it has to be a relationship of trust. The minister has got to know that the deputy is competent and is going to give him absolutely the best advice that he has in an unvarnished way, on all sides of any issue. Having given his advice, he will then take the decision that's rendered and implement it in a highly professional manner. That's the essence of that relationship.

How do you define success as a deputy minister? One way to define success, it seems to me, is how comfortable that person feels. Do you feel at the end of the day that you did a pretty good job? Closely related to that tends to be the esteem of your peers. There's always this penumbra of "old boys' club" around. That's a powerful motivator. This is a community of people working on these things. These aren't lone wolves.

Political Pressure from Above

I have seen examples where decisions came from sources outside my minister's office. I can recall at least one occasion when the prime minister of the day said, "This is the way it's going to be." My minister and I were both a little unhappy about it, but those were the rules.

The decision being taken was political. As a deputy I was called on to execute it, not to advise any further on its wisdom.

Influence of the Media

We used to refer to *The Globe and Mail* as a test of activity. If you were concerned about how to play some action, you asked yourself, how would this look if it were reported in *The Globe and Mail* tomorrow morning? Unless you had a happy answer to that, you'd better not do it. The government is like any other organization — what entity does like to admit its mistakes, particularly if they're going to be on the front page of the paper tomorrow morning?

I had a lot of experience with the media. For example, during the Oka summer (the standoff between the Canadian military and a small group of Mohawk at the Oka Native reserve lasted the entire summer of 1990) I was the deputy minister of Indian affairs. That was a pretty interesting national issue. The media reported what I had to say about it early on in the summer, and in a way that made me uncomfortable. Later in the summer it became clear to us on the government side that the way in which the media was reporting the story — and not what we were doing — was having more effect on how the Mohawk were responding to us and the public. The whole affair at Oka continued until the time that the people there no longer had easy access to the media. Once we realized that if we could cut off their cellphone use, we could cut off their access to the media, the effort collapsed fairly quickly.

Accountability: Dealing with the Parliament and the Committee System
A deputy is accountable to a number of different folks: to the prime minister who appoints him, to the clerk of the Privy Council, to his minister, to the Treasury Board, to all those parliamentary commissioners for information and official languages. So there are a lot of accountabilities here. But a serious one is to Parliament and its committees. I always took it seriously. I always went prepared, in depth, to answer any question that I thought they might ask.

I have to say I never had to breathe hard, yet the parliamentary committees should have made me breathe hard.

One of my regrets about my time in Ottawa is that I didn't deal with Parliament more frequently and more deeply. I found parliamentary committees disappointing. They would get you up there, ostensibly to talk about something serious, and then they'd divide their time into little 10-minute segments, the first six minutes of which was taken up by the member making a speech for his constituents. And just about the time you'd think they were going to pin you down with some interesting question, it was somebody else's turn. Parliamentary committees in that sense became a bit of a game — a bit of a nuisance. They weren't very substantial, usually.

The public accounts committee was usually a little bit different because the public accounts committee had in the Office of the Auditor

General a very serious staff who could prepare the most embarrassing possible questions for any deputy minister. That would usually keep you on your toes.

As for serious scrutiny by parliamentarians, of budget estimates, of policies, of past actions, the quality of your performance over the last year or so, it really was a disappointment. I think parliamentary committees are not as they presently operate a serious accountability mechanism. They don't have, in general, a staff that can prepare them with penetrating analyses or questions. Their individual members tend to play the partisan game more heavily, a substandard game.

It is rare to find a parliamentary committee taking a view, for example, on matters of administration or of the quality of program delivery, or of estimates, or spending, or any of that kind of thing. It was not impossible, but rare.

Now, the other side of that question is, do deputies prepare to avoid answering questions from parliamentary committees? Yes, to a degree we do — in the sense that a deputy owes a debt of loyalty to the government of the day. Those are the folks that were elected by the people to govern. So if a parliamentary committee member — let's say an opposition member — asks a question and you can keep your minister out of trouble by giving him a literal answer and not volunteering the next six paragraphs, it's probably wise to do so.

Are you getting value for money in your parliamentary delegate? Maybe. Let me put it this way. There's nothing in the system that says a parliamentarian cannot be highly effective in holding a department to account. In other parliaments, in other congresses, for example, it's normal for individual members to specialize — to be the real specialist on defence or regional economic expansion, to develop deep knowledge of the field and a close knowledge of the players in the field, too. Then on public occasions, like a parliamentary hearing, you are able to ask very difficult questions. These are the kinds of things that expose the dilemmas of politics and public administration and get the most penetrating kinds of answers. I wish our parliamentary caucuses and the opposition would specialize more and devote more time and attention to learning the fields that they're supposed to be critics for. I think that parliamentarians miss the boat on this account. It's wide open to them to do a better job. Nothing is standing in their way.

Power of the PMO

The Prime Minister's Office, some have said, is an extension of a prime minister who is a four-year dictator. That's an extreme view held by some friends of mine. I wouldn't go that far. But it is certainly true in our system that a prime minister wields a great deal of power, mostly through powers that are not written down. It's kind of interesting, but nowhere in the Constitution are the words "prime minister" or "Cabinet" even mentioned. The prime minister appoints all members of Cabinet. He decides what their jobs will be and how broad their powers will be. He appoints all deputy ministers. Well, right there you have everybody's attention. The people who work closely with him in the Prime Minister's Office, his political wing, are few in number but generally pretty high in quality and guile. They can wield an enormous amount of power if they want to.

I do recall one time being instructed to give a press conference by a senior member of the PMO. The normal question from the PMO is, "You did what? Why?" And then you have a chance to explain. A lot of central-agency work, both political and bureaucratic, has an emergency quality to it. "Stamping out fires" is one way of putting it. "Dealing with the urgent matters of the day" is another. Often these transcend the powers or interests of a particular department. The central agencies, which can bring together several different organs in government, play quite an important role there, and the PMO is among them.

DAVID CROMBIE

David Crombie was mayor of the City of Toronto from 1972 to 1978, and was elected to the House of Commons in 1978, 1979, 1980 and 1984, where he was minister of national health and welfare and minister of Indian affairs and northern development. He also held the post of chancellor of Ryerson University in Toronto. A member of many community organizations, Crombie is the founding chair of the Waterfront Regeneration Trust, chair of the Toronto 2008 Olympic Bid, chair of the Toronto Heritage Foundation and president of David Crombie & Associates Inc. He was also formerly president of the Canadian Urban Institute, based in Toronto.

TOPICS:
A History of Blurred Constitutional Jurisdictions
Cost-Shared Programs
Who Does What?:
Citizens Don't Care Which Level of Government Delivers Programs
Taxes

Sharing Tax Revenue
Shared Ownership
Uncertainty
The Blame Game
The Centralization of Power
Responsibilities of the Federal Government
Interconnected World
Collective Accountability

A History of Blurred Constitutional Jurisdictions
Even as a written guarantee in the Canadian Constitution, the division of powers among levels of government has always been blurry. It still is today. For the first 30 years of Confederation the federal and provincial governments fought over who did what; even over who could charge tax on alcohol. So it wasn't simply the question of what to do with cities that got blurred.

The division of powers among governments in Canada will never be fixed for all time because life changes. People change. Needs change. When a society is doing very well it has different needs than when it isn't doing well. So "who does what" will change. When the war came along in the 1940s everything changed. In peacetime, good times and bad times you have to respect those changes.

The Canadian constitutional system does an adequate job of providing a proper check and balance in the division of power between governments. I've been in a number of countries and seen how they work. It's probably no better in any other place. But it's no worse in any other place.

Cost-Shared Programs
No level of government is willingly going to give up money, power or exposure. What they will do is share them.

A cost-shared program is a way to spend more money than you have. It's helpful to municipalities because it gives them the opportunity to provide services which the public needs but that they cannot afford out of the property tax alone. The difficulty is that you're spending money that is not yours, and it's always easier to spend more of it and not be accountable for it. Most people in government agree that the old-fashioned cost-shared programs, with 20 percent here and 15 percent there, or a 25/75 split, institutionalize non-responsibility for the product (and programs) and usually inflate the costs.

If we walked into a grocery store and I said, "Get what you need and I'll look after 75 percent of it," you'd buy more than you could actually afford. And if you have a program where the other governments are paying 75 percent and you're only paying 25 percent, you'll also spend more, not because you're irresponsible or greedy, but because your municipalities have real needs. And those needs require far more money than the normal income of municipalities allows. So they're happy to get these programs.

We don't need episodic sojourns by federal and provincial governments into city life whenever they feel like it. The cities need the other levels of government to commit to publicly accountable programs for the long term. Cost-shared programs are most effective in cases where there's a clear commitment by a level of government to perform a specific task over a particular duration. Five or ten years is a commitment.

One example was the housing program that we had in the 1970s and early 1980s. We knew what we wanted and what we needed. We went to the federal and provincial governments and sold them on our program. We helped them change their legislation in order to accommodate it. We asked them to fund the program for five years. This was a predictable period of time so that it couldn't be changed whenever governments changed. We built a lot of housing in Toronto through that program.

My problem with cost-shared programs has to do with questions of accountability and extending costs. But one benefit is that you don't have three levels of government trying to deliver the same service. So at least they've diminished that kind of duplication.

Who Does What?:
Citizens Don't Care Which Level of Government Delivers Programs

Generally speaking, most people are uncertain about which level of government delivers the services that they receive. There are some organized groups of civic society in municipalities, such as business associations and ratepayers' groups, which do know. The people who do know what level of government delivers a program are a small number of insiders within the system.

Most people don't know what the federal government does. They know that the local government looks after the roads and the sidewalks, but they don't really know with any great precision. Secondly, they don't really care. They know that it should be done more efficiently and democratically, but beyond that, politicians and bureaucrats care more than voters and citizens do.

It isn't necessarily a problem if citizens don't know which government delivers their services. Just because you drive a car, that doesn't mean you have to know how to build a motor, right?

People should have some reasonable intelligence about how government works; that's part of being a citizen. But they shouldn't be expected to follow the vicissitudes of how much money is spent by this government on this part of a service; it's all very complicated, much more complicated than it was 100 years ago.

The best check is having public accountability through the media. It's a cliché, but the reason that it's a cliché is that it's true. You have to have constant exposure to the issues. The media should be given access to politicians, bureaucrats and community leaders so that they can explain themselves.

The problem now is that federal and provincial governments no longer think that they have a clear, specific responsibility to civic society in cities. But they do.

Municipalities have always been the responsibility of the province, as they should be. The province has to be involved because they have a custodial relationship with the municipalities.

You can't assume that cities' boundaries and borders will stay the same forever. And the federal government, meanwhile, takes a large chunk of tax dollars and gives very little in return to cities.

Taxes

Historically, the property tax has been the major vehicle for cities to control their earned revenue. But now most provinces have taken about half of the property tax.

Ontario takes a good chunk of it for education, which is supposed to be a municipal responsibility. Anybody who thinks that there's local control over education hasn't lived in Ontario for the past decade. It's now controlled and operated by the province.

Another form of revenue is dedicated taxes. We have some, but they don't go to the purposes for which they're raised. The hotel tax is a good example because everybody tries to use that money to do the things that will allow hotels to flourish. In Ontario that hotel tax doesn't go anywhere near a hotel. You might just as well increase the income tax or tax people for using the subways because it goes somewhere else.

If you took it and said, "Look, we're willing to take the hotel tax and use it for hotels," people would understand that. And those who use hotels would feel a lot better about it because they'd know that they were going to get better service.

Airports do that already with a user-charged private tax. It's called a levy. You walk in and they say, "We're building this wing of our airport. Please put in another $15." That's a tax because you don't have any choice, but it's a tax by a private government.

We have to find ways to link accountability and payments to services in municipalities. The more we do that, the better we will be. The current tax system has to be reformed.

Even if we do the right thing now, it will have to be reformed again in 25 years. I emphasize this because people think that if a generation solves a problem, then they won't have to solve it in the next generation. Every generation has to re-solve these problems because times change, opportunities change and costs change.

Sharing Tax Revenue
In the past 30 years the costs of the operation of cities, the constant reinvestment, repair and maintenance of infrastructure, have gone way up. The municipalities' share of tax money has gone down. It has gone to the federal and provincial governments.

Every time they stand up and say, "We've got a surplus," I yell, "Overtax!" What are they doing with a surplus when we have needs in the city that produces the most wealth in this country? The federal government has the wrong thinking.

A number of years ago the city was given a substantial amount of money by the other levels of government. The city spent all of the money building the National Trade Centre instead of on multiple projects. They made a judgment that it was the best thing to do. They were right to spend money on the National Trade Centre because at least they were saying, "We need to do something with economic development." Having a National Trade Centre is a really good idea in those terms.

However, the centre should have been built by the provincial and federal governments much earlier. The money that came in this time should have gone to civic needs, such as the transportation system, the education system and all of the infrastructure that we needed for public works, in terms of sewage and other environmental work. These are the guts of the place.

If you don't have the money to look after the hard services in the municipality (which we don't), then that's a clear indication that the system is out of balance. Cities need to have more money.

Toronto (and I could say the same about Montreal, Vancouver or Winnipeg) doesn't have enough money. Too much is taken out of it for the federal and provincial governments, and not enough is left for it to continue to be Toronto. That's the problem.

Shared Ownership

Major infrastructure programs, such as housing, can be set up for any area of responsibility. Programs can be created for transportation, or for pipes, sewers and other environmental work. But you have to make sure that the program is designed by a large enough team, involving the federal, provincial and local governments and whichever agency is appropriate so that they all have ownership of the program.

Gone are the days when every municipality said, "This is what I'll do, 100 percent. This is what you'll do, 100 percent." That doesn't work anymore. No family works that way. We're all in one another's pockets and living on one another's street.

You have to find a way to design a program so that everybody is onboard because they have ownership. Make sure that the financial commitments from the three levels of government are long term: five years, seven years, 10 years. Make sure that there is appropriate publicity for each of the partners. If you're willing to share the exposure, you'll find that people are far more willing to share the money and power.

Tapping into one's desire for publicity may sound like political gamesmanship for dollars, but that's human nature, and not just in politics. I find this with baseball players, businesspeople and actors. They want recognition for what they do.

Uncertainty

Everybody becomes cynical with funding from different levels of government because they can never be sure what the government is going to do. The federal or provincial government will say, "We're thinking about an infrastructure program." You have no idea what they're thinking or how much money that involves. They don't tell you. It's a lot of game playing, and it need not be so.

You need people who are willing to see that cities are a major, if not *the* major, basis of wealth creation in this country, not simply tucked away in a corner. That's what we've been saying for years.

The real problem now is that the chickens have come home to roost. Unless we put major investment by the federal and provincial governments over the next five to 10 years into transportation, the environment and so on, cities will continue to lose their edge. And this country will lose its edge in the global economy.

The Blame Game

To a certain degree one could say that local politicians are just blaming another government for their own problems. It's always easier to blame somebody else, and politicians certainly do that. The federal government blames the provinces. The provinces blame the federal government. The municipalities blame them both. That will go on.

You have to make sure that once in a while you get an opportunity to bring home a program. The municipalities get out there and sell their own programs, but not in a flashy way. You have to do the work and create a circle wide enough for everybody to have ownership in your project. It can be done. The problem is that often members of Parliament, and even Cabinet ministers, aren't involved in the decision making that can affect a city.

The Centralization of Power

One of the major differences between Canada and the United States is that we don't have party politics at the local level. Mel Lastman in Toronto and any other mayor can say what they like because they're not part of a political party.

It's far more democratic. When a Canadian mayor talks about whether or not he can get something through his council, he is by and large representing the community because he has no control over that vote.

At the other two levels of government, the party system increasingly delivers power to the Cabinet and even more so to the office of the prime minister or the office of the premier. Therefore we can have members of Parliament or members of the legislative assembly who have no idea what's happening in the government because they're less and less connected to it.

There's a great opportunity for reform. We need to hear far more from our MPs and MLAs, who should join with members of councils and school boards in fighting for the needs of their hometowns.

The first ministers of Canada basically run this country. And even there it's a small number of first ministers. We have far more centralization of power than the U.S. has at that level.

We know that when the Liberal caucus meets in Ottawa, or when the Tory caucus meets at Queen's Park, our people from our hometown, whether you're from North Bay or Toronto, are fighting for our needs. But we don't hear about any of that.

In Western Canada they have a great line: "Your job is to represent us to Ottawa, not to represent Ottawa to us." We hear the same cry right across the country. We need to hear from MPs and MLAs that they understand and will fight for our needs.

Responsibilities of the Federal Government

Just recently we've seen the federal government announce funding for scholarships and infrastructure. Some would say that these are all provincial or civic duties, but I don't have any difficulty with governments sharing responsibilities because we live in a complicated world.

No one ever said that the federal government isn't responsible for education. They've been involved in tertiary-level education for a long time, and their contributions have normally been very successful. For example, they gave money for technical high schools in the 1920s and 1930s.

I have no difficulty with their understanding that they have a responsibility to help people get an education in this country. If they want to have a program, they're clearly within their jurisdiction to do so. They should just work it out so that they're not taking allotted money away from the provinces or the municipalities.

With the issue of infrastructure it's more difficult to say who has responsibility. Even the word itself seems like a blur; no one knows what it actually means.

It seems to me that there are certain kinds of infrastructure that are essential for the future of the country and are therefore important to the federal government. Transportation is one. Regional transportation is a responsibility of both the federal and provincial governments, and I think that they can work that out. The federal government has been in transportation for a very long time, since the Canadian National

Railways. And indeed all regional transportation has to travel on lines over which the federal government had original jurisdiction.

You can't deal with an airport today in a major city and not see it as part of the economic power of that region in the future. That's a federal responsibility. They make some contributions for the costs of immigration and settling refugees, but not nearly enough. That's one area where they have a clear responsibility, and it would help if they carried it out.

I don't think that the federal government has to go into areas that aren't their responsibility or invent new jurisdictions. They just have to look carefully at those jurisdictions for which they already have responsibility and their programs that help cities, for which they are publicly accountable and for which they will make a long-term financial commitment.

Interconnected World

Life is blurred. When it comes to accountability for tax dollars, you can't impose a rationality on government that doesn't exist in reality. If someone says, "You are responsible for transportation," you can't be responsible for all aspects of transportation because you're connected to the world.

Who's responsible for telecommunications? The city has some part because they have to provide land where you can put the dish, for example. But that's a regulatory thing, and global, so it also has to be federal.

So life is complicated. There's an ecosystem, and not just in nature. If you try to impose a kind of logic of "who does what" on a constantly changing ecosystem, you're crazy. You'll go nuts. The only thing that you can do is understand generally who does what in your particular time and place. Then you can recognize that it will change. The key is figuring out who's doing what right now as we move to the future. Who should do what in the future?

It's hard for a citizen to know who does what. So it's up to politicians, bureaucrats and community leaders to try to understand what the divisions are. We know, for example, who's responsible for sending troops to the Balkans. The federal government looks after international matters. It's not Mel Lastman. He may be responsible for calling in the army for snow, but he isn't sending troops to the Balkans.

Who's responsible for the tough ones? Who's responsible for education? All three levels are. It's a question of knowing at what level you are going to take a certain responsibility. What parcel of obligations will you have? And those will change.

For example, how do you get buildings changed for disabled people? As they get older, between 20 and 50 percent of the population will have barriers to access through either age or disability. That involves buildings, education, research and so on. The costs are enormous.

All three levels of government have clear sets of responsibilities. When it comes to passing bylaws to insist that buildings become accessible, that's up to the local government. Should we have money for research? Yes; that's up to the federal government.

So you can take the whole field as an example and outline what those responsibilities are. People will be happy to know that the federal government will do this, the province will do that and the municipality will do that.

Where the divisions are now may change in 10 years. No one ever hands it to you, saying simply, "Forever and a day, this local level of government will do it and this one will not." That's not going to happen. Life is complicated. And we can use as many hands as we can get.

Collective Accountability

The question becomes, "Who is accountable when everybody is accountable?" Everybody must continue to be accountable. Politicians must be accountable at all three levels. Community leaders and citizens have to pay attention.

I don't have any difficulty with everybody having some part of the accountability because I regard that as part of the dynamic, interconnected world in which we live today. You can't simply give one major thing to one level of government.

There are things that the federal government can do. There are things that the provincial and local governments can do. There are things that independent non-government agencies can do. We can figure out what all of these things are, design a program and then hold people responsible.

With education, for example, although the federal government has a responsibility, they don't have to build schools. Generally people say that they don't build schools. But they do build some schools in areas where they're still dealing with language rights.

Should they provide money for people who can't afford to get a tertiary level of education? You bet. If it's worth being a Canadian, it's worth getting educated in order to make a contribution, not only to yourself but to the future of the country.

As a Canadian you won't be able to point at one level of government and say, "You do that and I want to know why you're doing it." No, life is more complicated than that. If you want to know who's responsible for the transportation system, you'll find out that three levels of government are.

It's true in every other country, too. Politicians have an obligation to design programs that allow the public to be served by a long-term commitment by all levels of government.

If you ride on the subway, take a trip out to the airport or go across the country, you're depending on more than one level of government. You want to make sure that all of those levels know which end of the program is theirs and make a commitment to it.

I don't blame citizens for being lost in the system. But the only thing that actually moves governments is people. Politicians live in a vote economy, and if they want to get re-elected, they're going to try to look after their citizens.

The job of MPs and MLAs is not simply to serve their constituents' federal needs. They need to serve the whole citizen. They need to participate with their MLAs and the local government people at the same time in order to design these programs.

Does that sound complicated? Yes, it is complicated. Life is complicated, and if you insist on simple answers, you'll get simple people.

BRIAN KELCEY

B rian Kelcey was a senior advisor to Ontario's minister of consumer and business services, working with stakeholders on the province's proposed privacy law and expansion of the LCBO's agency store system. He was the press secretary to Ontario's minister of intergovernmental affairs and government House leader in the provincial legislature from 1999–2001. In that capacity, he acted as a media spokesperson for the Ontario delegation at several national conferences, including the first ministers' meeting on health-care finance in 2000. He started his public affairs work by organizing talks between environmental groups and a logging union on Vancouver Island in 1991. He also served as Manitoba director and later as Ontario director for the Canadian Taxpayers Federation, from 1995–1999.

TOPICS:
First Ministers' Meetings: At the Prerogative of the Prime Minister
How the Prime Minister Dictates the Agenda
Making Decisions in a Time Crunch

The Pressure Cooker and Rushed Decisions
How Chaos Rules over Billions of Dollars
Accountability of the Premiers
Who Holds the Cards?
Role of the Media: How They Drive the Agenda
Role of the Provincial Press Secretary: The "Spin"
When All That Matters Is Public Perception
Cost-Shared Programs: Creating Tension Between Governments
Cost-Shared Programs as an Election Strategy
Provincial Priorities Versus Cost Sharing
A Case Study on Health Care and Cost-Shared Programs
The Ministry of Intergovernmental Affairs:
Overlap Between Provincial and Federal Governments
Overlap in Government and Citizen Frustration
Clarity and Jurisdiction:
Accountability of Provincial and Federal Governments

First Ministers' Meetings: At the Prerogative of the Prime Minister
A first ministers' meeting takes place in a formal meeting between the premiers of the various provinces and the prime minister where they resolve one particular issue or another. There is a common misconception that those meetings take place regularly. There are in fact regular meetings of provincial and federal ministers. But a first ministers' meeting is extremely rare because they only happen when the prime minister decides that there is something on his political agenda that he can actually convince all the premiers to agree to.

The key condition for these meetings is that they come about at the prime minister's desire. The premiers ask for first ministers' meetings on all sorts of other subjects. However, until the prime minister agrees and says, "These are the conditions and the issues that you're free to discuss at a table with me on a particular day," you can't convince the prime minister to have a meeting. Because the prime minister has a veto over the process, there has to be some reason or some excuse for the prime minister to want those premiers sitting at a table with him breaking bread.

How the Prime Minister Dictates the Agenda
Attending a meeting of first ministers is very different from ministers' meetings or premiers' conferences. One of the big differences, of course,

is the stakes. The first ministers' meeting I was at, as a press secretary with the Ontario delegation, was in September of 2000. Essentially, at that time the prime minister wanted to cover his vulnerability on health care because the provinces had been demanding or asking the prime minister to reinstate provincial health-care funding that had been cut from federal funding. The prime minister was politically motivated to get this done (due to the coming election) and the stakes of this meeting were very high. We are talking about billions of dollars changing hands from the federal government back into the coffers of the provinces.

The Ontario government knew what they wanted from the meeting and was lucky in the sense that getting a return of federal health-care funding to 1995 levels was in fact a campaign promise in their campaign platform in 1999. So we had a very clear mandate to ask for what we were asking for. On the other hand, what that actually translated to in terms of the real mechanics of government, what that meant for ordinary people, depended entirely on the federal offer, and as I've said, that only appeared that morning as the meeting started.

Making Decisions in a Time Crunch

The process of making decisions about billions of dollars at these meetings is bizarre to me. On the one hand, you see that the premiers, as individuals and as a group, and the prime minister are much smarter and much shrewder than I think a lot of the public gives them credit for. But on the other hand, the process is really very bizarre. To use a well-worn political cliché, it's like an episode of *Survivor* with a strange twist in that you pack all of the different premiers and the prime minister into a conference room with very few support staff. You are saying, "Look, we want a decision on this issue." In the case of the meeting I attended, the decision was how to fund health care in this country, within five or six hours of the beginning of that meeting. What was really unusual about the meeting was that the provinces had been asking the prime minister for a proposal to fund health care for several months. Yet they didn't see the actual multibillion-dollar proposal they were supposed to make a decision on until the moment they arrived at that table on September 11, 2000.

To give you an idea of how crunched the time is, typically the first day of the meeting is a dinner at 24 Sussex Drive, where the primary purpose is to have the prime minister welcome everybody. In fact, our understanding at the staff level was that during the first ministers' meeting in 2000, the substance of the deal that the prime minister was offering wasn't even put on the table on that first day. I don't think anybody would want to make a decision about billions of dollars or an issue that is as important as health care within a few hours. The province of Ontario had been asking for details for months from the federal government to make sure that we could discuss this thing intelligently and work out all the details. But frankly the way the process worked, which was in large part under the control of the federal government, we had no choice but to sit at that table on their timetable and work everything out. And we had to do it within a few hours with information that the premier and our government had only received moments before.

To an outsider or a citizen watching these events on TV, it may seem like these deals, in this case a $23-billion deal, were struck right out of thin air. But to a degree they are not. At a first ministers' meeting there are some support staff, crunched into cubicles, who are there to help advise the different premiers and the prime minister and whoever is representing each province. And you do have some information. For example, the Ontario government knew how much we were spending on health care. We also knew how much the federal government used to transfer when they made larger transfers to other provinces. We did have some idea of what was happening. When you are inside the room, where only a few very, very high-ranking officials are, or at lower levels, it's surprising how dynamic the atmosphere is. You could literally come out with almost any result. Compared to the Ontario government's ideal situation, the decision at this meeting was made so quickly that it might as well have been made out of thin air.

The Pressure Cooker and Rushed Decisions

In situations like the first ministers' meeting you have only hours to make a decision worth billions of dollars. That kind of time constraint doesn't make for great working conditions. Essentially you have support staff, I think there were seven or eight of us from Ontario, crammed into a couple of cubicles. Smaller provinces or territories got one cubicle. If you leaned the wrong way in a cubicle, you would find yourself in Nunavut or Manitoba. Within that space you have a laptop and maybe a speakerphone to work with. From the conference room where the premiers and the prime minister are meeting, you either get premiers wandering down with information about what they think the deal looks like or you will get an occasional note from inside the meeting. And on the basis of that information alone, and in this environment with just the laptop and the speakerphone, you must figure out, "Is this deal coming our way? Is this something that solves the problems we are looking at?" There is a great deal of confusion even within the negotiating process as to what the federal offer means because you haven't had the advanced time to work out what it is that's sitting on the table.

The dynamic of these meetings is one of junior-grade geopolitics, in the sense that alliances are important. The whole idea of having a premiers' consensus so it's harder to peel one or another off is extremely important to the provincial governments. You develop networks of friends and enemies. While I was at the first ministers' meeting there was one point where I wanted to get an idea of where the spin was going. If I'm going to do that, I just talk to my colleague from Manitoba or British Columbia. You have better relationships with some provinces than with others. Those relationships develop just as much on the basis of personality or political perception or partisanship as they do on the basis of whether you have a common interest at the meeting. It's a very chaotic dynamic, and a very chaotic process to work in. You have to treat everybody as an actor in that process that could mess things up or improve things for you by talking to the right person.

How Chaos Rules over Billions of Dollars
One story that I took away from that meeting is, roughly, a $2-billion story. You see, the other agenda item at the first ministers' September 2000 meeting was the so-called National Children's Agenda. In terms of the order of priorities to the premiers, it was very important, but it was still secondary to the health-care problem that had been on their agenda for a year or so. Yet because we didn't hear the federal offer until that very morning, we couldn't map out what that meant for the National Children's Agenda. By the middle of the day I was speaking to reporters who didn't know whether the roughly $2 billion the feds were putting toward the National Children's Agenda was in their offer for the Canada Health and Social Transfer (CHST) or outside of that. And that's $2 billion plus or minus the net sum.

There was a press conference midway through the meeting where the federal officials had to try and explain their offer to the media to counter some of the media spin and the rumours that were going around. At that press conference there were three different federal officials literally arguing in front of the media as to whether the $2 billion for the National Children's Agenda was in their own offer or out. By the end of the day there was rampant confusion within our delegation, within their delegation and within the media as to where this $2 billion actually was. I only found out days later that the money was in the CHST offer, which was a negative from our perspective.

Accountability of the Premiers

The group of people who are present at a first ministers' meeting is extremely small. In these meetings you tend to have the best form of accountability. Of course, it's very easy for premiers to come to these meetings and work these deals out because in the end they are the leaders of their parties. You get a sense at a premiers' meeting, in particular, that if a premier is cutting a deal, he or she has a pretty good idea that the deal has support at home. For the most part, particularly in meetings where the premiers are not making the decisions, the only real contact they have with their province is through a speakerphone. Usually officials from relevant ministries and the premier's office are on the phone, just checking to make sure that the premier is working within the negotiating parameters that were expected when the delegation left for that conference.

There are a number of ways you could make the criticism that these meetings are undemocratic. For example, there is often frustration from larger provinces, which are saying, "I get the same vote at such-and-such a meeting as the representatives from a new territory like Nunavut." In theory they do. Quite often the territories and the smaller provinces will watch the tennis match or chess game between the larger provinces and the federal government at the table and pick a side at the end. They usually will work with whatever consensus has been agreed to. But for the most part you have the chief executives (the premiers) of these governments at the first ministers' level, and ministers at a lower level, who are in a very good position to make a deal. If they really wanted to they could cut and then walk away from it and have no accountability. A classic example historically of this is the Meech Lake Accord scenario, where two provinces had not really sewed up the support of their legislature from the back end. And we saw the results of moving too far away from the position that your legislature or your caucus can support.

Who Holds the Cards?

The first ministers' meeting is a little unusual in that the federal government has a big home-court advantage. It's in the Lester B. Pearson Building (in Ottawa) and the provinces are told how many staff they can bring. Although the rules are fairly laid out by the federal government with some negotiation with the provinces, it's clear who the boss is. At ministerial meetings you can sometimes get fairly ridiculous groups.

I remember in Quebec City, for example, for a meeting of ministers of the environment. Ontario, the largest province, had an unusually large delegation of nine. It was about two or three people larger than normal because we had a replacement minister there who hadn't had time to be briefed on many of these issues. Meanwhile, David Anderson, the federal environment minister, who clearly had an agenda at this meeting, brought a delegation of 52, nine of who had some sort of title putting them in communications. David Anderson was sitting at the table as a minister of the environment, and behind him there was a huge phalanx of chairs of staff members who spent the meeting sitting there, waiting for the remote chance that the minister might have a question to ask them to help in his negotiating stance. Other provinces bring two or three staff members. Ontario usually brings five or six, and we're the biggest provincial government. Quite often the federal government treats these meetings as an opportunity to roll out the communications infrastructure. Roll out the staff. You have to wonder what the purpose really is of having 50 people in that room away from home for a couple of days.

Role of the Media: How They Drive the Agenda

In fact the media is much more central to the process in a first ministers' meeting than I think many of the premiers or ministers who are involved in these things would want. What you have is a situation in a meeting room where you often have abstract discussions about what a deal is going to look like or what should happen. But when the premiers and the prime minister or ministers at a lower-level meeting arrive, the first thing they do is speak to the media saying, "What are our objectives?" And when they leave the one thing they have to worry about is if there is no deal or no consensus, which will be the basis of judgment for anywhere from 30 to several hundred journalists, in the case of the first ministers' meetings.

To a certain degree the microscope of the media skews the decision-making process. I can't speculate on what everybody is thinking, but the key strategic element for a government in one of these meetings is how the result will appear in the media. Quite often first ministers' meetings or ministerial meetings are discussed over nothing more than a so-called communiqué, which is essentially an advanced, elegant form of a press release. In the case of the health-care deal that was worked out in September of 2000, the objective of the provinces was to get more health-care dollars into provincial coffers. But in our view the reason for the meeting was that the prime minister wanted to be in a position to stand up and say that he had brokered this deal to demonstrate that he really did care about health care at the provincial level.

Role of the Provincial Press Secretary: The "Spin"
The purpose of my job at the first ministers' meeting, and my job with the Ontario Intergovernmental Affairs Department, was to act as a channel between the ongoing negotiations and the reporters who were back outside. It's really troubling for a reporter. You feel some sympathy for them, in a sense, that they have to at the end of the day file a report on a big meeting that was supposed to be important. But they have virtually no information about what's going on inside. Really they are in a very dependent situation. It is the classic old meaning of the word "spin." They have nothing else to rely on but what a federal spin-doctor is saying on one side of the room and what I, as provincial media relations staff or spin-doctor, am saying to a reporter on the other side of the room. That is their sole source of information until the premiers walk out, and it makes it very difficult to judge what the final deal actually meant.

These aren't great working conditions for the federal government either. In these circumstances a lot of strange situations occur. For instance, I was standing in a media scrum giving background to reporters desperate for information. Across the room there was a federal spin-doctor selling a completely different message. At that point there was a chance that the deal would fail, and I heard her trying to downplay the deal's chances of success. The federal spin-doctor was saying, "Nobody came here because they have to sign anything. We are not expecting people to sign anything to go away."

And I turned and I couldn't help myself but to interrupt and say, "Then why are we here in the first place?" Here we had all of these staff crunched into these rooms, we had premiers running back and forth down the halls to these cubicles when they were taking breaks to negotiate. We had barely any information because we were working entirely off projections of what the federal deal meant. If we weren't there to sign something, why were we being crunched in here with a political deadline? Not a fixed deadline, but a real political deadline of what will be on the six o'clock news. What's the point? And of course I didn't get an answer to that question because she was probably just as frustrated as I was.

When All That Matters Is Public Perception

To a citizen looking at the system from the outside, it may seem to be irrational. It doesn't make sense that you would be talking about $2 billion in six hours. I want to make it clear from my personal experience, in all of the intergovernmental meetings I've seen, that it's not the players who are being irrational per se. The politicians there are better and smarter and more capable than many people in the public give them credit for. But when you lock any group of 13 or 14 people in a room to make a decision in six hours about anything, you're going to come up with a strange result. Particularly if they know that outside that room they have to justify how they came to a deal, often without knowing all of the details of the impact of that deal itself. It seems a little crazy. Many people I've talked to who were in that environment and have seen those sorts of meetings come away shaking their head and thinking it's some kind of a political hallucination to go through the experience.

Here's the most important point about the September 2000 first ministers' meeting — *this meeting was an example of a first ministers' meeting that we didn't need at all.* There was nothing stopping the prime minister from restoring the money he cut from health care in 1995. He could have stood in front of a microphone and done it on his own. But the beauty of this situation, from his perspective, was the premiers had asked him for this money, so why not get them all in a big room and trot them all out in front of the cameras a few weeks before the election? And the result is you have a headline that says, "Prime minister brokers health-care deal — nation builder." Instead of a headline that says, "Prime minister restores money that was cut by his government from health care several years before." It was a meaningful and interesting meeting for the provinces in that they got what they wanted. But the reason they got what they wanted was because they showed up for a necessary (from the PM's point of view) photo opportunity rather than a necessary meeting with the prime minister.

Cost-Shared Programs: Creating Tension Between Governments

There has been a lot of tension lately between provincial governments and the federal government and one of the reasons is cost-shared programs between the two governments. Quite often the federal government will say, "We're going to move into this area of jurisdiction," and they use their spending power to start spending in that area. Although this may interfere with a provincial program, there isn't always a debate over the program between the two levels of government. I think anyone who has been watching newspaper and news coverage closely will see that there is more and more resentment from the provinces when the federal government charges in with money into their political jurisdiction. In 1999 the provinces asked the federal government to sign the Social Union deal in order to prevent all these areas of jurisdiction from bumping into each other and creating conflicts. But at the time of the first ministers' meeting, our ministry's opinion was that the federal government was really leaving that deal out to dry in terms of actually living with the mechanics of it.

Cost-Shared Programs as an Election Strategy

Cost-shared programs between the federal and the provincial governments can involve billions of dollars. A provincial government can be left scrambling to figure out how they're going to implement the dollars that are being offered up to them. That creates a lot of cynicism in terms of negotiations between the provincial government and the federal government. In the health-care process leading up to that first ministers' meeting in September of 2000, there was a great deal of cynicism in the respect that many provinces spoke out, publicly and privately, that they felt that this was all part of the Liberals' coming election strategy.

Whatever you think about the partisan politics of that, in practical terms federal governments have often created cost-shared programs where they have said, "We'll come in. We'll pay half the costs for these new services or this new capital spending." The province is more or less obliged to come in and pay as well, otherwise they are declining free money from the federal government. So the provincial minister will sign the deal. The election happens. The cupcakes are rolled out and the announcement takes place, with the federal minister there cutting the ribbons. And a couple years down the road the federal money trickles away and goes toward a new cost-shared program. This is what creates the cynicism.

During the lead-up to the health ministers' meeting there were a lot of finance ministers telling the public and telling each other in meetings that they were beginning to see cost-shared programs as liabilities as much as assets. They didn't know if the federal government would be carrying its share two or three years down the road when it actually mattered.

These cost-shared programs skew decisions in many cases. In the lead-up to the first ministers' meeting in September of 2000 on health care, you would hear this opinion time and time again from other governments. Our government was certainly concerned about this. Cost-shared programs can be productive. But if they are not carefully designed to fill a specific need, they can be dangerous. They can lead provincial governments to spend money on areas that are not a priority in their particular region or province simply because the money is on the table. One of the premiers came out of the first ministers' meeting saying, "Look, it's hard for a politician to say no when there is money on the table." That is the problem with the cost-shared program when the federal government makes an offer. If you say no to a cost-shared environmental program, absurd as it is, it looks to the public, or at least to the media who's reporting it, as though you are refusing the environment. The clear implication — and the federal government feeds this implication — is that you're saying no to the environment in general, instead of saying no to working on this set of priorities on the environment. Somehow you're some kind of fool for not taking the federal government's money.

Provincial Priorities Versus Cost Sharing

When the federal government sets up these cost-shared funds, quite often its priority is to get visibility and impact in different provinces. This is a real problem. For instance, at the September 2000 meeting Health Minister Allan Rock presented a cost-shared program to buy new MRIs (Magnetic Resonance Imagers) for the provinces. But at that meeting you have a province like Saskatchewan that has problems just maintaining its basic hospitals. Their first priority is not more MRIs. They need basic facilities. They need nurses. They need to cover their

308

basic budgets. However, when the federal government says to a province like that, "We're going to provide funding for MRIs," the public expectation is that of course the provincial government is going to accept free MRIs. In the end the province is left holding the bag, paying the operating funds for these MRIs that may not have been what the province actually needed in the first place.

That's a representative example, but there are many provinces who are saying the same thing. "We have different priorities. If you force us into a cost-shared program that does a specific thing, you are essentially putting us under political pressure to take resources away from things that are our priorities and move them over into an area that you think is a national priority. These things are clearly provincial areas of jurisdiction for a reason, and we know best how to deal with them." Quite often I think the cynics among us in intergovernmental affairs look at a lot of federal funding offers as carrots.

Cost-shared programs and blurred divisions of responsibility between the different levels of government waste money on administration by transferring dollars back and forth. Our government's position, especially during the lead-up to the health-care conference, was that money was being wasted and badly prioritized in cost-shared programs or programs that weren't tailored to what was necessary. When I was in Intergovernmental Affairs in Ontario, we fought hard over the issue of labour and training. Both the provincial and the federal governments are working to try to train unemployed people and workers at risk of losing their jobs. But these two different levels of government are working at cross-purposes in spending training dollars.

Labour markets are different across the country, and the provinces can deliver the programs to exactly where the unemployment is. We have been asking the federal government to do that in Ontario for years. When we went to speak to them on this issue they wouldn't even discuss that kind of agreement with us. There are so many government MPs from Ontario that the federal government is losing ribbon-cutting opportunities if they put that program into the hands of the provincial government. However rational it may be to allow the provincial government to deliver the program, the federal government does not want the Tory provincial government to get the political pop from providing the training.

A Case Study on Health Care and Cost-Shared Programs

I can tell you one interesting story that relates to cost sharing. While I was with the Ontario government in 1999, they made a decision to take ads out against the federal government's involvement in health care. That was a very controversial decision, and I know for a fact that it was something the provincial government thought about a great deal. But the situation was this: we had a cost-shared program with the federal government, and they were not holding up their end of the bargain. In this type of disagreement there is no mechanism whatsoever to force the two sides to come to a resolution, whether it's the provincial government or the federal government that isn't holding up their end of the agreement. This is a major problem with Confederation. There is no court that will say, "You didn't keep your deal, so you will be punished." Or, "You are the side that has to pay up."

The provinces and the federal government tried to create such a process through the Social Union deal, yet every time the provinces have come to the table and tried to get that process in place, the federal government has said no. For a very good reason: when you have no dispute-resolution mechanism and the federal government has most of the taxing power and few of the responsibilities of program spending, it's a great deal for them. The only way you are going to persuade them to come to the table and talk to you about your cause, no matter how just it may be, is politically. Since nothing else was working in terms of trying to politically persuade the federal government that it was time to restore the cuts that they put into health care, we had only one political tool remaining. We bought some advertising and squeezed the federal government to the bargaining table by convincing voters that those cuts should be restored.

The ads were successful from the provincial government's point of view. We were happy to know that if necessary, you could use ads to get the federal government to the table again, if it was something you needed to do. Our ministry and our government made all sorts of proposals at the time to try and do things in a more intelligent way through a mediation process, but the federal government said no. So the ads worked for us then. I think it's entirely possible that you will see more of that in the future. There will be a point some day when an ad is going to be the solution.

Why did the ads work? Because the public doesn't really know who is supposed to deliver health care in Canada. Now, I don't blame the public because health-care financing, which is really the issue here, is very complex. The provinces in theory are the ones who are supposed to be delivering health care. Yet the federal government is moving into more and more "grey areas" of delivery. I think it's pretty clear that citizens believe the provinces are better at delivering health care because they're right there on the ground seeing the needs of people. So I think the pure educational value of getting that "provincial message" out is what got the federal government scared enough to come and meet with the provinces and discuss the needs of funding health care in this country.

The Ministry of Intergovernmental Affairs:
Overlap Between Provincial and Federal Governments
Increasingly governments in Canada, certainly our government, are finding that they have to have staff whose job it is to be an intergovernmental "staffer." I worked in a ministry called Intergovernmental Affairs for a couple of years. If you ask ordinary people to describe what it is we are doing on a daily basis, they scratch their heads. Intergovernmental Affairs is a very small ministry in the Ontario government, with about 40 staff who identify areas of overlap between the federal government and the provincial government.

Virtually everywhere there is a ministry there are different kinds of overlap. There is minor overlap in terms of provision of Aboriginal services. There is increasing overlap in health care, transport and infrastructure. There is overlap in terms of the environment and environmental issues. These are a big source of tension because provincial and federal governments have different policies and priorities in that area. If there is an area of government in the Canadian federation where there isn't overlap, that is a rare thing to find. There are departments and units in the Ontario government like the Intergovernmental Finance Unit, which is in the Ministry of Finance, just to figure out how all the money is being transferred back and forth between the governments. It becomes a considerable drain on people's resources just to understand what relationships they are committed to, as opposed to focusing on the delivery of programs in one way or the other.

Overlap in Government and Citizen Frustration
To a certain degree all of this overlap is very frustrating for people working in a level of government, as I did in Intergovernmental Affairs, but

it's much more frustrating to the citizen. As a citizen, if you're looking to find out who to complain to, for example, that your hospital isn't working or you are worried that there isn't enough funding of roads for the expanding City of Ottawa or if you are complaining that there are problems with your environment because you're a resident living on the Great Lakes, you don't know who to pick up the phone and complain to. In some ways it provides advantages to those governments because it allows them in desperate situations to finger-point at one another and say, "It's not my fault."

Clarity and Jurisdiction:
Accountability of Provincial and Federal Governments

It has certainly been the official view of the Ontario government that we could use some clarity in how things are run in this country when it comes to accountability for dollars. And while I'm sure the federal government will point back and say, "Ontario has invaded our jurisdiction now and again," I think more and more governments, like the Ontario government, are standing up and saying, "Let's try and get some clarity. Let's work out who does what."

Let's say there is a natural disaster or something like this. The Canadian public just wants someone in government to fix the problem, regardless of who has it in their area of jurisdiction, and politicians realize this. So until our system of government in its entirety learns to say no — and mean no — areas of jurisdiction will not be clear. Until the lines of control and communication are clear you will always have the temptation for one government or another to step in and say, "We can get more political mileage out of solving this problem more quickly than the next level of government." I think this is the source for a great deal of the government overlap that has been created.

I don't believe that the provincial government is to blame for the problems that we have with clarity. The belief of the federal government is that we have invaded several areas of federal jurisdiction, for example, justice and law enforcement. But I think, genuinely and objectively as a citizen as well as a political staffer, that the provinces are much more the honest partners. I have seen the federal government step into areas where it makes no sense, time and time again. Certainly there are complaints both ways, which is the frustrating point for citizens. When there is a problem, the first thing they have to do is to navigate through a group of people who are saying it's somebody else's fault. Sometimes it is somebody else's fault. But in the end, wouldn't we all like a country where we can at least figure out whose fault it is?

RITA BURAK

Rita Burak is a 30-year veteran of the Ontario Public Service (OPS), rising from a secretarial position to the most senior public servant in Ontario. As chief operating officer within the Ontario Public Service, she spearheaded a restructuring to transform the public service into a more effective, customer-focused and performance-driven organization, while maintaining its reputation for professionalism. She was the first woman to serve as Cabinet secretary.

TOPICS:
Biographical Information
Role of Cabinet Secretary
Politics Versus Public Service Neutrality in Decision Making
Political/Media Perception of Civil Service Neutrality
Public Servants' Motivation
Federal-Provincial Jurisdictional and Priority Conflicts
Federal-Provincial Relations
Role of Legislature in Federal-Provincial Agreements

Health Care
The Federal Structure of Canada: Division of Powers
The Public Service and Policy Mistakes
Ministerial Accountability
The Public Servant and Post-Rationalizing Decisions

Biographical Information
I left the public service in June of 2000, a 30-year veteran. I began my career as a secretary and ended up as the head of the public service and secretary of the Cabinet — so from secretary to secretary. I worked in a variety of ministries: Labour, Agriculture and Food, Housing, the Management Board of Cabinet. It was a wonderful time.

Role of Cabinet Secretary
A secretary of the Cabinet, whose official title is clerk of the executive council, has three roles. First, you are the deputy minister to the premier, which means you must advise the premier on a daily basis about the issues that are in front of him.

Second, you are the head of the public service, and when I left in June, there were approximately 64,000 public servants in Ontario. That is a very important role because you are entrusted with ensuring that the merit principle in the public service is maintained. That means no political interference in hiring and firing of public servants. You can be fired for incompetence or reasons like that, but not because of your political beliefs. The important principle of maintaining political neutrality in the public service is entrusted in that position.

The third role for that job is to oversee the decision-making processes that Cabinet undertakes and to help with the structure of government, those sorts of things. This means ensuring that the decisions of Cabinet are carried out. It's a bit of a dual role. The secretary of the Cabinet is in the pivotal position to help translate to the public service, the politically neutral public service, the will of the duly elected government of the day. At the departmental level that's done by the deputy minister.

Politics Versus Public Service Neutrality in Decision Making
At one level it's a very complicated process, and then at another level it's really quite simple. In the Harris government, for example, the government came in with a very firm political agenda with the Common Sense

Revolution. They had a clear policy and fiscal agenda and the premier was personally determined to ensure that they carried out the initiatives that they said they would.

Here's how it works: the civil service works with the incoming government to help them translate their political agenda into a policy and legislative agenda. An idea of one of the first pieces of legislation that the Harris government dealt with when they came in, in 1995, was to change labour legislation. What happened was a process of the public service working up some ideas based on what the minister of labour told the public service the interpretation of that initiative was. This resulted in a policy paper that would have gone through a policy committee, which all Cabinet submissions do. Finally it would get through Cabinet after everybody's had a kick at the cat. That would have led to a piece of legislation that gets put into the legislature, gets debated and passed.

Again, I talked earlier about a very important principle — the political neutrality of the public service. This means that you serve the duly elected government of the day. For example, in my 30 years in the public service I served the PCs, the New Democrats and the Liberals. In all three governments there were policies that I might have done differently, but I knew my professional responsibility and all public servants know this. Their professional responsibility is to help that government carry out their policy, even if it's not something that they personally agree is the best thing to do for the province or the country. If you can't accept that political neutrality, then quite frankly you should think twice about being a public servant.

Political/Media Perception of Civil Service Neutrality

Certainly first-time ministers, newly elected governments, people who have never worked in government and who have skewed perceptions of the role of the civil service, often come in with expectations that the civil service is going to thwart their every political wish. But usually once they come in and they start working with real, live, breathing, hard-working civil servants, they find that this isn't true. They really are supportive. The vast majority are professional and are trying to do the right thing.

The other influence on ministers in how they perceive public servants, if I may expand on this, is the media. Throughout my career I have been absolutely enraged at some of the ignorance I've seen in some of our journalists about the role of public servants. One journalist, who shall remain nameless, and who wrote an article just a few weeks ago about the federal public service, quite appropriately disagreeing with something the federal government had done, referred to federal public servants as being "co-opted." This is a person who doesn't understand the role of the public service and assumes that because they were helping the federal government carry out this particular policy, that they were somehow co-opted. They weren't co-opted; that's their job. Their job is to help the politicians get their policies through.

Public Servants' Motivation

Again, the vast majority of public servants understand that and not only understand, but want to serve the public. If you were to ask the average public servant, "Why did you join the government?" as opposed to earning, particularly at the senior levels, a lot more money in the private sector, he or she will answer with one of two responses: "I genuinely wanted to make a difference" or "I wanted to influence public policy in an important area." The vast majority of public servants feel that way and that's what makes it work.

Federal-Provincial Jurisdictional and Priority Conflicts

We have a great country, but we have a pretty interesting and complex federation. If you were to line up all of the departmental responsibilities that are shared between the provinces and the federal government, you would see a pretty complex picture of how we operate. Environment is a good example. Agriculture is another example and there are many more. So within that context of in some cases blurred responsibilities, and in the worst-case scenario, duplication of effort, there's a lot of natural tension that will come about when one level of government or another decides on a priority.

If you were to take the example of the infrastructure program, the provinces are looking at it from one perspective, the federal government from another. The federal government is trying to ensure that this expenditure is going to make sense on a national basis. Individually the provinces might have very different priorities for how that money should be spent. It will certainly be roads in Ontario, and in other provinces it may be water. In some provinces it may be local cultural facilities that need upgrading. There's a lot of give-and-take in how these things come together. A lot of work is done first at the civil service level, as programs are being developed — federal public servants and provincial public servants talking about what the criteria might be and trying, although not too early, to get into "How much is my province going to get?" This would lead to ministers speaking and ultimately some framework agreement on how the money should be spent.

Why do we have different jurisdictions working in the same area, or some of the overlap or sharing? Let's be professional and say some of the areas where we're sharing responsibilities are written into our Constitution. Agriculture is a good example. It was in the BNA Act that this would be shared. In other cases the joint responsibility for these subject areas has come about by agreement — federal-provincial agreement. And in each case it's been done for the best of reasons.

It's not the most efficient system in the world. Personally, as a public servant who has worked in a number of these areas and has had to help a government take very difficult decisions in the face of budgetary deficits, I believe that there is work to be done sorting out who is doing what and in cutting back some of the overlap and duplication. The challenge is, if you're going to enter into that kind of an exercise in Canada, that there are different views among the provinces. The political situation in the province of Quebec is a perfect example of where we might run into some difficulty if we were to embark on a wholesale reconfiguration of responsibilities.

Federal-Provincial Relations

I'm speaking to the fact that we have a separatist government in power. And would they even be willing to have a rational discussion about responsibilities at the federal versus the provincial level? I suggest to you they probably would not. As to how Ontario and Quebec have aligned themselves more recently on some critical issues, if you step back from the politics, there's a lot of logic in that the provinces are both large, in terms of the number of people combined and their contribution to the national economy. After all, we are neighbours, so there's a lot of practical reasons why we find ourselves aligned with Quebec on a number of issues that we have to deal with the federal government on.

Role of Legislature in Federal-Provincial Agreements

I think you have to look at the issues that are being dealt with at the first ministers' conferences. We certainly don't have the time to get into

Meech and Charlottetown conferences, but when I think of premiers' meetings that I've attended over the years, I know that there's an awful lot of work that goes on before those meetings come together. There's a lot of work and discussion at the bureaucratic level, at the level of ministers responsible and at the political staff level before the meetings ever take place. There has to be an agreement on the agenda and everyone will want to know what everybody else is thinking about a particular topic before they go into it.

There are a lot of federal-provincial meetings on a lot of topics. For example, the environment ministers meet quite frequently and the federal and provincial counterparts get an awful lot of work done that is of great benefit to the country. What is the role of the legislature in these meetings? Well, one of the biggest topics that we saw at the last first ministers' meeting was the agreement on what additional funds would be put into the health-care budget. That decision, I think, at the end of the day, is one appropriately made by the prime minister and the premiers. You remember the context — the provinces setting out what the real cost of health care was going to be in the coming years and requesting that the federal government share the revenues that they were enjoying as a result of the economy. The legislature certainly gets an opportunity to discuss and debate the health-care budget in each province, as those budgets go through the estimate process in the legislatures. The same applies at the federal Parliament level.

Health Care

We would need another whole series of discussions to do justice to the current health-care issue. As someone who's worked inside the public service, I know the tremendous amount of money that is being spent and will be spent on health care. In Ontario we are spending this year about $23 billion on health care. That represents 44 percent of the provincial budget and the projections are that it's going to continue to increase. That is a tremendous public policy issue that the public should be aware of and have some input in, have some debate about how we are going to deal with this and all the other things that we want to get done.

In respect to a clear constitutional provincial jurisdiction in this area, we should remember that at the time when we decided that (remember, it was the post-war years) growth was tremendous. We were terribly optimistic. We thought we could do this and there would be no problems in continuing to fund this forever and a day. Now we're finding out that perhaps it's a bit more difficult than we thought. It's not as easy as saying, "This is clear, why don't we just have one government or the other do it?" It's going to require a lot of thought and a lot of discussion, although it will continue to be delivered through the provincial governments. Because of our tax agreements, we're going to require that the federal government continue and, moreover, increase its share in health-care spending.

Recently there have been ad campaigns by the provincial and federal governments on their respective roles in the current health-care debate. Even though I've left the public service, I'm still a public servant at heart, and I make no judgment call on the expenditure of moneys for advertisements. But here's the context and it may help you understand the expanding health-care budgets, the tremendous worry that we have about the growth of health-care expenditures in the provinces, a bit better. Provinces really didn't get too upset about this until they found themselves being criticized by other levels of government about why they weren't doing better, why they were not rationalizing hospital amalgamation, for example. Suddenly they found themselves being criticized by, wait a minute, the federal government. They want to get the explanation across to the public that one of the reasons they've had to take these steps is that the transfer payments that the provinces relied on to help fund this tremendous expenditure were being cut back by the federal government.

The public really wasn't hearing that part of it. The public was seeing some things happen in the health-care system that they didn't like. They knew that the provinces were responsible for money going to the hospital sector, to doctors, for example, and so would focus their anger on the provincial level. On top of that the provincial government was getting some scorn heaped on them by another level of government. Wait a minute, we better just let folks know that part of the problem here is the federal government pulling back. For example, I'll bet the average person in Ontario assumed that the federal and provincial governments were funding, equally, health-care costs in the province. So the province took out those ads and explained, "Guess what? The federal government is only funding health care to the tune of about 9¢ on the dollar." Personally I think it is important for the general public to be informed about who is paying for what in this.

The Federal Structure of Canada: Division of Powers

One solution here would be to say, for the federal government to say, "All right, we will pull out of this. Let's change the tax arrangement, whereby we will take less money in taxes from you, the provinces, and you're going to deal with health care, 100 percent." But if I were the federal government, would I want to do that? What is the rationale for our federal government, if it's not to be a part of some of the fundamental issues that make us Canada, makes our social framework. If the federal government is no longer an important player in the social framework of our country, what is the role of the federal government?

If you say, "Let's go back to the way the country was supposed to be made," I would answer that obviously we are still a federation. A program like health care was not envisaged over 100 years ago when the country came together. There will be other programs, as we go forward, that we will not know today and that might be relevant in the future. There's nothing inappropriate in the country deciding at some stage of the game that it wants to embark on a new social program or a new program involved in the resources area. But we should do a better job. We can do a better job of working together and ensuring that we're doing it efficiently and effectively. I think there's still hope for doing that.

The Public Service and Policy Mistakes

I think it's pretty clear, assuming there is a reasonable level of resources to carry out programs, that when things, administratively and operationally, go wrong the public service does have to answer for problems. I think the situation has not changed dramatically over the years, and I'm thinking back over the last 30 years.

When it comes to policy issues, in recent years there has been a bit more scape-goating of the public service when great policy ideas go wrong. That is unfortunate, at both the federal and provincial levels, because the way our governments work is that Cabinets are ultimately responsible for approving policies. To then blame a public servant for something that didn't go over very well or that wasn't successful is not terribly fair. There has been a bit more of that recently. That's unfortunate because public servants are responsible for ensuring that politicians receive good professional advice, and helping the minister get all of the facts that he or she should have before a policy decision is made.

Once a policy decision is made the whole point of democracy is that you hold the elected officials accountable for those policies.

Ministerial Accountability

There have been a couple of instances where we have seen ministers try to put the blame on public servants. I can remember in Ontario, in the 1970s, that one of the most famous examples of a minister taking responsibility for a problem was Darcy McKeough. I can't recall what the issue was, but I think he was at the newly formed Ministry of Energy at the time. Something went wrong and he immediately said, "I'm the minister. I'm going to resign." And he did.

As we got into the 1980s and into the 1990s we don't see as clear-cut an acceptance of ministerial responsibility in every case that we'd like. Having said that, I think it's important to keep in mind that the world that governments operate in today is complex. I think it's really unfair to hold a minister responsible. A minister is responsible for a large department where on any given day any number of things could go wrong that the minister might have no knowledge of — some operational issue at a local level. The minister would have no personal knowledge of it and might not even have directed a particular operational policy. If something goes wrong, does he have to resign? Well, I think we have to think about that. I think we have to find a balance between the political backbone to stand up and say, "I'm the minister responsible. This didn't go very well," versus, on some fairly localized issue, expecting and having the opposition calling for the minister's resignation at every turn. I think somewhere there has to be a better balance.

The Public Servant and Post-Rationalizing Decisions

Let me give you a talk that I've given to public servants who've worked with me over the years. I hope it doesn't sound like a speech. It goes like this: Nobody elected us. We're there to help governments carry out their mandates and once a decision is taken, even if it's one that we don't think is the best decision that could have been taken, or if we disagree philosophically or personally with the way it's going, our responsibility is to help them carry it out to the best of our abilities.

At the senior level it also means helping the government explain their programs. Again, this is once a decision is taken. Is it a problem for a public servant to post-rationalize a program once there was a political decision? Is that the right thing to do? I see it this way. Nobody elected us, and the public is going to hold the politician accountable at the next election for what he or she does. Our job is to help them. It's a judgment call. I mean, if it's something that you find so offensive to your own personal principles that you couldn't possibly explain it or help rationalize it, then there are lots of jobs out there; you could go look for one of them. If you want to be a professional public servant, then you have a duty to help the elected government and to help the public understand what it is that this elected government is trying to accomplish.

PAUL TOUSENARD

Paul Touesnard is a civil servant and senior policy analyst. He worked on The Atlantic Groundfish Strategy within Human Resources Development Canada. During debates on what to do with the Atlantic fishery he was called to testify in front of several parliamentary committees.

TOPICS:
Biographical Information
Impressions of the Public's and Politicians' Interests
Politicians' Concern with the Short Term
Short-Term Thinking: TAGS
Program Design: Implementation
Length of Public Service Employment and Program Influence
Political-Bureaucratic Interface at Higher Levels:
Parliamentary Committees
"Planted" Questions in Parliamentary Committees
Types of Committee Questions Asked of Bureaucrats
Political Pressure and the Public Service

Bureaucratic Origin of Policy Options
Ministers: Representing Government or Bureaucracy?
Do Bureaucrats Get a Bad Rap?
Political Promises and Program Delivery
Government Transparency

Biographical Information
At the present time I'm a policy analyst for Treasury Board. I've worked for 20 years for the federal government here in Ottawa. I did a variety of jobs along the way, working on a number of different projects. The most notorious of those is probably the TAGS (The Atlantic Groundfish Strategy) program. And so I have some experience in terms of the dealings of the federal civil service.

Impressions of the Public's and Politicians' Interests
One of the things that I found amazing, in my thinking, is the way in which people seem to think that the issues which affect them are the most important issues, and that the issues which affect other people are not important at all. This sort of narrow-mindedness, if you want to call it that, is very usual. In fact, for someone to think of the whole picture is very rare. That's the first issue that you might want to keep in mind. The second is that people will freely accept handouts from other people. Over time they will become accustomed to these handouts and will even think they are entitled to them. But the efforts that people make to avoid paying their fair share are quite remarkable as well. There's quite an imbalance in these two extremes, and the efforts that people make to get out of paying taxes, for example, compared to how freely they'll accept government handouts is quite interesting.

Also, people are far more concerned about the present than they are about the future. They put a great weight on things that are happening in the current environment, as opposed to things which may or may not occur in the future.

What I've noticed as well, and I'm sure that you would come to the same conclusion, is that this also tends to be a cross-generational issue. It's that the older you get, the more interested you are in the present. And of course those people in power are usually older, right? So what could you expect they're going to be interested in except the present?

The final point that I would like to make is that partisan politicians are just that. They're partisan politicians and I think it's wrong to expect them to be anything but partisan politicians. From my observations, the interests that they serve are primarily their own. These include the people that are closest to them — that is, the party whose support they need in order to get re-elected, their constituents and, finally, the general public. To think of politicians as being interested in the general public first is kind of unfair, both to them and to the people who have these expectations.

Politicians' Concern with the Short Term

I think there are two reasons that politicians are preoccupied with the present. One is that the term of Parliament is approximately four years and it tends to follow a particular cycle. The first half of that mandate is usually made up of fulfilling promises that you made during the election. In proving that you're able to govern a country and do a good job, you have to fulfill your promises. Then in the third year of that mandate you have the time when you want to maybe think about the future and do something longer term. So maybe you have some tough pills that you want to give to the populace during that period. The fourth year is usually when you're building up for your next term in power and once again making promises and fulfilling obligations that you have. So it tends to follow a particular cycle. There never seems to be a good time, really, to do anything tough. Maybe in that third year, if things are going well. If not, then there's lots of time to do things, to hand out goodies, but not very often a time when you want to give the people tough medicine.

Short-Term Thinking: TAGS

I think that one of the best examples of short-term thinking was the TAGS program. This was an East Coast fishery program that was instituted in 1994. It was an attempt to appease the fishermen when the fishery had collapsed as a result of what was believed to be a combination of industry greed and government mismanagement. It was an annual, continuous, short-term solution in which quotas were set at the highest possible levels in order to appease the fishermen and the industry. Concern for the environment and the state of the fish stocks were generally ignored.

The program that was brought in, in order to help them, first NCARP (Northern Cod Adjustment and Recovery Program) in 1992 and then subsequent programs, generally tended to be income support payments to fishermen to sit around and do nothing. There were some elements of training for those people who wanted it, but there was no real enforcement mechanism in order to make people take the training to get the benefits. Typically it was just, "Here's the benefits, and we hope you take training." The bottom line was that it was an incomplete work program, which was rather shortsighted, even at the time.

Program Design: Implementation
Public servants are concerned with programs on at least two levels. One is the way in which the programs are designed, and then the other is the way in which they're implemented and used. You could have the best possible program design which takes into account all things, like job creation, economic development, retraining and other types of elements which you know would contribute toward a better solution. But if in the end the vast majority of the budget gets devoted to income support, then that's the way it works. You do have a certain amount of leeway in order to make the best possible suggestions, but the final design is one that rests with the ministers. These are the people responsible for that portfolio.

I suppose from time to time public servants may feel themselves in conflict with political decisions which are reached. I think that most people deal with that either by finding another job or by finding some aspect of the program that they can support. They work toward developing and enhancing that aspect of the program and hope that it's what gets implemented. I can't think of too many instances in my career where I felt a complete opposing view of what ought to be done. When that happens people move quite freely. There's lots of movement around in the public service from one place to another.

Length of Public Service Employment and Program Influence
Some people have been around for 30 years, but they haven't advanced through the ranks as others have. I think that the length of time that someone has been here isn't always an indication of their influence, nor is the position they hold within the organization. Some people at lower levels of the organization may be consulted. For example, while working on the TAGS program I met regularly with deputy ministers and associate deputy ministers, even though I wasn't at a significant

level within the organization. It was because I had the expertise in that particular program.

I think that part of the difference is that those people who rise through the ranks of the public service are those people who consider that to be their goal, as far as the career is concerned. Personally I've never had that as my goal. I like to do interesting work in interesting projects, but I've refused, several times, jobs at higher levels because it would be an imbalance in my work and personal life. I think that those people who serve at a higher level in the public service do so because that's part of their career goal. But I would add to that, that those people who serve at the highest levels are those people who are most comfortable with the connection between the political and the public service. Those people who are not comfortable with that connection either don't rise to those levels, or they refuse to take jobs at those levels.

Political-Bureaucratic Interface at Higher Levels: Parliamentary Committees

I've never worked in the deputy minister's office, but I've had a significant amount of dealings with them. At the highest level in the deputy minister's office, for example, they have to wear two hats because they have to serve and run their ministry and they have to deal with the minister's office. There are very frequent dealings with the minister's office, and so along the way it gets very difficult to separate what's political and what's simply administrative. These things come to a head, for example, when you have to meet before a parliamentary committee.

At parliamentary committee meetings, generally what happens is this. I've been to a few parliamentary committee meetings, as a witness at some, and what you do is try to prepare yourself for all the possible questions that some people might ask, not counting the ones that you've planted among the government members. Usually you're well prepared for those, but it's among the others that you're not sure what's going to happen. So you do research to find out what kind of questions the opposing members, particularly, might ask, or even some which the renegade members of the government party might ask. That is a little more challenging. Basically you put together a book and hope that you can flip quickly to the question that they've asked and provide a reasonable answer. You hope that you can provide an answer on the spot because if you can't, then you probably have to submit a report later on, which you don't necessarily want to do. It's a very interesting experience that I'd recommend to anyone at least once. After that you can see whether you like it or not.

The political realm is the political realm, and you certainly don't want to give the impression that the government doesn't know what it's doing; or can't answer their questions; or gives misleading or misinforming answers or answers that appear misinformed. The political realm will usually try, and on some occasions with success, to scope out what the possible challenging questions might be. If they have some intelligence, they (hopefully) might pass that on to you so that you're not caught out by difficult questions and don't make the whole department and/or the minister look bad. But that doesn't usually happen. They are usually questions that are more specific about the program that you are managing, or supposedly know something about, and to which you should know most of the answers.

Of course, they may ask some very obscure questions about some particular member of their constituency who had this or that experience with your particular program, and why did this or that happen? In such a case you may not be able to answer those types of questions on the spot, and you may have to get back to them. You are there as a representative of the minister, in some way, because the ministers do occasionally get called before these committees. That's not unheard of and happens from time to time. If you're supporting the minister or you're supporting the deputy minister or some other senior bureaucrat, then you hope that you have something enlightening to say about the question.

I think that in general the civil service does not look forward to appearing on parliamentary committees. It's looked at as being a lot of work because you have to prepare for a lot of questions that may never be asked. You also have to track what questions people have previously asked and how you responded to them. You often have to follow up with questions that you can't answer completely on the spot. So it's viewed as being a lot of work, but it's also viewed as being necessary because that is the link that the civil service has with Parliament and, indirectly, with the people of Canada whom they represent. It's looked upon as an obligation maybe, but not one that you often look forward to.

It is a risk every time you go before one of these committees that in answering honestly somebody's question, you will let the cat out of the bag or implicate some other aspect of the government policy, either in your own department or in some other department. There are risks that people face every time they go before one of these committees. So you hope on the one hand that the answers that you give are truthful, in that they do answer the questions that have been asked, directly. On the other hand you hope that your answers don't have any other implications that are unforeseen.

"Planted" Questions in Parliamentary Committees

Questions are planted all the time in the House of Commons. For example, the questions that are asked by backbenchers are often suggested by the ministers' offices of those respective departments. As part of Question Period there are questions that are asked by the government side as well. Those are often what you could call "planted" questions. The same thing happens in parliamentary committees where each member of the committee has an opportunity to ask a question while the witnesses are present. Some members of the committee who aren't particularly interested in the issue that's being discussed at that time may be open to the possibility of asking a question that the witnesses easily will be able to answer. This also may either strengthen or enhance the minister's particular view on that program or send a message that the minister would like to convey. Usually the members of the parliamentary committees are not the most senior members of the party or the most visible members of the party. They're usually backbenchers.

Types of Committee Questions Asked of Bureaucrats

I think there are several types of questions that committee members put to bureaucrats. There is the standard sort of question from the opposition members, where they're looking for fault. They're looking for somebody to blame or a flaw in the program that they can flog and make some political mileage out of. In some cases they're asking very honest questions because they just don't know, and they're simply trying to find out more about what's going on.

In some cases there are people who ask the most outlandish questions that would require absolutely perfect knowledge of everything that ever happened or could possibly happen. They think that the person who's sitting there on the spot is going to be able to answer that question. This is of course ridiculous, but these questions do come up from time to time. Usually those are questions that have to do with individual cases. I'll use the TAGS program as an example. The program had 40,000 clients. For example, a member might come up in a committee and ask a question about one particular client out of 40,000 and expect the people there to know the case that they're referring to, and then be surprised that they can't answer that particular question on the spot. It's actually quite funny when you think about it. You just say, "That's kind of a strange question. I don't know why anybody would think that we would be able to answer it." Then you take that under advisement and promise to get back to them with all the full implications and details of the particular case and go on to the next question. You hope they don't rant and rave too long about it.

Political Pressure and the Public Service
I don't find that political pressure affects my current job that much. When I was working with the more political programs, like TAGS, there was a lot more. It's not so much direct pressure, but maybe a pressure to be aware of what the political realities are: to second-guess or anticipate what the politicians are going to be thinking or feeling when you make presentations to caucus, for example, or presentations to some of the Cabinet committees. There's a lot of to-ing and fro-ing among the bureaucracy as to what will be acceptable to ministers. There is a lot of, "Well, this minister feels this way about that, and so you can't say this or that. Based on what they said at the last meeting, we think that they might support this or that."

It is up to the departments or the agencies, like the Privy Council Office, for example, to try and broker some of these issues, especially when there are several government departments and several ministers involved. They must try and broker some kind of an agreement between the respective elements of the different departments and come up with something that ministers, as a whole, will want to accept. At the highest levels, when you bring something before Cabinet, it becomes very political. It can't help but be because the political masters are the ones who are going to decide yes or no, or how much or how high you're going to do something.

These political considerations come back to the people who are involved in making that policy. For example, you may do 30 versions of a particular policy. You may do 10 on the way up, 10 on the way back down and 10 more before it gets back up to the Cabinet committee to try and get it right. Getting it right means it passes through a number of filters. Those filters are up through the levels of command in the civil service, from the various levels to the deputy minister who will have to make the pitch before the Cabinet committee and have the support of the minister's office. How this gets done, along the way up, is, of course, partly a political process because you have to know what the ministers will accept. It has to be partly an analytical process because you have to know what makes sense, from a policy perspective. In the end, every policy that gets adopted by Parliament is some combination of these two.

Bureaucratic Origin of Policy Options

Maybe there is a myth about the politicians running everything. I don't think that's necessarily true. I think that every policy that reaches the level of a minister, for example, has to have some kind of rationale behind it. Now, maybe it's not the policy that those people who worked on it would have favoured, but it can't be something that is without basis. There has to be some support for it in order for it to reach that level.

I don't think that there is ever a situation where a minister just decides something offhand and then everybody has to scurry around to decide what it is. I think that would be a very unusual situation, certainly from my experience. It may be that you present several options and you believe the analysis supports option A better than option B. The politicians in the end pick option B, which is not necessarily your preferred option, but it's one which there is some support for. Otherwise you wouldn't have offered it as one of the options. So I think that it's a question of degree, rather than a black-and-white situation where bureaucrats are suddenly forced to scurry around trying to figure out how to implement something.

Ministers: Representing Government or Bureaucracy?

I think that the Cabinet ministers more often represent the government than a particular department. I mean, they are the ones who are usually elected on a particular platform. I think that in a new mandate for a new government that's definitely true. Over time the situation changes, and if a government is re-elected for a second or third time, then the two become more or less entwined. It becomes difficult to see the separation between the government and the bureaucracy in that case.

Some ministers may be accused of defending the bureaucracy, although I think you have to think about what a Cabinet minister's interests are. A Cabinet minister is a politician who wants to advance his or her own political career. This is often the case, so I don't think that serving the bureaucracy would be necessarily something that would advance their own political career that much. Based on a number of factors, they probably consider that a certain approach is better than another one, whatever those factors are and whatever weighs on their mind at the particular time. Sometimes it may be some urgent, pressing need to address an issue that affects their constituents or a constituency that they support or represent. In this case they may favour some short-term solutions as opposed to longer-term ones.

In general, not very many decisions are made hastily. If you had one thing to take from this, it is that decisions generally are not made hastily and are made based on analysis. The analysis would address what is the best decision to be made; what is the best from the perspective of that backbencher, from the perspectives of the minister, the civil service, the public and various interest groups. That's a very complicated process and it's a very difficult one to find a balance between all of those different and competing interests. Normally the people who are the most vocal are the ones who have the most to gain or lose from the particular decision that's being made. Oftentimes they oppose it because it doesn't serve their particular interest.

Back to the first point that I mentioned, about people not considering other people's interests or the interests of the country as a whole. I think that is often where the press is coming from. They do not consider the interests of people as a whole. They are just looking for something that they can flog and will keep them going for a couple of weeks selling papers or whatever.

Do Bureaucrats Get a Bad Rap?

I think that in general, although they're more or less protected from it by the civil service, bureaucrats do get a "bad rap." I think that's probably true in a lot of cases. They are the nameless, faceless people behind the scenes who can be blamed when things go wrong but are usually not given the credit when things go right. Credit is usually reserved for the people who are in the limelight. It's always easy to say that this or that process was wrong, or this or that program is not being implemented

333

the way it should be, or if I were doing this, I would do it differently. People in the limelight can say those sorts of things because they're not going to be called to do any of those things. It's easy to say things that you'll never have to do in the end. I think that the civil service does get a bad rap because they're the ones who have to go on. They're the ones who have to face the clients day after day. They're the ones who have to explain things to other people.

Political Promises and Program Delivery

Promises that are made by the politicians and the bases from which they arise are not usually that outlandish in terms of where the civil service happens to be at that particular moment. It would be unusual for something to come down which is at odds with the prevailing bureaucratic direction. Occasionally that might happen, in which case it would be up to the government to try to find some kind of middle ground. If something is not feasible and it can't be implemented, that will certainly be fed back up through the chain of command. Oftentimes that will introduce a check on what can or cannot be done. The system does work in that particular way. However, there is an element that is introduced — in terms of politicians serving their interests, the interests of the party, and how they view those as being aligned with the interests of the country and the various interest groups represented in different ways. Does it make life more difficult? It makes it more complex. Sometimes it makes the choices easier because civil servants may be prone to argue with one another for a long period of time as to what has to be done or what ought to be done.

Oftentimes within departments there will be groups of people who will see things one way and other groups who will see things in a different way. There will be differences between people who view things from a policy perspective and those who will view it from a program or implementation perspective. So the kinds of programs that they would come up with would be quite different. Some would be very simple to implement and maybe miss the mark, whereas others might be very complex to implement.

Government Transparency

In terms of transparency, citizens probably think that government is not very transparent. The show they see in Question Period each day doesn't serve their interests; the questions that people ask are not answered; the reports that they receive are too complicated to understand. Citizens likely feel there isn't a mechanism whereby they can get their questions answered, whether it be from the political process or some other process. So from that perspective it probably is not seen to be transparent.

I think the point that people are missing is how complex issues really are. Issues are not so black and white as people might think. If you just compare, for example, an issue that you know a lot about. You see how that issue is portrayed in the press, then you wonder if how it is portrayed in the press is on a normal, everyday basis. Then you may wonder, what about the issues that I don't know very much about? How are they being portrayed? Are they being portrayed any better than the ones that I do know something about? Probably not.

People have a tendency to underestimate the complexity of issues and perhaps overstate what is in their own interest to believe and how they see the world from that particular angle. This goes back to what I said about valuing the present more and wanting a solution to a problem now. That's as if to say, "I want somebody to solve my problem now. I don't want to wait because somebody else's problem is more important than mine." The civil service has to balance all of these. So does the political realm, to a certain extent. It's a very complex process. The older you are, the more you tend to value the present as opposed to the future. This argues in favour of having younger people involved in decision making. I think that's an obvious solution to the problem. I don't know if this necessarily would work in the political realm, not if you look at how old people are who are members of political parties and at what stage in their career they attain influence. Having youth advisory groups or some other mechanism whereby people in whose interest it is to value the future can have a greater impact on how decisions are made would certainly be an advantage. It would be an enhancement to the system that we have today.

Chapter 9
The Press

MICHAEL HARRIS

Michael Harris is an award-winning journalist, author and national affairs columnist. For years he was a frequent host of the CTV political affairs program *Sunday Edition*. He also hosts a daily show on News Talk Radio 580 CFRA. He is the author of numerous books, most recently *Con Job*, a book that is critical of the Canadian correctional system and calls for a tougher approach.

TOPICS:
New Realities of Political Coverage
Concentration of Power and the Powerless MP
Easy Journalism and the Parliamentary Buffet
Harmful Effects of TV
Investigative Journalists: A Rare Breed

New Realities of Political Coverage
If you look at the 2000 election, most commentators felt that all of the important developments in the election were media-driven. Every time

a substantial debate began, it was quickly tripped up by some sort of personality issue or confrontation over that particular day's faux pas. As far as the city of Ottawa goes, I don't think there's any question that it's the story that gets picked up, rather than a story that's occurring, that gets all the play. It becomes a sort of a self-feeding ethic. You begin to believe that what you're reading in the paper is what's going on.

I think it's pretty disgraceful when you have a Parliament of 301 members and it's only the Cabinet members who get the coverage every day. Even that coverage is like unlinked items on a grocery list. There's never any follow-up in a scrum. Someone's pressing to ask their question because they have an editor to feed, and to that one reporter a minister gives out 10 unconnected tidbits of information. The MPs who are getting the committee work, who have really looked into an issue, are often the ones that never get any interviews, let alone an in-depth interview. And let's face it: very little committee coverage is done in this city.

Concentration of Power and the Powerless MP

I don't think much has changed for backbenchers since Trudeau said MPs were "nobodies 50 feet off Parliament Hill." I think that the backbench MP who can't get on a committee, who can't become a parliamentary secretary, let alone end up in the Cabinet one day, is a person who is basically a pawn in the game of chess. He's pushed up the board and down the board according to the party whip, and his own views on matters are rarely, if ever, heard. So it's really a recipe for frustration to sit in the back bench for your career in Parliament.

What I've seen over the years I've been in the business is a gradual concentration away from the elected member, away from the minister, right up to the top level. I don't think the power is held in Cabinet. I think the power is held in the PMO, and that's not just a function of our federal politics. If you look at what's happening in Queen's Park, no minister of the Mike Harris government moves without approval through the premier's office. In fact, here in Ottawa someone like Senior Policy Advisor Eddie Goldenberg has a lot more power than several Cabinet ministers. It's the people who make a full-time job out of the politics of our public life rather than public administration who decide when elections are called and who will be the spokespeople on the really sensitive issues. The people who are closest to the seat of power enjoy the ear of the prime minister.

For example, when the original Donald Marshall story broke in 1983 and 1984, Marshall had been in prison for 11 years for something he hadn't done. It was under the jurisdiction of the Government of Nova Scotia, but I found it impossible to get an interview with the justice minister of the province because the people around him closed the door. The ordinary members of that legislature understood what a potentially explosive issue it was, but the response of the people in power was to control the information. MPs are powerless for a lot of reasons. One reason is they are not privy to the top-level information of their own government. So you can imagine what it must be like on the other side of the House.

Easy Journalism and the Parliamentary Buffet

I think one of the poverties in journalism today is that taking a subject to book length is hardly ever done. Most news agencies can't afford it, and it's questionable whether it would hold the public's attention. There is the 15-second clip that everyone reads, but there's no follow-up story the next day. It's partially lazy journalism, but it's also easy journalism. It's like coming out and having your lunch from a buffet that someone lays out every day. A recent example is the whole thing about there being no prices in medicare. The very next day I did an in-depth interview with Allan Rock for two hours about whether or not that was true, and if it wasn't true, what had to be done to have things fixed. He gave very substantive answers, but I think the story only made page nine in my newspaper. In another newspaper we were on the front page one day, but the next day's latest rage had nothing to do with medicare. The norm has become this daily buffet of going from one subject to the next and covering mostly personality-driven stories. So yes, it's easy, it's lazy, and it's also the kind of *People* magazine ethic come to television.

Harmful Effects of TV

Television, I must say, is the hammer that most people use to pin down the news these days, not reading. You know, if you ask yourself, "Who is the most powerful journalist in the country?" I think you'd be hard-pressed to come up with an easy answer. It used to be people like Jeff Simpson — the commentary people, people of substance who knew the system, knew Ottawa and had a cultural memory. Now it's basically a dogfight every day to see who gets the best clip. I don't think any journalist individually is powerful. It's the medium of television, one medium out of the many that we have covering Parliament, which is the most powerful.

Some of the best journalism pieces I've ever seen have been television documentaries. Some of the worst I've seen is when people are, you know, wielding their vomit-cam and looking for the 15-second inane clip of the day. It totally depends on how the television people approach the task. It depends on who is doing the thinking behind the camera. When television works, it's the most powerful. When it doesn't work, it's the most destructive and dysfunctional, and most days unfortunately it's the latter.

Investigative Journalists: A Rare Breed
I'm not sure who started the process, but I think the end result, that the news has been dumbed down, is irrefutable. As a person who's essentially a writer, I would like to think that we have a chance to change that, just as the MP has a chance to change their now impotent role in our parliamentary system. It comes down to individual journalists working hard and selling stories to editors. So far I haven't seen a lot of examples of that. You can count on the fingers of one hand the number of investigative reporters whose work has made a real difference in this country. Andrew McIntosh has done some fine work. Jim Bronskill of the *Ottawa Citizen* is another example. But they are not the norm of the hundreds of journalists who work Parliament Hill — these two people are the exception, and surely to goodness one would think that there's a little more room for some others.

It's a harsh judgment of some of my colleagues and they probably wouldn't make me president of the Press Club tomorrow, but I wasn't in danger of being that anyway. I think that the business of journalism is about the reader, the viewer or the listener. I don't think it's about the people who purvey the news, who come in every day and purport to cover the news. It's about who's looking at it, the end user. I'm more concerned about their judgment — expressed in the number of books sold, number of letters to the editor or the number of mistakes they point out — rather than how many kudos you get from your buddies.

Don Newman

Don Newman was appointed senior parliamentary editor for CBC Television's national news in 1988, after 13 years working as a reporter, editor and anchor of *This Week in Parliament*. Newman came to work for CBC's parliamentary bureau in 1981, following a two-year stint as *The National*'s senior Western correspondent, based in Edmonton. In 1997 Don Newman was honoured with the first ever Charles Lynch award for journalism and received the prestigious Order of Canada in 1999.

TOPICS:
Power of the Member of Parliament
MPs' Influence Is in Caucus
Party Discipline: Why the Reform Debate Won't Amount to Much
Influence of Public Opinion on Accountability

Power of the Member of Parliament
There hasn't really been an erosion of power for members of Parliament. What has happened is, particularly after the 1993 election when a lot of

new MPs came in, many thought they would have more power than they actually did. In our system, for most of the 20th century and certainly since party leaders have been chosen by the parties themselves instead of by the party caucuses, power has drifted off to the Cabinet and then to the leader's office.

Members of Parliament still have power, but they have a different kind of power than perhaps they would like to have. When the Reform Party (now the Alliance) came in, I think a lot of them thought that the House of Commons operated like the House of Representatives in the United States, which of course it doesn't. We have a responsible form of government, not a representative form of government. I think that some of them were surprised to learn that, and since then they've been agitating for more powers. The backbenchers on the Liberal side kind of like that idea since the Cabinet has changed relatively little during the Chrétien government's seven years in office. They think if they can't become a Cabinet minister, then, hey, maybe the backbenchers should have a little more power.

MPs' Influence Is in Caucus

One of the difficulties in our system is that the one place where MPs do exercise a fair amount of power is in the party caucus, but the party caucus of course is private. Now, if the MPs really want the public to see how effective they are, maybe they should lobby to have the party caucus open. The caucus is where the backbenchers get a chance to talk to the Cabinet ministers and voice their opinions. At the end of the caucus meeting the prime minister sums up what he has heard, but he doesn't necessarily have to follow their advice. The best example of that is last fall's election. At the Liberal caucus about two weeks before the election was called, 31 out of 155 MPs went to the microphone and most of them — in fact all but one, I'm told — said, "I don't think a fall election is a good idea." The prime minister said, "The polls are good now. If they're not as good in April, you'll be telling me a different story and it'll be too late then." And then of course he went ahead and called the election anyway.

The bottom line is that MPs, while they don't have as much power as they would like, do have power in the caucus and the public just doesn't get to see them exercise it. Certainly within the parties the caucus has replaced the House of Commons as a place of open discussion.

When legislation comes to the floor of the House of Commons, you only have to listen to the first speaker from each of the five parties and you have a pretty good idea how the parties are going to vote. You don't have to listen to the other speakers.

Party Discipline: Why the Reform Debate Won't Amount to Much
There's no doubt that parliamentary reform is at the moment a hot topic. With the Alliance and Liberal backbenchers pushing hard for more power, I think there will be some parliamentary reform, but it will probably be around the edges. One of the biggest parliamentary reforms in recent memory was the election of the Speaker of the House of Commons. Until 1986 the prime minister appointed the Speaker after consulting the opposition parties, but not his backbenchers. Now that the MPs get to elect the Speaker themselves, it has happened, perhaps as recently as the last elected Speaker, that the person perceived to be the prime minister's favourite didn't win. It probably tells you why there won't be many more free votes in the House of Commons.

The government considers most votes a question of confidence. The ultimate confidence test is of course the budget. But the fact is, the budget is *the* confidence motion, and even if we move to more free votes, we will never have a free vote on the budget. The system just doesn't work that way. If the government cannot get the support of the House of Commons on how the money is going to be spent, well, then it has to resign, there has to be an election or the governor general has to invite someone else to form a government. It was the no-confidence motion on the budget that finished the Joe Clark government in 1979.

Members of Parliament can put their ideas forward in the finance committee and in caucus. They can also lobby the advisors to the finance minister and the advisors to the prime minister. The Prime Minister's Office has a lot of power. There are a lot of people who work there; it's just not the prime minister and his secretary. That's how MPs try to make their voices heard. But there's no doubt that on the budget they'll never see a free vote.

Influence of Public Opinion on Accountability
Some members of Parliament say that there is accountability and it's imposed by the media and polls. I'm not sure that the polls do hold

politicians accountable; in fact, polls tend to drive what politicians think. Public opinion has really changed political life and not for the better. Instead of leadership, we find followership.

GORDON LOVELACE

Gordon Lovelace was an editor at the *Ottawa Journal* from 1973 to 1980. He served as the director of information services for the Senate of Canada from 1984 to 1995. He is an award-winning humour writer for newspapers and television and currently works as an independent public affairs and communications consultant in Ottawa

TOPICS:
The Role of the Media
The Nature of Politics: The Importance of Image
Limits of Legislation
Public Frustration with Process
Flexible Finance and Options to React
The FAA: Flexible Instrument of Fiscal Accountability
The National Interest and the Bottom Line
The National Interest and Local Concerns
The Senate: Problems with Sober Second Reflection

Experience and Fiscal Responsibility in the Senate
Function and Benefits of the Senate

The Role of the Media

Does the media do its job in educating the reading public to a very high level so that we can fully understand and better participate? Oh God, I hope not! It appalls me when they occasionally try to get into this mode of educating the public because I spent so many years in school with somebody trying to educate me; I was very happy to get out. The first time that anybody puts a newspaper in front of me that tries to do the same thing as my teacher back in Grade 6, I for one will burn down the newspaper. I don't want to be educated and as a journalist I don't want to educate. I don't mind telling people what happened, but I'm not going to go out and start giving them Grade 3 economics so that they can understand what I'm talking about.

Let's remember the fundamentals. People want to be left alone; they don't want to be educated to a level so that they can participate in politics. Now, this may cause a certain grief to people because they see lobbyists and action groups grabbing hold of the political agenda and of the public purse and running with it, and occasionally they will come back and voice their displeasure through a vote and drag them back in a bit. But I can assure you that the media doesn't do a good job of even covering Parliament. The reason why is, first of all, they don't know anything about it, and number two, Parliament is excruciatingly boring.

The Nature of Politics: The Importance of Image

This is a town which is based on image. This is a company town, as you might have noticed, a factory where politics is used to manufacture legislation and laws. So certainly image plays a role; otherwise you don't get to be a player because nobody votes for you. For example, the way to get rid of somebody in this town is not to criticize them, slam them or hammer them. The real way to get rid of somebody is to embarrass them. To give you a case in point, the recent solicitor general and his little conversations on the plane. It wasn't the hammering of the opposition that really got to him. As a matter of fact, he denied it and everybody said he should stay on, but once the routine started getting on radio and TV and in the newspapers, actually making fun of him, he became an embarrassment. As soon as he became an embarrassment and indeed got embarrassed (and it's pretty hard to embarrass a politician) then he disappeared.[1]

Limits of Legislation

There's a fundamental law which was never passed, and that fundamental law is called the loophole law. It's actually more of a theory, a constitutional seesaw as old as our history which dictates that politicians, parliamentarians and legislators shall not be subject to their own laws. It's quite simple when you think about it. They should be above it because only by being above the law can they can go and create laws. Now, if we were to take a look at why we require such a thing to have politics and Parliament function, we see it's extremely difficult to put so much legalistic, regulatory pressure on politicians that they cannot manoeuvre enough to change their mind and therefore get elected again.

Let me give you an example to clarify what I'm suggesting. Imagine I'm a politician. I tell you I'm going to abolish the GST. If I don't abolish it, I could be in a lot of trouble, one would assume. But on the other hand, if I twist it enough, I can figure out a way to say that I'm going to abolish it and still not do it. That's a fundamental in politics. I think it was John Crosbie, in his book, who said, "Of course we lie to the electorate to get elected because if we told the truth, we'd never get elected." So that's part of the fundamentals of politics in itself and the overriding theory — that politicians should not be subject to their own regulations — comes from exactly that. There has to be leeway to allow politicians to react to changing political pressures, to react to changing times.

Public Frustration with Process

I think every little person who pays taxes, no matter what benefits we may derive from them, feels frustrated and the fact is, they can't have input or an attachment to government. It's the old line, I guess, out of an old stage show, *My Fair Lady* or something: "If only everybody were exactly like me, wouldn't it be a wonderful world?" I think we all think that way. You've seen the frustration of people saying, "This is how I would run it if I was running the infrastructure program." It's a great frustration to me, but you wouldn't be happy with the way I'd run it because I'd say, "The hell with the sewers, let them drink mud."

Once again, this is the division between the two things we want here. We want instant political action and we want to see the results tomorrow, so we want our politicians to bring in whatever it takes to do that: policies, legislation, regulation and the accompanying money. On the other hand, the same people who want this also want a bureaucracy, an accounting system, everything tightened right down to the last doorknob, that will administer and keep an eye on every dime.

Everybody wants goodies. The fundamental theory is that on one side you have the political and on the other side you have the bureaucratic and the overseeing which keeps an eye on the political. Your big frustration is you've tried to track down the proof of that and you haven't found it, and it's not surprising you haven't found it. The reason you haven't found it is because much of it is an illusion. Yes, there are systems in place, but how effectively can they all work in all their stages if we're going to get specific action on an issue by a certain date?

In politics it's like in so many other things: watch what you wish for because you actually might get it, and that's the difficulty. The political process, particularly the electoral process, is very much part of a wishful-thinking process. If we follow through and give power to our representatives, why should we be surprised when they take the fastest, but perhaps not the most efficient, route to fulfill our wishes? So should there be less government? By all means. Everybody wants less government. They haven't got around to the fundamental part of having less, which is having members of Parliament sitting less often. Let's have them meeting less often, never mind fewer politicians. Give them less time to do the work and the work will diminish. That means there will be less regulation, less legislation, less government and hopefully less money spent.

Flexible Finance and Options to React

We have parallels in Canada now with the United States, in which jurisdictions are trying, constitutionally, to attempt to make it impossible to bring in a deficit budget. It seems to be a very moral, ethically minded idea, but out there is still the concern of what happens if armed conflict breaks out, as with World War I or World War II, and as usual we have to refurbish the Canadian navy? We might have to go into the hole to do that. So even in a country as wealthy as the United States there is still an awful lot of political pressure not to have the lack of that option engraved in the constitution. We've got the same thing here and need that kind of leeway for politicians, so that if tomorrow suddenly something happens there's always the provision to do something different politically to respond to the winds of change.

I wonder what kind of narrow criteria a politician should use in this case? Should one indeed say, as many business concerns do, that government should be run as a bottom-line business. "Corporate governments." It's got a wonderful sound to it. Now, that of course would be very simple to administer. All we would say is that if your jurisdiction, let's say your province or your part of the province, isn't profitable, we'll shut you down.

I can assure you that if I were a politician trying to get elected in the next election, I would consider it an emergency if I were so narrowly held by financial strictures and good corporate management of government that I couldn't possibly get re-elected. Politicians survive because they are elected and re-elected. They need the leeway to react to the political forces that often run counter to good management. If we had good management, we wouldn't be talking about closing mines in Cape Breton today. We would have closed them 50 years ago; and of course Cape Breton would not exist anymore, which is maybe the way to go at it, but unfortunately in a political system, that's very untenable. So you can see the need for flexibility.

The FAA: Flexible Instrument of Fiscal Accountability

The FAA (Financial Administration Act) is a blueprint that wouldn't be a surprise to any accountant anywhere in business, or in government or in administration. It's there as a basic foundation of rules and I don't think you'd find very much in it which would be shocking. It's mainly a heavy-handed tool that operates like a kind of a conscience, which allegedly keeps everybody on track. In terms of being a great philosophical bible that politicians would consult, however — for example, before coming up with ideas — it just doesn't serve that purpose. The concept is that the FAA is out there as kind of a cornerstone or a touchstone supporting all the little manuals that you may have sitting in your accounting office. But I don't think everybody sits there and analyzes every piece of legislation with a view to whether it's going to pass muster with the FAA. No, I think bureaucrats can sit there — or anybody else — and say to you as a politician, "I don't think this is going to fly." If you start asking too many questions in your haste to get through what you want, maybe they'll wave the FAA in front of you; but I'm speaking figuratively because I don't think either you or I would be able to track down a copy very easily in this town.

Everybody talks about the wondrous Financial Administration Act. They seek it here, they seek it there, they seek it everywhere but they can't find it, mostly because I don't know that too many people have a copy of it. I don't know how many copies there are and I've never seen one myself. I don't think the Senate ever had one. I inquired some time ago and nobody seemed to be able to track one down here. It kind of drifts around, out there in the background as kind of a bogeyman, and that's what it is. It's used by bureaucrats like myself to scare politicians so they don't go too far in fulfilling their promises.

It's sort of like the old Soviet Union's constitution, which was definitely one of the best in the world. Even today most legal experts will tell you that it's beautifully crafted and beautifully drafted and obviously if any country had followed every one of its rules properly, it would be absolutely a paradise on earth. The FAA is the same thing and I think you've got to remember what lawyers do and why they cost us so much money. When we insist, just as we insist with our politicians, to a lawyer that we want an ironclad contract which won't let anybody wiggle an inch, of course at the same time we also want a way to get out of it ourselves, if need be. So the FAA can be understood in exactly the same fashion, which once again brings us back to leeway and flexibility. Sure it's out there, but it's like a bookend that can fall off if we add one more volume.

The National Interest and the Bottom Line

I think this comes down to the great fundamental here, to quote an old adage, "We have seen the enemy and he is us." We deserve the government we have, we deserve the politicians we have and we deserve the political and financial administration we get because that's what we insisted on.

It's interesting to me, many of these debates that go on across Canada about the national interest and the bottom line versus our national vision. What happened in the case of the CF-18 repair contracts years ago was that there was a choice. The contract was either going to go to Winnipeg or to Montreal, and despite the fact that Winnipeg perhaps would have been a better deal economically, it went to Montreal. Why did it go to Montreal? The government wanted more votes in Montreal and it worked; they got more votes. Now, they did some polling asking Canadians how they felt about this, and they said it should always be the bottom line when it comes to this sort of contract. Then they asked Canadians if they agreed with this even if by following such a method your town or city were to lose business. Would they still support what they just said? They all said no; the bottom line is to be the absolute criterion in good government — until it takes away something from me locally and then we totally disagree with that.

So the fact is, that's what politics is. We all think it's dirty, until the time comes that we're going to lose something or we want something that we don't have, and then we insist on it, we revert to politics.

Already you can see in just one issue everything that we're talking about here, in the massive movement in Canada over the past few years to become fiscally responsible and to let that translate into political action. Things did change and now we have almost every jurisdiction in Canada showing a surplus. The aim was to get rid of the deficit and, after getting rid of the deficit, use all of those surpluses to pay down the debt. This sounds correct and you and I would do this at home; however, when we apply that same good home reasoning to the political system we see something different. What happened as soon as we started showing our first surplus was that the same frugal, reasonable Canadians, you and I, wanted to forget the debt and wanted our money back through tax cuts, more money for health care and more money for pensions. As soon as the first little bit of financial heat was off, we wanted to get back into spending. So once again our fundamental problem is balancing the fiscal responsibility we say we want with the reality of what we turn around and ask for from our politicians.

The National Interest and Local Concerns

I don't think it's a matter of weighing the good of the country versus somebody's short-term political preferences. The good of the country, I always thought, ends at the end of the driveway that belongs to most Canadians. That's just about as far as they look in terms of national vision. I don't think too many Canadians think very much in terms of great national concerns because we are not an international world-playing power that foments much national concern. This is not so much a country, in terms of a great huge place, either spiritually or geographically, so much as a great long, skinny, narrow little piece of real estate that follows railways and highways along, huddling to the U.S. border.

This does not really encourage national vision, does it? So the fact is, wherever we are on this little chain, that's where we pick up our little pieces of the pie and a good politician is the one who takes care of his own backyard.

When politicians come to Ottawa, what they're doing is looking for something that's big at home, and all these little things to you and me from outside are big at home. Eventually these little things become part of a huge outlay of funding, they become extremely complex and that's where we get our deficits. I think people will support each other's projects simply for the reason that they know that all of these little projects are important. I mean, a good politician is one who knows the value of a culvert out on a local highway. He knows that issue is going to get him a lot more votes than any long, involved speech he might give about human rights in a foreign location.

Big news back home will get him re-elected and that's not a sad statement at all. I mean, we created a federation so that we could bring our local concerns to Ottawa. It's very simple; that's why Ottawa's here, as a kind of halfway spot between all the hagglers. That's exactly what our politicians are supposed to do: take our little local concerns to Ottawa and try to sell them, and I don't think anybody should be ashamed of that. I think what the electorate wants and what the resident in any governmental jurisdiction wants is, fundamentally, to be left alone. Their priorities are, number one, don't bother me and, number two, plow my roads, remove my garbage and make sure the drinking water is clean. Those are the main concerns and they don't give a fig or a fiddle for most of the issues which are generally created by political science majors or people who probably never work for a living.

The Senate: Problems with Sober Second Reflection
The political veterans in the Senate here ironically are probably closer to the business administrators that everybody claims they want in government. These are bottom-line people and perhaps that's why we have a Senate and why it was created: to be that kind of overseeing body.

They do a pretty good job of overseeing, but that causes political problems. I've been here in the Senate for 15 years and I've seen an awful lot of occasions of political pressure from Canadian national-vision people who come up with an idea, but no conception at all about what the economic consequences would be. I remember one occasion, back in the 1980s on a beautiful, lazy Friday in June, when one MP stood up and put forward a private member's motion that it will no longer be Dominion Day on July 1; it will be Canada Day. By golly, it went through because nobody was paying attention. Whip! All three readings in one afternoon.

We know it must have been an important thing because the next day *The Globe and Mail* announced that from then on July 1 would be Canada Day. Now everybody was cheering this great movement away from our colonial past, we would be Canadians on Canada Day and act like great national Canadians. The only trouble is, they didn't examine an awful lot of the bottom-line material that might be created by this citizens' movement. But the Senate did and they found something like 14 separate acts, regulations and related legislative ephemera which might cause problems.

If the Senate had acted very quickly on the Canada Day issue, the prime minister at the time, Mr. Trudeau, might have been standing on the front lawn saying, "Isn't it wonderful? Welcome to your first Canada Day," with nobody else there because under some of the related regulations and acts we as Canadians don't get Canada Day off, we only get Dominion Day off. All of this legislation would have to be changed, otherwise the bottom-line businessman might take a look and say that he doesn't have to give anybody the day off on Canada Day. The law says employees get a day off on Dominion Day, but now they won't because they changed it. We prevented this from happening in the Senate. These changes didn't occur for a year but life went on just as it did before. The country did not fall apart because they had to wait another year for Canada Day, which we now enjoy exactly the way we always did as Dominion Day, and we get the day off to celebrate it.

Believe it or not, legislation is not generally pushed forward by people who want it in 10 years. Most Canadians, as the people ultimately who initiate the need for legislation, have the patience of a boiling tea kettle. So I don't think anybody comes up with a policy concept or an idea for legislation with the idea that we're going to spend years debating it before we pass a law. Generally we're in a bit of a hurry and certainly things often need a little more thought, so they push it through in the House of Commons where they can have their debate. They have a fairly hurried debate and they send it to the Senate where it's supposed to go slower, but as soon as it goes slower the public gets outraged and accuses the senators of stonewalling the legislation for whatever purpose. If on the other hand they put it through in a hurry, which is what the House of Commons wants, then they're accused of rubber-stamping.

Experience and Fiscal Responsibility in the Senate

Having been here in the Senate for many years, I've seen some of the talent down in the other chamber that we elect and they scare me. When the Senate takes in a great spate of MPs, they pretty well ruin the place because they double our budget. In 1984, for the first time in our history, we actually did get an awfully large number of MPs who were shipped down by Mr. Trudeau on his retirement. He filled every seat, bench, crevice and windowsill he could with these people and they were indeed extremely demanding. Rather than having three of them share an office, they all wanted a lot of things and our budget went crazy. I think their freewheeling and free-spending ideas must have come from a different philosophy because the Senate has always traditionally been an excruciatingly cheap place. I think it's because the MPs were elected and had got used to demanding to spend money. I think it's the ones who are appointed and never were elected who were always penny pinchers.

I think the Senate's going to survive because after a popular election, that's when we're all involved: voters, volunteers; even if we read about politics we get involved. This involvement often brings sweeps of change and that fills up the House of Commons with all these fresh-faced, very local people, trundling in with a new mandate and new ideas, who have to start suddenly taking care of business. They've never been here before and they're not really in a position or in a mindset that would lend them to fiscal responsibility and the proper running of our finances. They had to run little budgets at home, but they didn't get elected by running out on the hustings and making speeches about taxes, deficits and debt. They came in here on a wave of local promises.

So now suddenly we form committees and these folks not only don't want to be on the fiscal responsibility committee, they aren't trained to do that. Moreover, it isn't banking, accounting or bookkeeping acumen which determines whether a person is going to get on the House of Commons finance committee. People are placed because of the need for diverse and varied representation on committees from the specific communities and/or positions elected persons represent, no matter how narrow and regionally specific they may be. It's done according to politics and we know that politics doesn't have very much to do with good fiscal management. Often they don't go together: if you're a good fiscal manager, you may never get elected. So we have all these new people running around trying to find the washrooms in the House of Commons running the country!

Function and Benefits of the Senate

Recognizing this, the Fathers of Confederation came up with the idea to take a group of very wealthy, old, white males and appoint them to the Senate so they can keep an eye on the elected members down in the green room, and that's what senators have been doing for years. People may complain about it, but senators have done this in their own funny little way by stalling, by putting things on a backburner and very often by quietly going up to their House of Commons colleagues in the back corridor and dissuading them from unwise or ill-advised courses of action. The Senate has been doing that very quietly, very effectively for 130-odd years. People don't talk about it because they don't like to be embarrassed in the House of Commons when somebody points out that they're not able or expert on many of these fiscal things. On the other hand, the senators aren't elected, so they have to relent once in a while to allow the will of the popular electorate to hold forth.

They're here when they're needed and unfortunately that's the type of government we used to have, the type the Fathers of Confederation created, which was a government when we needed it. Now we have this factory where politics is used to manufacture legislation and laws, and as a factory it has become self-fulfilling, self-aggrandizing and self-sustaining. But actually our system of Parliament was set up based on the bottom line. Why would you bring an MP to Ottawa during haying season, for example? He might lose his farm, so of course they didn't. Instead they would bring them here in things called "sessions": a couple of weeks to take care of pressing issues, pass a couple of bills, pay the three civil servants. And then go home to plow. The Senate reflects how Canadians have voted over the last 50 years; the House of Commons reflects how they voted a few months ago. And that's always going to be the case because that's what the Senate was designed to be.

Now, however, that has changed everywhere else in the electoral system. We've got elected officials around all the time and that's dangerous because they're in a sandbox filled with the potential for legislation and politics, and trust me, they're going to play in it! We want to keep them away and that's why the Senate is good. All we do is bring them in once in a while, when other members have really fouled up, and let them fix things by delaying or killing a proposal. The more they stay away, the fewer problems they can cause. Believe it or not, this is probably one of the first discussions that has ever been held in this country in which somebody actually suggested not lowering the number of politicians, but lowering their opportunity to get together and cause damage, allegedly on our behalf. So maybe it'll expand from here, who knows? But I for one, like a lot of Canadians, was very happy during a period from about early 1979 right through until almost two years later. What happened during that time, of course, was that the Joe Clark government came in, for the Conservative summer vacation in power. Then, of course, they fell on a budget, so that budget never came in. And then the Liberals took a long vacation after they got in, so we didn't have a budget for almost two years. That meant taxes on cigarettes didn't go up, taxes on beer didn't go up, taxes on gas didn't go up. This was a very happy country for two years because we didn't spend a dime. Everybody was happy. You see what happens: if you keep them away from any possibility at all that they can get near that money pot, your problems are largely solved.

NOTES

1. Lovelace is referring to an incident involving Andy Scott, who resigned his position as solicitor general of Canada in November 1998. Mr. Scott was on a small flight around the beginning of October 1998 and was overheard by opposition MP Dick Proctor (NDP) discussing, with his seatmate, the APEC inquiry into how demonstrators were treated. Proctor took notes and made public in the House of Commons that Mr. Scott was "prejudging" the outcome of the inquiry. The resulting media scrum and pressure on Mr. Scott resulted in his resignation.

Chapter 10
The Executive and External Mechanisms of Control

Patricia Adams

P atricia Adams is an author, editor and economist, and the executive director of Probe International, an independent think tank and environmental watchdog. Her books include *In the Name of Progress: The Underside of Foreign Aid* and *Odious Debts: Loose Lending, Corruption and the Third World's Environmental Legacy*. She has worked on a variety of international development projects and is a co-founder of the International Rivers Network and the World Rainforest Movement, as well as an associate editor of the British magazine *The Ecologist*.

She has appeared before congressional and parliamentary committees in the U.S. and Canada, has written numerous editorials for major daily newspapers and has appeared on many of Canada's major radio and TV news and current affairs programs.

TOPICS:
**Nature of the Export Development Corporation and Disposition
of Funds
Political Interference**

Access to Information
The Auditor General
Lack of Parliamentary Scrutiny
Self-Disclosure Policy
Loan Problems and Borrowing on the Taxpayer's Credit Card
The Canada Account: Loans Too Risky Even for the EDC
Problems with the EDC: Harm Caused by Unsound Subsidy
Subsidy of Foreign Interests
Subsidy of Social Injustice
Subsidy of Social and Environmental Degradation

Nature of the Export Development Corporation and Disposition of Funds
The Export Development Corporation is a Crown corporation that subsidizes Canadian exports and foreign investments in other countries. It does so virtually in secret since it is not subject to the Access to Information Act. It supports approximately $45 billion a year in Canadian exports and foreign investment. Of that $45 billion, about $18 billion is guaranteed by the Canadian public, so it is operating on Her Majesty's credit card and putting taxpayers at risk.

The Canadian government essentially uses the Export Development Corporation as a slush fund. It is not subject to public scrutiny and Parliament does not have adequate controls over it. Moreover, the auditor general is legally bound to not disclose details discovered about the Export Development Corporation. As a result, it's an institution that can be used for cronyism and it creates an environment that can lead to corruption. Essentially it amounts to an avenue that can be used for corporate welfare. Funds are delivered to corporations that are politically well connected or that are in constituencies that are politically important to the government.

For example, suppose an exporter wants to build a hydro dam such as the Three Gorges Dam project on China's Yangtze River. The private sector won't touch it because the project is far too risky and much too expensive. Politically the project is causing problems in China, causing great instability and social unrest. It's not even economically efficient since it's going to produce power that is three to four times more expensive than the competition. Canadian companies that want to build the project will get subsidized funds from the Canadian government through the Export Development Corporation, which will lend the money to the Chinese government. The Chinese government will then promise to hire the Canadian companies to actually build the project.

Political Interference

The EDC is hiding its cronyism by hiding politically motivated loans. By all accounts, there is regular political interference in the lending decisions of the Export Development Corporation, but the public, at the moment, is not allowed to know the individual projects that the Export Development Corporation is supporting. In the future we will be allowed to know those projects, but that's it. We can't see their reasons or economic analysis for financing a project. We will only be able to see some of their environmental analysis, which will be too late by the time it's disclosed. We can't even know which particular loans have failed, and the Export Development Corporation has actually lost lots of money. Their loans to many Third World governments were not paid back, but we are not allowed to know which countries have not paid those debts back. We're not allowed to know, for example, which cost subsidies the Export Development Corporation is using within the corporation to make money on some projects to subsidize others, for example, nuclear reactors to China.

The motivation of the Canadian government in supporting the EDC boils down to vote-getting. It's supporting politically well-connected firms in important constituencies. By all accounts, Bombardier is a major recipient of EDC funds, and nobody knows for sure exactly how much they're getting from the EDC because it's not disclosed. Many people have called the EDC Bombardier's bank. One of the reasons why Bombardier is a major recipient is because it is politically important to subsidize firms in Quebec. The prime minister has made numerous statements in which he has said that one of the ways we're going to keep Quebec in Confederation is by playing the international trade card. When you look at the statistics, there's a disproportionate share of EDC funding going to firms in Quebec. These regular subsidies to Bombardier amount to raw patronage for political purposes.

Access to Information

The Export Development Corporation is not subject to the Access to Information Act. When the public defines what sort of information it would like to get about EDC's activities — for example, which hydro dams or coal plants it is building or which companies are receiving money to support their exports — we do not have the right to find that information out. The citizen knows very little about the Export Development Corporation because the EDC is not obliged to disclose information regularly. When the public decides what sort of information it would like to know about the EDC's activities, it simply has the door slammed in its face. The EDC can say that they are not subject to the Access to Information Act and are therefore not obliged to disclose this information.

The World Trade Organization has sided with Canada, saying that these subsidized loans to Bombardier and Northwest Airlines aren't subsidies. But part of the problem that the World Trade Organization has had, too, is access to information. They have complained, as has the U.S. government, that Canada is being too secretive. Canada is not disclosing the necessary details to adequately assess what the EDC is doing.

The Auditor General

The auditor general does a financial audit of the Export Development Corporation every year, but only submits a one-page letter that is reproduced in the EDC's annual report and gives no detail at all about its operations. The auditor general also does what is called a "special examination" of the EDC every five years. This essentially looks at the economy, the efficiency and the effectiveness of what the EDC is doing, as the auditor general would do for any other government institution; however, the auditor general is not allowed to disclose this to the public. He must give the report of his examination to the board of directors of the EDC. If he feels that there is something in the report that the minister responsible for EDC should be aware of, then he can bring it to the minister's attention and he can request that it be given to Parliament. But he must consult with the minister and EDC before he discloses it to Parliament.

When we asked for the auditor general's reports that were done in 1999 and in 1994, the EDC responded that these are private documents. Neither document has been submitted to Parliament, so Parliament has not seen them either. We also did an Access to Information request for the 1994 report, to the ministry for international trade, and they reported that they did not even have it in their office.

Lack of Parliamentary Scrutiny

Parliament, too, has only marginal oversight over the activities of the EDC. At the moment it can review the proposed future plans of the EDC, but members of Parliament have no powers. They can occasionally review proposed changes in legislation but all they can do is comment. At the end of the day, if the committees review a proposed legislation and those committees are dominated by the government, then they simply approve it, the actions of Parliament amounting to that of a rubber stamp. The EDC is already is a very secretive institution and it is arguing for even less disclosure and less scrutiny by Parliament. The EDC is actually arguing that its status be changed under the Financial Administration Act so that Parliament would lose even the right to examine the EDC's proposed plans.

Self-Disclosure Policy

Currently the EDC has introduced what they have called a disclosure policy. It is essentially no better than the status quo since it gives total discretion to the EDC to decide what to disclose and what not to disclose. One of the main arguments that they make is that the corporation should decide what is disclosed because this is commercially private information that should not be available to the public. Our argument is that the EDC has got its priorities backwards. Since it is a public institution operating on the public purse, it has first and foremost a responsibility to the public. It should tell its corporate clients that if they do not want to borrow money from a public institution like the EDC and accept those rules of disclosure, then they could borrow the money from private financial institutions instead.

Loan Problems and Borrowing on the Taxpayer's Credit Card

The Export Development Corporation operates on Her Majesty's credit card. It issues bonds that are guaranteed by taxpayers, in effect borrowing money at a lower rate than the private sector financial industry can. It automatically gets subsidized money and also does not have to pay taxes or reinsurance premiums. It gets a number of subsidies this way and also gets compensation from the government when it writes off any loan that it's not able to collect on. So there are a variety of subsidies that allow it to make itself look profitable when it really is not a commercially viable institution, given its loan structure.

Since the EDC can raise money to finance projects that are not economically viable and which the private sector would not lend money to, taxpayers are essentially taking on the risk of bad loans. In some cases the EDC can apply pressure through the Canadian government to get repayment. For example, for many of the Third World debtors who were not able to pay the money back, the government simply renegotiated their loans or cancelled them through an institution called the Paris Club. The government then compensates the EDC to the sum of about $800 million by simply making a transfer of funds from the Consolidated Revenue Fund and propping up their books.

It is not a healthy institution financially because its debt-to-equity ratio is too high. It has far more low-quality loans than a private sector financial institution would, and yet it can continue to operate because it has access to the public purse. In fact, if you made the Export Development Corporation act like a private corporation that pays taxes, accepts its own losses and borrows money at private sector commercial rates, it would be losing money.

The private sector is far better at investing money efficiently and in creating jobs than the government is. The EDC argues that it's creating these jobs, and if it didn't fund these projects the jobs wouldn't be created. The premise behind this claim is patent economic nonsense because every time the Export Development Corporation borrows money, it raises interest rates for the private sector. It raises the overall borrowing cost for the government and ultimately for taxpayers. It would be far better to just leave the Export Development Corporation out of it and let the private sector make these investments. What we have found is that the private sector is much better at internalizing environmental risks and social risks than the government is.

The Canada Account: Loans Too Risky Even for the EDC
There are some projects that even the Export Development Corporation is too embarrassed to fund or would adversely affect its financial standing. Generally they are projects that even by the EDC's relaxed standards are much too financially dubious for the EDC to carry on its corporate account. For support of these the government uses the Canada Account, a $13-billion fund that Cabinet can use to spend on projects that it deems to be of national interest. This account gives Cabinet the right to support projects for any reason it wants to. These projects include

nuclear reactors in China and in other countries as well. Cabinet decides by decree whether or not to support a project and the EDC administers the fund for Cabinet.

The EDC is uncomfortable with the Canada Account because the Export Development Corporation raises funds on international capital markets by issuing bonds and maintaining a façade of financial soundness. That means that they have to keep certain projects in certain countries off their books because even by the EDC's standards they are much too risky. These are hidden in the Canada Account and Cabinet makes decisions to finance them, but the EDC administers that fund and gets paid by the government for administering it. Although such projects are said to be in the national interest, it's very difficult to get information about them. Also, the public is never able to properly scrutinize the operations of Cabinet when it comes to the Canada Account or the Export Development Corporation when it's spending money on its corporate accounts.

Problems with the EDC: Harm Caused by Unsound Subsidy

Although the Canadian government may claim that Canadian exporters depend on the EDC, I disagree. The Export Development Corporation's involvement in this sector has stifled the development of the private sector's financial industry to finance exports and foreign investment. The insurance and banking industries have made this case to the government time and time again. It's really a fallacious argument to say that Canada would not be exporting without the EDC. If anything, it's quite possible that EDC is actually stifling the development of the export sector. In any case, if it turns out that some of the firms that the EDC is supporting are simply not economically viable firms, then it doesn't make any sense for Canadian taxpayers to be subsidizing them in the first place.

The Canadian government is a leader in financing bad projects. For example, in the case of the Three Gorges Dam in China, nobody would finance that project. Neither private nor public foreign investors would go near that project until the Export Development Corporation decided to fund it in 1994. Since then other public institutions have reasoned that if the Canadian government is supporting this project, maybe we will too. This project, the Three Gorges Dam, is going to create an enormous cesspool and lead to the forced displacement of two million people. A variety of academics writing for the *Far Eastern Economic Review* have predicted that this is going to lead to social chaos well into this century. This is by all accounts one of the worst projects in the world, and the EDC led the way with their endorsement and with the permission of the Canadian government to go ahead.

Subsidy of Foreign Interests

The Canadian public would be very surprised to discover that U.S. multinational corporations like Amtrak and Northwest Airlines were getting subsidies from Canadian taxpayers. It's ludicrous and there's no reason in the world why we should be subsidizing American corporations. The EDC tends to fund large corporations, although it brags about the number of small and medium enterprises that it lends to. Eighty percent of its operations are supporting the operations and the exports of large companies like General Electric of Canada, SNC-Lavalin, Bombardier and General Motors. These loans are essentially subsidized loans that are helping institutions and companies in other countries.

Subsidy of Social Injustice

The Canadian public has a responsibility to act accountably for the way our public funds are used. In the case of China, which is one of the largest recipients of Export Development Corporation funds, that government is not accountable. It arrests people who oppose the projects in which it is investing, for example, again, the Three Gorges Dam. The Chinese government has arrested people who were simply trying to get compensation for lost land. These people are in detention without trial and without due representation; however, if we in this country protest the construction of this dam and its financing with Canadian funds, we are not going to go to jail. We are not going to suffer arbitrary detention, or worse, and because our government makes projects like this possible in the first place, we have a responsibility as citizens and as taxpayers to make sure that the money is spent in ways that are consistent with public values in this country. If we don't, then even more of these bad projects will proceed at the expense of the environment, individuals and economies.

One of the other cases that I remember was another dam project in Colombia from which a lot of civil unrest resulted. There were a lot of paramilitary groups that were terrorizing the local indigenous community who had been displaced by the dam. We received a letter from the minister one day, saying that the minister's colleagues and the

Colombian government have it under control and everything is fine. The very next day one of the leaders of the indigenous community disappeared and it was largely believed that he disappeared because of the paramilitary groups. The Canadian government is not really on top of this, nor are the governments that they're lending money to.

Subsidy of Social and Environmental Degradation

As an environmental group, International Probe scrutinizes the environmental effects and the financial effects of Canadian government activities overseas, and corporate activities. We have been approached by other citizens' groups in other countries who, like us, are concerned about projects in their countries that are financed by our government through the Export Development Corporation. For example, the EDC has supported the Chamera Dam in India. We have, thanks to the Access to Information Act, just managed to get some documents from CIDA (the Canadian International Development Agency) about this EDC-supported project that showed that the dam has been built in a geologically unstable area. There have been, over the last 10 years, incidents that show geological instability and the possibility of catastrophic events like a dam failure. This information was secret until the last four or five months. This is extremely important information to the hundreds of thousands of people living downstream of this dam. They need that information, and since their lives are at risk, we feel they have a right to that kind of information. We don't think the Canadian government should be putting other people's lives or environments at risk without those people being fully informed and having a say in what goes on in their environments and their communities.

The Canadian government is causing a lot of harm in other countries through institutions like the Export Development Corporation. We think that this is irresponsible spending and, as a result, we do research to try to expose what the Canadian government is trying to keep secret about these projects in other countries. Our 20,000 supporters across the country write letters of concern to their members of Parliament expressing worries about the way the Export Development Corporation is operating. They usually get responses from the government that essentially say, "Don't worry, everything is under control. We have taken action."

CHARLIE PENSON

Charlie Penson was first elected as a member of Parliament for Peace River (Alberta) in 1993, and was re-elected in 1997 and 2000. He was appointed Opposition critic for industry and elected as the vice-chairman of the Standing Committee on Industry. He has been Reform Party critic for international trade as well as a member of the Standing Committee on Foreign Affairs and International Trade. A former chairman of the Northern Alberta Rapeseed Processors, Mr. Penson has also served as a director of the Rural Electrical Association and the La Glace and District Agricultural Society, including two terms as president.

TOPICS:
Crown Corporations: Little Transparency in Government
Crown Corporations: Lack of Accountability in Spending
Parliamentary Scrutiny: Limits and Systemic Obfuscation
No Access to Information
Regional Development Agencies and Subsidies
The Canada Account: Need for Accountability

Cabinet Control of Subsidies
Business Will Take What It Can Get
Subsidies: A Lose-Lose Proposition
Remedies: Transparency in Government
Remedies: Dissolution of Crown Corporations

Crown Corporations: Little Transparency in Government

Members of Parliament deserve the right to be able to ask government agencies if public money, taxpayers' money, is being wisely spent. In the areas of Crown corporations, regional development agencies and programs like Technology Partnerships Canada, the government cannot answer or refuses to answer questions about public money. They don't make the commercial transactions transparent so people can see if their investments are good value for money spent, if there are bankruptcies, or what has happened to those commercial loans.

Examples of Crown corporations we are referring to include the Export Development Corporation (EDC), which has assets in the range of $35 billion. They do a lot of commercial transactions. There is also the Business Development Bank of Canada (BDC) as well as Technology Partnerships Canada at Industry Canada. They dish out hundreds of millions of dollars in repayable contributions every year, which is ironic since these are long-term loans and we don't know if they ever get paid back.

Why isn't the government transparent? There's no reason why they shouldn't be. If this were a commercial bank, it would be a different situation and of course there would be no transparency. But this is taxpayers' money, and we have to know whether it's being spent wisely. There are many other programs out there that need government money, and if it's not being spent wisely, these current programs should be terminated.

Crown Corporations: Lack of Accountability in Spending

The Government of Canada is spending billions of dollars that it is being unaccountable for by allowing Crown corporations to exist as arm's length agencies from the government itself. Parliament has no authority to work in this area, even though in the Liberals' *Red Book* of 1993 the prime minister talked about installing an ethics commissioner who would report directly to Parliament. Instead, the ethics commissioner reports to the prime minister, which makes a big difference. We're saying that instead of the EDC reporting to Parliament, the EDC should report to the minister of industry.

Parliamentary Scrutiny: Limits and Systemic Obfuscation
Parliament has minimal oversight of billions of the dollars spent in this fashion. Members of Parliament can ask agencies like the Export Development Corporation or Technology Partnerships Canada or the BDC about their operations, but they don't get any answers. The difficulty is that there is no method to get these answers. For example, members of Parliament ask the Export Development Corporation questions about its loans and they say, "Well, we don't answer to you. We answer to the minister of industry." We go to the minister responsible and ask the question. He says, "Well that's an arm's length agency from government, and I can't give you that information." So we're caught up in this triangular process where you can't get the information you need to make decisions.

No Access to Information
As a citizen you can apply to an Access to Information officer for information about the activities of an agency, but in most cases you won't get an answer. They use a lot of "whiteout" at those departments, so if you get any answers at all, they're very limited.

It's very difficult for taxpayers or anyone else to find out under what terms this money is being lent and even more difficult to find out if it is being repaid. As a citizen you can find out how much has been paid back in loans, but you can't tell which companies have paid it back. A global amount is shown in the yearly figures on how much is repaid, but as a taxpayer or as a member of Parliament, you can't see which individual companies or countries that money has been loaned to. Even parliamentary critics in different areas and in the opposition parties have no way of knowing who has not paid back a loan. This is a real problem because we could have a failed loan to a company here in Canada or another country and nobody would know how that particular transaction turned out.

Regional Development Agencies and Subsidies
There are dozens of programs that the government uses to subsidize. The regional development agencies are probably one of the worst. The

government would claim that we need these programs to create jobs. I disagree. In fact, if citizens knew the cost of these programs, they would be in violent disapproval of them. There's an old saying that the government can't pick the winners, but losers can sure pick government. We find all the time that there are a lot of failed programs where the company is gone as soon as the government money is gone.

It's far better for the government to set the proper business environment in place. They need lower taxes, less regulation and less interference to get an interprovincial trade agreement between the provinces. We have better trade agreements internationally than we have between provinces here in Canada. An interprovincial trade agreement would be a better type of system to encourage business to do well in Canada, rather than trying to pick winners and losers.

The Canada Account: Need for Accountability

Another program the government uses to make subsidized loans is the Canada Account. The Canada Account is financing that is mostly to foreign countries or businesses in foreign countries. The Export Development Corporation administers it on behalf of the government of Canada, and it's real risky financing. That's why it doesn't get done through any commercial agency at all. For example, a couple of years ago Prime Minister Chrétien went to China and announced that he had signed contracts worth $4 billion. Most of those contracts were for nuclear reactors that were financed by the Canada Account through the Export Development Corporation at below-market interest rates. Quite often financing from the Canada Account is quite a bit below market interest rates. That's why the Canada Account has to have special approval from the Cabinet.

Cabinet Control of Subsidies

A lot of industries ask how Cabinet makes a decision to subsidize a company. Here is an example of one of the subsidies that Cabinet approved. In January 2001, before the House of Commons resumed its session after the election, the industry minister announced a $1.7-billion subsidized credit to Air Wisconsin so Bombardier could sell a large amount of regional jets to them. They sold this idea to the Canadian public as a one-time deal to stop the trade war with Brazil. They hoped that we would drive Brazil to its knees. Unfortunately it hasn't happened just as we predicted. Bombardier came back again less than five months later asking for $1.5 billion to sell regional jets to Northwest Airlines of Minnesota. Now, Northwest Airlines is the fourth largest airline in the United States and we Canadians are loaning them money at low interest rates to buy regional jets.

This is the new standard, in which large American corporations are benefiting from the Canadian taxpayer's money via subsidies.

Canadians are basically subsidizing American multinational corporations at lower-than-market rates of interest. We are guaranteeing $1.5 billion in the case of Air Wisconsin, and loaning Northwest Airlines $1.7 billion in lower-than-market interest rates. Now, apparently, there's an Arizona company that Bombardier had sold jets to earlier that is complaining that they didn't get the same deal.

Business Will Take What It Can Get

In these situations Bombardier seems to be using the Government of Canada and taxpayers' money as a sales pitch. But I'm not faulting Bombardier. Any corporation, any company, would take the subsidies offered by the federal government. If the government is stupid enough to offer those kinds of terms, people are going to take advantage of them. We are really faulting the Liberal government for having that kind of policy. The trade minister and the industry minister will argue, and I think the prime minister will as well, that we should be proud to have these national champions in business and we have to promote them. Well, I say it's easy to be a national business champion if you've got the Government of Canada as your banker.

Subsidies: A Lose-Lose Proposition

I think Canada has a limited ability to be able to compete against subsidies, which I think is the wrong form of action. We have to take a much more aggressive approach toward the World Trade Organization and NAFTA; we have to negotiate down subsidies and tariffs. However, the government picks industry favourites all the time and that's why they have no enthusiasm for talking about reduction of subsidies at the World Trade Organization. Canada has traditionally been a world leader in trying to get these kinds of rules put in place, but there's been a lot of slippage under the Liberals in the last eight years since they came to office. They love using the Canada Account instead and really don't believe in the market economy or free trade, and it's really starting to show. After 50 years of negotiations, first under the old General Agreement on Tariffs and Trade and then with the World Trade Organization, the conclusion the government, prior to the Chrétien Liberals, came to is, the subsidy game is not winnable. Subsidies should be stopped, but Canada is back in that game because the Liberals like the kinds of tactics which permit them to promote their political friends.

The general policy of the Liberal government, especially through the Department of Industry, is one of picking winners in industries that they want to promote and then throwing money at them to accomplish that goal. The biotech and aerospace industries are their two "new economy" industry favourites. For example, 15 years ago the Canadian government of the day decided to privatize Canadair, so they put development money into this regional jet. They wrote off nearly $2 billion and sold it to Bombardier for about $150 million. The idea was that we would cut the flow of subsidies and losses to the aerospace industry. That was a good theory, but 15 years later we're back into subsidizing the aerospace industry.

The government is hopelessly behind the business sector in realizing what the trends are. In any case it should be listening to business rather than trying to pick winners and then subsidize them with government money, but that's what they tend to do. For example, the prime minister has said that we're not going to lose jobs at Bombardier in a trade war, that these are very important jobs. Well, people in agriculture or mining can argue that their jobs are equally important. A job lost in agriculture or a job lost in aerospace or shipbuilding is an equal loss.

The new economy versus the old economy is poor thinking. There's a real irony here and there's no consistency. We need to focus on our traditional strengths and traditional industries. Western farmers or shipbuilding industries don't have access to the same kind of loans as the government's big favourites and we would be far better off if instead of the current state of affairs, we just had a level playing field for all industries. Then businesses will make decisions to stay in Canada. Lower taxes and lower regulations make it easier for businesses to operate in Canada, so they won't have to go elsewhere. Subsidies are a failed policy and should be discontinued.

Remedies: Transparency in Government

We must have transparency in Crown corporations and regional development agencies that subsidize businesses. We must also allow Parliament to oversee their decisions and actions, or else most of those programs should be cancelled altogether. We'd be far better off just letting the commercial banks do the commercial business and commercial insurance companies do the insurance. Then we could reduce taxes for taxpayers. There would be a level playing field. We wouldn't have special customers that get special favours because they know the Liberal government of the day has a key to the House of Commons.

Remedies: Dissolution of Crown Corporations

We don't think there's any compelling need for Crown corporations in Canada. We maintain that Crown corporations should be privatized or if there's no need for them at all, they should be just dismantled. The private sector of the economy will offer those services and the taxpayers will not be involved. If a company goes broke, it would be a market sort of situation in which the taxpayers would not be required to pick up the tab and that's what we encourage.

There are lots of examples of Crown corporations that have gone into the private sector or have been sold off and are now very profitable. The Mulroney government privatized a number of them in the late 1980s. Air Canada is one example but CN Railways is probably the best example. CN Railways was taking $200 million of subsidized money per year out of the taxpayers' pockets; now it's making hundreds of millions of dollars in profit. Petro-Canada is another. At one time we had the government in the oil business. That was privatized and now they are doing very well.

Either Crown corporations will have no reason to exist or else they should be able to function and operate effectively. I think most of them could operate effectively if they were privatized — the EDC is a good example of that. They offer two services, offering loans like a bank and export insurance. There are groups out there that are telling us that they have no room to operate because the EDC takes all that area. They don't pay any taxes at all so it's unfair competition. They forced others in the private sector out of the business.

Parliament does not discuss the privatization of Crown corporations because the Liberals like the system just the way it is. The Liberals use Crown corporations for their own self-interest and have been doing things this way over the last 100 years. They're very much an interventionist government that likes to keep their hand in the economy and keep control over how things work. We, on the other hand, want to get as far away from that as we can. We'd like to let the market look after the market sector and let government look after things that we have to do in the social areas.

FRED BENNETT

Prior to his retirement in 1993, Fred Bennett was the director of financial and economic analysis at Industry Canada. He worked in government from 1975 to 1995, briefly interrupted by a four-year term in the private sector. During his time at Industry Canada he analyzed loans and contributions under the Defence Industry Productivity Program (DIPP). He is now completing his doctorate in political theory at the University of Ottawa.

TOPICS:
Background
Subsidy Provides Program's Rationale
Impact of Public Relations
Access to Information
More Than Just Economic Considerations

Background
I was Industry Canada's director of financial and economic analysis in the special projects branch here in the Department of Industry for

about 10 or 12 years. I certainly was involved in a number of DIPP (Defence Industry Productivity Program) cases during my time here, anticipating the negotiation of repayment project.

When DIPP first started — and it's supposed to be different now with the new TPC (Technology Partnerships Canada) program, but I'm not sure whether it is or not — it wasn't expected that there would be a lot of repayment. A lot of the repayments were listed as something the company would repay after they'd earned a fair and reasonable profit. But who knows what a fair and reasonable profit is? It's a term that is open to interpretation. In some of the larger deals we were instructed that the repayment terms were to be calculated in such a way that it wasn't likely any money would ever be repaid. In other words, if you're going to repay them over the total sales of the product, we would start our repayment terms after unit 500, when we really only expected they'd sell 400. The theory behind it was that the company would use the money for further investment.

In the aircraft business Bombardier and Pratt & Whitney have done exceedingly well. They're good marketers, they sold their product and the repayments did come into effect — even though on some of those earlier arrangements that was not our intent. There's nothing in the guidelines saying you have to make structured repayments as tight as you can get them because if you made it too close to normal commercial funding, there would be no point to the assistance. You could do other things. For example, what are they going to repay us? Are they going to pay us the dollars they received? Are they going to pay us the dollars they received, plus interest? Are they going to pay us the dollars, plus interest *and* inflation? So there were a variety of parameters you could play with to make the repayment terms heavier or lighter, depending on what your goal was.

Every contract could be opened up and renegotiated depending on the terms. There were always provisions. These were contracts between the department and companies and any contract can always be reopened. So when repayments were due, it was quite appropriate and acceptable for the company to come in and say, "Well, instead of repaying you, we would like to direct this money toward a new project." Then you could reopen the deal and renegotiate the terms. Whether that's still possible under the TPC program, I have no idea, but there wasn't anything illegal about it.

Subsidy Provides Program's Rationale

These are subsidies. If they weren't subsidies, there'd be no point to them. Even when they talk about the TPC program as providing risk capital as if they're venture capitalists — then why don't the companies just go to a venture capitalist? The reason is because they presumably want terms that are not as strict or as heavy as what a venture capitalist would impose on them. If we weren't providing terms that were better than venture capitalists or banks, there'd be no point to the program. The whole point is to give a subsidy in one way or another. Loan guarantees are a subsidy. There's a cost to the Crown of guaranteeing a company's debts. Repayable loans have a cost. Even if you get the money back, you're probably not charging the interest rate of a normal commercial transaction. If it's a high-risk project, they're not going to get prime or prime plus one or prime plus two at the bank. They'd be going to some junk-bond financier and paying a whole lot more. So if there's not an element of subsidy in there, it's a waste of time. That's what they're about because if there were no subsidy, nothing would happen.

There are legal differences among contributions, repayable contributions, loans, loan guarantees and all the rest, which I'm not qualified to talk about. That's a lawyer's business. There are certainly legal differences among the various kinds of instruments the government has at its disposal. If you think about it logically, if it's not structured in such a way that the company is going to receive some kind of financial support that it wouldn't have otherwise, what would be the point? The whole point is to provide subsidy. That is the point of an industrial development program or a technology development program. You can dress it up how you want, but it's not going to have any impact unless the government is transferring money.

Money makes companies do things — good things or perhaps bad things, depending on how you look at it — but money makes companies do things they wouldn't have otherwise done. So if there were no element of subsidy, what would be the point? If the department were offering loans on the same terms as the Bank of Montreal, what would be the rationale for it? There wouldn't be one. I know they don't like to say that there's still an element of subsidy, but if there weren't, there'd be no rationale for the program whatsoever. It's only the element of subsidy that makes the program have any sense at all.

It's a misnomer to call the subsidy a loan or to compare them to the loans in the private sector. These are loans that are contingent on the company making profit or the company achieving success. When you go to your bank to borrow money for a house, the banker doesn't much care whether it's a nice house or not or whether the house goes up or down in value. The banker just wants the money back. But in this case the whole point of the program was to provide funding for companies to do things which they might not have been able to do otherwise (without government money). If it was a loan on strictly commercial terms, what's the point? So when they talk about there being loans on commercial terms, in my view that's nonsense. Basically what they are is disguised ways of conveying a subsidy to the companies. That's what they're supposed to be.

I don't know much about the rest of the public service. I spent my entire career in either the Department of Industry or its predecessor department, Regional Economic Expansion. That's the way things worked then. Sometimes there were contributions given for which there was not even a hint of repayment. Other times they were set up as repayable loans or repayable grants and contributions, in which case it was possible there would be repayments. Now my understanding is that there are some more repayments coming in; they're a little more diligent about structuring repayments and collecting the money. But during a large part of my time here it just wasn't expected that there'd be a lot in the way of repayments under the old DIPP program.

To be fair, in recent years, to the best of my knowledge, they've become much more precise in drafting the repayment terms. During the 1980s they were quite often drafted as the company made repayments, after they'd earned a fair and reasonable profit on this project. That opens up all sorts of accounting issues as to what constitutes the profit for the project. My belief is that the deals are now structured in such a way where, under the new TPC program — and I think it's supposed to be this way — the repayment terms are clear. At the very least you can ascertain whether or not the threshold has been reached in order to make the repayments. Under the old DIPP programs there were only maybe one or two companies that ever made significant repayments.

The only one that ever paid back reasonable amounts of money was Pratt & Whitney in Montreal. I think its initial rationale for DIPP was military production. In later years it became a program to aid the high-tech industries, particularly the aerospace industry. It was supposed to aid them with research and development and initial production costs to get up to speed. I don't think the rationale has changed a great deal. There's still the idea that somehow the companies wouldn't be able to compete in the world market unless the government helped them, or that through government aid we would help them develop faster than they would otherwise. Those were the supposed rationales for much of the DIPP program. To the best of my knowledge, the rationale hasn't changed.

Research and development is so diffused. One of the reasons why it presumably requires aid from the government is because there are many bad projects that are supposed to be made up for when you have one big one. It's like drug companies. When they research 10 medicines that don't turn out or make any money, the 11th one is supposed to make enough money to recoup everything, plus profit. In some sense all R & D is like that. So it's harder to put down objective terms that tell you whether or not the deal has turned out to be good or not. You would be more likely to measure the return on research and development in general, rather than on specific projects.

The threshold test is done in increments. It's a measurement you need to find out whether you've actually made anything happen, besides give money away to the company. Unless your money is going to cause the company to do something that it wouldn't have done anyway, then you haven't done anything. If they would have done it anyway, common sense says you can't attribute any benefits to the project because the company would have gone ahead and built that airplane or built that car or researched this or developed that — because it was a good, sufficiently profitable project.

So if the money has merely topped up the rate of return and it was already a rate of return they would have had in any case, in my view you can't attribute any benefit to the assistance. Unless there was some sort of demonstration that the project was not viable on its own, without the government assistance, or that the company would be able to do the project offshore and get assistance from another government, there is no benefit whatsoever that could be legitimately attributed to the project. It was only after it passed the incremental threshold that you could start to wonder whether there were any benefits or not.

When government tried to influence economic activity by way of subsidizing or assisting a company, we were supposed to analyze whether or not the money we were going to give them, in the form of a repayable loan or a contribution, was necessary. In other words, if the company would have gone ahead and done some activity in any case, there was no point in giving them taxpayers' money because that would just be a transfer of wealth from the taxpayers to the shareholders of some company.

First we asked, "Is this the sort of project that wouldn't go ahead unless we put in the government money?" You could do that through a variety of financial analysis techniques. Is the project going to earn a decent rate of return even without the government grant? What would the rate of return be with the government grant? The second aspect was that even if they went ahead with it — with or without our money — was it a good project from a purely economic point of view? Was it creating jobs? Was it generating foreign exchange? Was it generating tax revenue for the government? So those were the two perspectives to look at.

When we would contribute to a project — by giving it a loan or whatever you want to call it — the project would generate, let's say, 1,000 jobs. The idea was generally that we would claim 1,000 jobs as being the result of our activity. Plus, we would claim the jobs that were created in the company supplying the company to whom we were giving the grant. And they would quite often claim what's called the multiplier effect, which is just basically the effect of people spending money. If the government spends money, people will get the money and they'll spend it on something else, which will create economic activity. From an economic perspective, I think most economists would agree that that's overcounting any potential benefits from a project because most people would have been working in any case.

When you create a job for an engineer or a high-tech specialist, those aren't the sort of people that are lacking work. Quite often we have to fill those jobs with immigrants. We have to specifically go abroad to look for people to fill the jobs. On the other hand, it's quite true that some of these jobs would go to people that otherwise might not be working. In reality, it was always my belief — and I think this is the belief most economists have — that the number of jobs that fall into that latter category, the category of incremental activity jobs, was much, much smaller than the numbers we would claim.

As an example, if you give a grant or a subsidy to a new restaurant, let's say, it's not necessarily true that there will be any more people working because the people that are now going to eat in that restaurant would probably have eaten in another restaurant nearby. So there will be more people here and less people there. You have to try to keep track of those effects to come up with an honest number as to what the true economic impact would be.

The justification for such programs is supposed to be that they create jobs and that they create economic activity that wouldn't otherwise take place. I tend not to believe very much in that. I think that most of the time government programs don't achieve the objectives they're supposed to achieve — but that was never my problem in doing the analysis because I regarded that as a political choice. I might have objected in my role as a citizen, but I didn't object in my role as a bureaucrat. My role was to do the analysis. It's true that government encourages economic activity in various parts of the country for social welfare or political reasons.

Impact of Public Relations

When government makes an arrangement with a company — a subsidy or a loan or one of the other instruments the government has — there's a natural tendency that they want it to look good. It has to be justified to the public, which is obviously the role of the minister and the role of the public relations people. So one way or the other they're going to justify it — there's no question about it. The department or the government never undertakes a policy and then has their PR people come out and say, "Well, it's really stupid, but we did it anyway." They just don't do it.

There is a need for the internal analysis, for the bureaucrats to justify their justifications. In other words, I had no problem with the idea of the PR person getting out front and saying that it was a wonderful deal, that it was going to create a million jobs and generate billions in tax revenue. That was the public justification. But what I didn't see the need for — and I think it was counterproductive — was to try and make it look that way in the internal documents through the internal advice we gave to the senior bureaucrats and the ministers. In some sense I saw that as a subversion of the system.

I had this quasi-naive view that analysis was analysis and politics was politics, and that the two don't necessarily meet. And that the analysts should be doing their work first. The politicians and senior people would then take the analysis into account while making a decision. They wouldn't necessarily pay attention to it. There might be other good reasons besides financial and economic matters. But what I objected to was the idea that the financial and economic analysis had to be brought into line with the ultimate public decision and the ultimate public defence of the project.

When people would say, "You should make this analysis look good because the minister wants to do it," how did I know that the minister did want to do it? How did *they* know that the minister did want to do it? The minister certainly never talked to me. He undoubtedly talked to more senior people. But when there's this idea that the analysis has to be fitted to the decision, it seems to me that the politicians and senior bureaucrats aren't going to get the good analysis and the good advice on financial and economic matters to which they're entitled. So in some sense I thought it was counterproductive, but that wasn't the way it was generally viewed.

I think this is the norm. I can only talk from actual experience and things that I worked at here, but it's quite natural that people that are going to make decisions don't want to have documents floating around that say the decision was a problem from the financial and economic perspective. My guess is that it's quite common that bad things tend not to get written down. Sometimes they do, of course, and then they do become public.

All that was asked of me was to provide the numbers or the economic and financial commentary that would make it look good. On the average I would try and put down on paper what I thought was the actual financial and economic circumstances. Most of the time it was for internal documents. I never did quite understand why they were so concerned to have things look good from a certain perspective when these weren't documents to be released to the public; these were documents for internal advice.

Access to Information

I'm of two minds about Access to Information. Presumably one of the reasons why people didn't want to have negative things written on paper, even for internal documents, was that they were afraid it would eventually become public, either through the auditor general, Access to Information or somebody would leak it. In theory, at least, I was always of the view that the politicians, the ministers, the deputy ministers could do what they wanted to do within the limits of the programs. But people should have the correct information to be able to assess that after the fact. Of course lots of government documents never get out because they're classified as commercial or confidential.

So I did find it frustrating that the deals put forward in the newspaper as wonderful things for the economy were, in a purely economic and financial point of view, not great at all. On the other hand, I have some sympathy with the view that if every document or every piece of paper were put out to the public, people would just stop writing anything down. You wouldn't give advice to anybody — financial, economic or any other kind of advice on paper — if you thought there were a risk it would be made public. There has to be a balance. In some ways, from the citizen's perspective, everything should be out there. But taken to the extreme that would interfere with government functioning.

Government decisions still have to be justified on paper. There's still Cabinet memoranda and briefings for the Treasury Board, memoranda to the Treasury Board, the Department of Finance and to ministers. So things are written down. But there was always a tendency or pressure not to write down the negatives, for fear it would at one point become public.

I distinctly recall being asked on at least one occasion, after having written something negative, to destroy it. "Destroy" wasn't the word used, nor was I ordered to. The exact phrase was, "The assistant deputy minister strongly requests that you withdraw that memo." It would be against the law, in my view, if the information was not already in various places on paper, but I never questioned it. I did withdraw the memo. I suspect I kept a copy in my own internal files that is probably still here in the department somewhere. Let's put it this way: I don't think I went so far as to rip it up, but I did withdraw it.

One other time I distinctly remember was when the government was going to assist Bombardier in buying the De Havilland plant in Toronto. There was an analysis that indicated that it wasn't necessarily such a great deal. Now, the analysis was very controversial because it's difficult to be certain in those circumstances. Subsequent events probably proved the analysis wrong in the sense that Bombardier has done an ace job with both those plants. But I was asked by somebody in the sector branch to prepare an economic cost-benefit analysis of the transaction, which I did.

When I sent it to the higher-ups, I got a phone call saying, "Why did you do this?" I said, "Well, because somebody asked me to do it." The guy just said he was going to send it back to me. I said, "Fine," and he sent it back to me. It remained, of course, in my files if anybody ever wanted to look at it. The deal was going to go ahead. It was clear that that deal was on the way. If they hadn't asked me to do the economic cost-benefit analysis, I wouldn't have done it. So it would have never existed. But in this case somebody asked me to do it, so I did it. I wasn't about to change it once it was done. If they hadn't asked me, I would have been quite happy not to do it — I didn't get paid by the piece of paper.

More Than Just Economic Considerations

There were lots of deals where nobody bothered to do an economic analysis because you knew very well that it wouldn't look good from a purely economic point of view. But there were other considerations. Political considerations, regional development considerations, or however you want to phrase it. For example, my recollection is, I don't remember ever doing any specific cost-benefit analysis on some of the shipbuilding arrangements that we entered into. From a purely economic point of view they probably would have come out negative. But it was clear that for various reasons the deals were going to be done. So we focused on making the deal as good as we could make the deal under the circumstances. Because it was going to be done.

So what's the point of pointing out that it's going to be a bad deal when it's done? We spent our time trying to make it as good a deal and as tight a deal, given the circumstances, as you could make. Once again, that didn't bother me particularly either. I was happy. Some of the least attractive deals or the sleaziest deals, if you will, were the most fun to work on because they were high profile. There were always meetings, you'd be back and forth with the company, there were deadlines and they were controversial. They were fun to work on. As long as nobody asked me to write a justification piece for it, I was quite happy to work on it. It was only when I was asked to put down on paper that it was a good deal when I didn't think it was that I had any problems.

How did it affect me? I was happy if somebody would instruct me to do a deal or to calculate a repayment formula where, as such, there'd be no repayment. I had no problem doing it. If my employer gave me an instruction that he wanted it calculated that way, fine, I would do it. What I had problems with was when they wanted me to then write a report that there would be repayment when I knew that the possibilities or the chances weren't all that great. My view is it was the politicians' choice as to how they organized their affairs. I was willing to do the negotiations, the contracts or the analysis in such a way as to help them do what they wanted to do. The only problem I had was when people wanted me to pretend that something was what it wasn't.

I was never particularly idealistic. My view was that they hired me to be the director of financial and economic analysis. I quite often got the impression that what they wanted was a director of financial and economic justification. And that I objected to. I was more than prepared to analyze this or analyze that, provide the results, good, bad or indifferent, in support of a good deal or in support of a bad deal. But I was not prepared to write down on paper or say that a bad deal from the financial and economic perspective was a good deal from the financial and economic perspective. I had no objections if they wanted to go ahead with the deal, even though it was bad from the financial and economic point of view. That's somebody else's business. That's the minister's business and the deputy minister's business. But from my perspective, what I objected to was the idea that no matter what deal was going down, it had to look good on paper, whether it was or not.

I certainly wasn't important enough to get instructions from the minister. I would get word from the assistant deputy minister or from the people who worked in the sector branches — they are the branches that deal with each individual industry sector. Somebody would say, "We have to make this look good because the minister wants to do it or the PMO is interested in this." So it would be sort of a general belief by most people that the politicians wanted to do this deal for one reason or another.

I did hear one or two ministers say that this deal had to go ahead, in certain cases. Senior public servants have influence; there's no question about it. Ministers are busy people. They're not necessarily expert in all the arcane details of finance and economics and law and all the rest of it. So the advice that the senior bureaucrats give has influence. There's no question about it. But to be fair, most of the deals I saw where I thought there was influence, I had only the strong feeling that it was true that the pressure was coming from the top. I have no way of verifying that, but that was my sensation.

Certainly on things such as the Westray coal mine. In that case politicians and people in the PMO did apply direct pressure on me. But in most of the deals there was more atmosphere pressure. I do believe that most of the time it was probably the politicians that wanted the deal done, but the senior bureaucrats certainly have influence in (a) how the deals are presented to the ministers, and (b) how they're structured. A lot of it is in the details. Just because you're going to do a repayable contribution with company X, there's a lot of room to make that repayable contribution agreement hard for the company to live with or easy for the company to live with. A lot of that is within the area of the bureaucrats to influence how it works.

The theory is that political things are the minister's responsibility. The department, the ministers and the politicians decide, and the bureaucrats implement. The deputy minister is supposed to be the link between the two. But it's naive in the sense that the government is too big and too complicated for the division to be made that clearly. In my view bureaucrats will, as long as these are discretionary programs, influence how the money is spent. There will always be political influence on how the money is spent.

The idea that you can draw a clean line is somewhat naive. Now, whether or not bureaucrats should be more resistant to political pressures is another issue, but you have to realize that when you work in the government, if you see a career path in the government, you want to fit into the culture. Maybe I'm too cynical. I just think it's foolish to try and pretend that people aren't going to act in their best interest most of the time, and for most bureaucrats, their best interest is to serve. What makes for a successful bureaucratic career is to keep your minister out of trouble.

By and large there's a culture inside a department. There is a culture inside any business and your career is more likely to go well if you fit well into the culture. The culture in the Department of Industry and the aspects I was involved in referred to the people looking for money as clients. So if Bombardier is your client or if Pratt & Whitney is your client, what you do is you try to be nice to clients, you try to serve your clients. I always had problems with the idea that our product was money. To me they were people that were looking for taxpayers' money. And it was more up to them to demonstrate that the project they had was going to give the taxpayer a return than it was my job to facilitate their getting the money. I didn't see my job as facilitating the giving away of money. I saw my job as analyzing to see whether it fit the rules of the program. So to the extent that the department was service-oriented and client-oriented, I didn't fit very well into the culture.

Promotion is obviously motivation for the bureaucrats. Also being close to power. To be the person who gives the advice to the minister or the Cabinet. Obviously when you get a promotion you make more money. But the salaries in the public service have never competed with the salaries in the private sector, at least at the executive levels. So I think most people here are not money-oriented. There may be some that couldn't get the salary in the private sector, but in general terms I don't think that's fair. I think most of the executives I met here are fairly capable people. Everybody wanted more money if they could get it, when the raises came out. But the real incentive is to progress up the hierarchy and to participate in big decisions — to be a player in the major decisions.

The voters are the people who presumably live in the places where the companies who are receiving the money are doing their work and hiring the employees and spending their money. The voters have the opportunity to throw the politicians out if they don't like them. Any sort of public opinion polls that I've ever read indicate that Canadians tend to expect their government to be an active participant in economic development, job creation and redressing economic disparities amongst the regions. So I think there are large numbers of voters who don't like it, such as myself. I don't agree with those programs. But my own feeling is the majority of Canadians expect their government to take an active role in economic development and regional development. That's just the way Canadians are.

It's not as if Canada is unique in this regard either. The Americans tend to have a much more skeptical attitude toward government than we do. But if you look closely — more so at the state and municipal level than the federal level — you'll find the same thing is going on. They have a sort of industrial development bond where the municipalities in the United States can issue tax-free bonds. They issue the tax-free bonds and loan the money to the company at the interest rate, which takes account of the tax cut. So it's by no means something that's unique to Canada. People will compare us to the Americans and say that we're much bigger sinners in this regard — we spend much more. I think a closer look demonstrates that we are, but it's not a difference in magnitude, it's a difference in degree.

From a taxpayer's perspective, in general terms, I was not in favour of industrial assistance. I can show my age by saying that I still remember David Lewis, the socialist NDP leader in the 1970s, referring to "corporate welfare" and "corporate welfare bums." I had a certain degree of sympathy with that particular aspect of David Lewis's policies. As a citizen I didn't really think that industrial grants or assistance to industry made a lot of sense because I didn't think it worked most of the time. As a bureaucrat I was prepared to work on whatever was required of me. It wasn't for me to try and influence government policy in that regard. As far as conflict goes, I'm not given to conflicts. It didn't bother me. I didn't feel any sort of moral quandary or anything like that.

There's no hard set of rules or criteria that says if you spend the money this way, it's wise and good value, but if you spend the money that way, it's not. Purely from the financial and economic point of view there might be rules that would indicate that this is a good deal. But the government is not a business. Political considerations enter into what is wise and just — to use a philosophical word — if you will. In my view it's part of the thing that politicians are supposed to take into account.

So how would you ensure that the money is wisely spent? I think you can ensure that the politicians or the senior bureaucrats, the ultimate decision makers, have all the information of both the objective factors, such as the economics and the financial analysis, the political factors, the social factors and all the rest. They then are the ones who are elected by the people to make the tradeoffs between all those factors. What I objected to was it seemed to me that by asking me to fudge the financial and economic analysis, one of the pieces of information that should go into making a wise decision was not going to be there the way it should be.

It contributed, I suppose, to the fact that I hated my job. I retired on the day I turned 50, which was the earliest date you could retire at the time when the government was doing the cutbacks. It contributed to the fact that I didn't find it a very pleasant place to work most of the time. I certainly quite enjoyed lots of the people I worked with; there's no question about that. But in terms of it being a satisfying job — it was a hassle. I was no longer interested in it and when it became financially feasible to move along, I moved along.

INDEX